"...The materials included are logically and effectively organized. The sequence of topics flows very well....practicing principals and other administrators, as well as persons in training for administrative positions, will respond well to the style of writing....There is a real need for the [book] since other materials on the same general topic tend to be more exclusively theoretical and not so well addressed to the practitioner. The [book] will make a genuine contribution to the practicing school administrator."
Professor David A. Erlandson
College of Education
Texas A & M University
(from a pre-publication review)

"...The [book], while very comprehensive, would enable the administrator to constantly keep alert on what is happening in the school and would enable him [sic] to have a continuous and thorough understanding of the program. With all the evaluative instruments available herein, he could carry on a constant evaluation and be able to remain up-to-date and on top of the school while keeping abreast with how the school is keeping up with the latest developments in education. The ideas are refreshing and can be adapted as the times change. [The book] applies to both elementary and secondary school administrators and the material could be adapted to fit the particular needs of each individual administrator and school. It has basic universal appeal and would apply to large schools as well as small schools, urban schools as well as rural schools...."
Professor Samuel Ersoff
Department of Educational Administration
University of Miami
(from a pre-publication review)

"...The list of additional resources at the end of each chapter is extremely helpful. The checklist suggested to evaluate school materials for sex-stereotyping is especially timely and helpful. I think that thousands of principals will welcome a guide that promises to make them central to the 'change-evaluation syndrome' and key to the accountability process...."
Professor Ned B. Lovell
Department of Educational Administrations
and Foundations
Illinois State University
(from a pre-publication review)

Printed in the United States of America

AN ADMINISTRATOR'S GUIDE FOR EVALUATING PROGRAMS AND PERSONNEL

AN ADMINISTRATOR'S GUIDE FOR EVALUATING PROGRAMS AND PERSONNEL

Edward F. DeRoche

Dean and Professor, School of Education
University of San Diego

Allyn and Bacon, Inc.
Boston • London • Sydney • Toronto

Library of Congress Cataloging in Publication Data

DeRoche, Edward F
    An administrator's guide for evaluating programs and personnel.

    Bibliography: p.
    Includes index.
    1. School management and organization—Evaluation.
2. School supervison—Evaluation. 3. Community and school—Evaluation. I. Title.
LB2806.D435   371.2   80-22367
ISBN 0-205-07252-6

Printing number and year (last digits):
10 9 8 7 6 5 4 3 2 1   85 84 83 82 81

Printed in the United States of America

CONTENTS

6

EVALUATING TEACHERS AND TEACHING 141

8

EVALUATING THE STUDENT ACTIVITIES PROGRAM 203

7

EVALUATING CURRICULUM: PROGRAMS AND MATERIALS 173

9

EVALUATING PUPIL PERSONNEL SERVICES AND PERSONNEL 225

10
EVALUATING AND IMPROVING
SCHOOL-COMMUNITY RELATIONS

PREFACE

I can never find permanent answers to any problem. I can only produce temporary solutions and hope for the best.

Winston Churchill

"It's What's Up Front That Counts" may be a slogan for a product, but anyone who has seriously studied the research in school administration knows the truth behind the slogan. The key factor to school success or failure is generally the school principal. With the aid of this book, principals may become professional leaders who show the community, colleagues, and parents that school principals want to know how they are doing (evaluation) and to be held responsible for what takes place in their schools (accountability).

Therefore, this book is based upon three assumptions: (1) school administrators are educational leaders, or at least want to be; (2) determining the effectiveness of a school begins with a self-examination by principals, teachers, and staff; and (3) progress toward quality education begins at the building level; that is, education is only as good as an individual school's principal, faculty, and staff. The challenge for today's educational leaders is to set an example that clearly demonstrates that schools can be the one institution where human relationships are enhanced while meeting the demands of society in general, and communities, in particular; and that a school can be a human and humane enterprise as it deals with internal and external evaluation processes and accountability requirements.

Determining the effectiveness of the school's programs and personnel is one of the major tasks faced by principals. They, more than any other educators, must respond to the public's pleas for quality education, for finding ways to enhance teaching and learning, and for helping parents and the community cope with the problems of raising children in a dynamic, rapid-paced society.

The ideas in each chapter in this book suggest that determining the effectiveness of any aspect of the school's programs and personnel is a team effort. Evaluation requires the understanding and cooperation of all school personnel. Determining teacher effectiveness without involving teachers in the process is a futile effort. Evaluating student achievement, attitudes, needs, and interests without involving students in self-evaluation is failing to capitalize on a basic tenet of the teaching and learning process. Assessing community attitudes toward a school without input from parents and other citizens is a waste of time. The school administrator has to establish procedures that create a feeling that evaluation is important, that the process for determining effectiveness is a worthwhile and valuable learning experience, and that the results will help everyone in the school do a better job.

While this book provides many examples, ideas, illustrations, and suggestions, most suggestions are not all-inclusive, but intended to generate further ideas. For example, as a school principal shares the ideas in the chapter on curriculum with teachers, other suggestions, maybe better ones, will result. If this happens, then the purpose of this book has been accomplished because the underlying intent is to encourage individual school personnel, guided by the leadership of the school principal, to take an active role in evaluating and determining the effectiveness of what is done in the day-to-day operation of the school.

This book is filled with useful ideas in conducting assessments and self-evaluations. But self-evaluation and the use of survey instruments, opinionnaires, and questionnaires, by themselves, are insufficient for decision making. The use of additional data to supplement what you find out from using the instruments in this book is also necessary. For this reason, each chapter provides you with descriptions of evaluation instruments that have been found valid, reliable, and helpful in gathering additional data for making decisions. The detailed, step-by-step assessment methods and procedures, coupled with the numerous evaluation instruments in the text and references, will help you to better determine what works and what doesn't work in your school.

Another feature of this book is that each chapter is designed to promote a team effort utilizing a problem-solving approach. A plan of action (Chapter 1) is carefully described that includes problem identification, data collection, data reporting, drawing conclusions, and making recommendations. Over the past twenty years, I have witnessed the frustration of teachers and others serving on innumerable committees trying to decide the best way to get the job done. Much time is wasted. Enthusiasm is drained. Frustration results. The suggestions in this book, properly used, should alleviate this problem.

Throughout this book, I have attempted to be positive, practical, and realistic while at the same time using research and theory to support the major themes described in each chapter. Each chapter examines the major evaluation responsibilities of administrators and teachers at the building level. Some of the material will have to be adapted by those implementing these ideas because of the school climate, the level of education (elementary, middle, high school), and other unique situational factors. To provide a well-balanced and useful guide that may be used with confidence by those that value evaluation, and in an attempt to meld theory with practicality, numerous charts, scales, inventories, forms, and checklists have been included for the purpose of duplication and testing in each school.

Thus, this administrator's handbook on evaluation, this ready to use reference, is designed to help today's school principals carry out their evaluative responsibilities in nine major administrative tasks: school climate, office and budget management, plant and facilities management, instructional leadership, teachers and teaching, curriculum, student activities programs, pupil personnel series, and school-community relations. It is a book for administrators who believe that it is important to know where one is before one can determine where to go and in what direction; in other words, evaluation for decision making. It is a book only for those administrators who want to assume responsibility for the effectiveness of school programs and personnel, and who have a positive attitude about evaluation particularly self-evaluation. Therefore, this book may not be for all administrators.

Although the focus is on principals and teachers at the building level, superintendents, assistant superintendents, assistant principals, supervisors, curriculum specialists, board members, and all others who wish to assess programs and personnel will find the material indispensable. The book is also recommended for those studying to be administrators. Experienced administrators and teachers as well as graduate students will find ideas, suggestions, and strategies which will help them solve many problems found in today's schools.

In one sense this is a very personal book. It has to be because school evaluation is a private affair made public. This personal factor requires the use of personal pronouns, a rarity in educational texts. Because of the case presented in the first chapter about the importance of evaluation at the individual school level, it just didn't seem appropriate to keep using impersonal phrases like "the principals should," "teachers should," or "school personnel should . . . ." I felt that since I was writing this book to *you,* sitting in *your* office, or to *you,* surrounded by a classroom filled with active youngsters, or to *you,* in *your* graduate class, the use of personal pronouns seemed appropriate. Perhaps the attempt to personalize the content of this book will clearly illustrate the personal-human aspects of the evaluation process and, more important, of education itself.

Recognition and appreciation go to all who helped type and critique the manuscript. A special thanks to Jackie, my wife, and Sue, Mike, Mark, Carolyn, and Dave who were so understanding, cooperative, and patient during the writing of this book.

1

EVALUATION: VIEWPOINTS AND PLANS

Time is not measured by the passing of the years, but by what one does, what one feels, and what one achieves.

Jawaharlal Nehru

The basic, most fundamental element of education is the interaction between a group of students and their teacher. All other school services, be they legislative, judicial, or administrative, are supportive and hopefully rendered in the context of enhancing the quality of teaching and learning.

Evaluation and accountability are usually interpreted by many teachers and administrators as an attempt to lay blame, to find scapegoats. This position is not supported in this book. Systematic evaluation may help you find out how to improve the quality of instruction and services provided teachers and learners.

Therefore, the ideas for organizing and administrating a plan for evaluation at the school building level and the viewpoints expressed about accountability have at its core the interest of classroom teachers with their twenty-five to thirty youngsters. However, before implementing evaluation plans, before you try some of the ideas, tools, and strategies presented in the chapters of this book, you must understand and appreciate the nature, purpose, and procedures for evaluation at the individual school level.

EVALUATION AND ACCOUNTABILITY: A VIEWPOINT

As a school board member, parent, and educator, I am convinced of the sincerity of the public's demand that educators be held accountable for what takes place in each of their schools. The public's plea is that we do a better job. Some want the best education possible as long as it does not cost too much. But the majority want the quality of education they feel they are paying for.

The public view of accountability focuses upon the essential element of schooling—what children learn. And, in the public's view, what they learn does not take place at home, or in the central office, or in the principal's office. What children learn results from "the quality of everyday life in school," the quality of relationships between student and student, student and classmates, student and teacher, and teacher and class.[1]

There are two central questions related to accountability. First, for what are the schools accountable? We are accountable for the goals and objectives that we publicly promote. These can be found in the literature of most school districts and/or in school board policies. We cannot tell the public what we will do for their children and young people (goals and objectives) and then suggest that we cannot be responsible or accountable for what we do. This position is certainly hypocritical. As Theodore Black writes:

> . . .We have those to battle to dispel the notion that the schools can and should erase the ills of society. The best that should be asked of our schools is that they produce citizens so well grounded in the fundamentals of knowledge, so adept in the proper use of logic, and so well versed in the system of values that is the glue of our society that they will be equipped to work out solutions to American's problems for themselves in due time.[2]

The point is that we should be careful about what we promise (goals and objectives) or at least qualify the promise; that is, explain to the public that these are promises (ideals) we strive for but for varying reasons may not accomplish.

The second central question is to what extent are school personnel accountable for the results of schooling? There are limits to accountability, particularly that aspect of accountability that deals with pupil performance and achievement. Any analysis of the research on pupil achievement reveals that a great deal of variance results from out-of-school factors (socioeconomic status, home environment) and the affect of the peer group. We should educate the public in this regard. These fac-

tors do not provide an excuse for any of us. They do suggest, however, that within certain limits and with caution, school personnel can be concerned and responsible for (accountable for) their clientele's academic achievements, attitudes toward school and learning, self-concept, and peer group influences. In addition, they can certainly be at least partially accountable for school and classroom climate, absenteeism, truancy, the drop-out rate, the vandalism and delinquency rate, the quality of instruction and school services, and the evaluation of programs and personnel. School personnel can also be accountable for explaining to the public what the school's problems are, what the highlights are, what is being done, why it is being done, how it is being done, how much it is costing to do it, and what needs to be done and the cost for meeting these needs. Sitting hour after hour at board meetings and talking to parents and educators across the country, one sometimes wonders about the effectiveness of the communication between the school and the public it serves.

There is little sense debating whether or not educators should be held accountable for what takes place in schools. Like it or not, the public wants it, the press promotes it, it is professionally advantageous and necessary, and thus we should accept it. One should not view the demands for accountability negatively. There are few parents or groups who are "out to get" the principal or teachers in their school. Rather the desire is simply to find out how schools are doing and, if need be, how to do a better job educating youngsters. What most parents want to know is whether their child or teenager is getting a good education (whatever that means). Their focus is on the school their son or daughter attends. This is one reason why this book on evaluation focuses upon programs and personnel at the building level, knowing full well that there are tremendous political and social influences bearing on the principal, faculty, and staff from the community and school district. But one has to place accountability somewhere, and I prefer to place it with the teachers, parents, principal, staff, and students. The implication of accountability is reponsibility, and the principal and teachers must respond by saying, "We are responsible, all of us who work, attend, and participate in this school." The personnel in your school and the public your school serves must be held accountable—responsible for the education children or youth receive.

Finally, it may be wise for you to consider the words of John Goodlad regarding accountability:

> My major objection to accountability based only on outcome measures of behaviorally defined competencies and proficiencies is that it takes one's attention away from all those qualitative elements inherent in the educational process.
>
> . . . What [has been] . . . largely ignored, however, is the word "value" embedded in "evaluation." We need to know much more about the values being promoted in school at any given time, where they come from, and what effect they appear to be having on the health of the school's ecology. Finally, we need to know a great deal about how individuals and groups both inside and outside of schools can best contribute to and be held accountable for their efforts on behalf of that ecology.[3]

A major purpose of this book is to encourage principals and teachers to examine and study that ecology—their school and classroom programs, environment, interactions, and community.

INDIVIDUAL SCHOOL AUTONOMY: A VIEWPOINT

I am convinced of the need for more autonomy for each school. That is why the focus of this book is on evaluation at the individual building level. There are several reasons for this view.

First, educational organization is not what it appears to be. When the educational literature, the press, and the public talk about "the schools," they tend to view it as a large, bureaucratic system. Certainly some are, but more are not. Consider the evidence. In this country, there are about 16,000 school districts with varying enrollments, the av-

erage being about 3,000 students. About 11,000 school districts enroll 300 students or less. The state of New York, for example, has 730 local districts excluding New York City and only 50 of these have more than 10,000 students.[4] Wisconsin has 436 districts; 409 have less than 5,000 students and only 27 have more than 5,000. The pattern is similar in most states. The Census Bureau counts every community with a population of over 250,000 as "urban." Yet less than 10 percent of us live in cities with a population of over 1 million; fewer than 30 percent live in cities of 100,000 population; 53 million live in rural areas; and 100 million live in suburbs or small cities "where the schools are far more successful than those in really big cities."[5]

Second, even where the educational organization is large, there is a plea for decentralization. Allan C. Ornstein provides an excellent review of panels', commissions', and advisory groups' reports recommending greater decentralization or community control in large city school systems. He also puts the problem in perspective by asking whether decentralization or community control will improve the education of students. The merits are implied, but little empirical data are available.[6]

Ray Cross, in discussing the merits of team management or decentralization, opts for the latter for several reasons; one of which is that when a system decentralizes, the principal takes on leadership of the professional staff and becomes "the chief administrator of an attendance center, not just an extension of corporate management."[7] In decentralized organizations, the principals, like colleagues in smaller districts, are closer to the clientele the schools serve, which increases their decision-making authority. In addition, schools in each community serve different clientele and need to adopt their programs accordingly. Teacher problems, parent problems, and student problems are all local in nature, to be solved in the individual school. Of course, school autonomy requires leadership by the principal, quality teaching by teachers, expert service by the staff, and great accountability by all.

Experience and common sense suggest that if education is to do the things we say it should do, it must be accomplished at the building level. For example, in critiquing the findings on the effectiveness of Project Follow-Through (a school-based extension of Head Start) House et al. concluded that "local schools do make a difference" and that "the peculiarities of individual teachers, schools, neighborhoods, and homes influences pupils' achievement far more than whatever is captured by labels such as 'basic skills' or 'affective' education."[8] Studies reported in *Looking Behind the Classroom Door*[9] clearly subscribe to the view that educational change will be most effective when it resides with the principal, teachers, students, and parents in the individual school.

Francis Roberts states it best:

> Nearly a quarter century of regular contact with the schools, including six years as a public school principal and nearly seven years as a school superintendent, leaves me thoroughly convinced there will be no early reform of American elementary and secondary education until the individual school is freed from system-wide entanglement of curriculum sequences, staffing patterns, and bureaucratic routines. Until the school, each school, is acknowledged as a separate and significant social institution, real, meaningful, no deep reform can take place. . . . Whereas the "school district" is an abstraction existing only on paper (maps, policy manuals, tax bills and the like), the school has significant reality. In short, it forms a community, for better or worse, and its catalyst, also for better or worse, is the principal.[10]

Finally, research studies suggest that large, centralized organizations tend to place reliance on codification of tasks and observation of rules (formalizing the organization). As a result, its members find little autonomy over tasks they are to perform and little participation in decision making, all of which tends to lead to alienation from work and from relationships with colleagues. Such a malady seems to appear in some of our large school districts.[11]

DEFINITIONS

The purpose of evaluation is the improvement of instruction and factors that influence instruction; namely, climate, program, teaching style, and personnel interrelationships. There are, therefore, several words used in this text that need defining. In addition, certain basic principles that serve as a guide to the proposals, ideas, and suggestions found in each chapter need to be outlined and highlighted. Let us first consider the definitions:

Evaluation

Evaluation (assessment) is the process used for determining the value, amount, or worth of something. "Something" refers to that which is to be evaluated—a program, a procedure, a product, an objective, or any school factor—which in the judgment of principals and teachers is worth the time and effort for data collection, analysis, and decision making.

There are two kinds of evaluation: formative and summative. *Formative* evaluation refers to gathering and using information during the process of doing something. It is on-going, requiring continual feedback for decision making and change along the way. This book suggests the use of formative evaluation because I believe that principals and teachers benefit more from feedback during on-going evaluation processes, during which they can change or redirect something, rather than waiting for the completion of a program or project.

Summative evaluation refers to gathering and using information at the end of something. It is popular in research studies. It has been used in determining the effects of a program, project, or procedure. Summative evaluation leads one to three kinds of decisions at the completion of something—to continue it, to change it, or to cancel it. For example, many teacher evaluation plans are "one-shot," end-of-the-year evaluations. D. Stufflebeam suggests that there is a relationship between formative evaluation and decision making and summative evaluation and accountability.[12]

Quantitative-Qualitative Measures

There are three kinds of tests used in schools: objective-referenced tests, criterion-referenced tests, and norm-referenced tests. Objective-referenced tests (sometimes labeled "diagnostic tests") are designed to find out what students know about a particular subject. Criterion-referenced tests examine how much students know in relation to criteria set by teachers. ("If you want an A on this test, you'll need to answer 90 percent of the questions correctly.") Your driver license test was a criterion-referenced test. Norm-referenced tests are standardized achievement tests. Achievement test results usually are published by the local newspaper with the implication that these results are a measure of the school's success—the quality of education one can expect while attending a particular school.

Each of these tests will be recommended for use as you go about collecting quantifiable information to help you make judgments about the quality of instruction and learning. But *quality* is an elusive word, and educating children and young people may be more an art than a science. To this end, attention should be given to other kinds of measures (for all subjects and activities, but particularly for the arts).

Educational criticism is a term coined by Elliot Eisner which suggests that faculty and administrators use the art form of evaluation—an artistic model of evaluation, namely criticism: "the illumination through penetrating critical description" of what in fact goes in school classrooms. Eisner suggests the collection of data and its critical analysis using student work, teacher logs, student activities, video-taping of activities, student essays, color slides, graphic displays of student work, tape-recorded interviews, and the like.[13]

Responsive evaluation is characterized by three criteria. First, those teachers and administrators engaged in responsive evaluation should be responsive to actual program activities. (Who is doing what? Concerned about what? Values what?) Second, evaluation that is responsive meets the infor-mation needs of a variety of audiences. There are many publics your school serves, each with varying information needs and ideas (see Chapter 10). Third, evaluation is responsive to participants and audiences' value perspectives.[14] Stake and Hoke write, "we who take the 'responsive evaluation' approach complete our studies without strong proof that the program was a success or failure and even without hard data for making good comparisons—but we often end up with people understanding their program better."[15]

Curriculum

The curriculum includes those programs, subjects, and experiences designed specifically for children, youth, and adults who participate in the school. The curriculum finds its content in the needs of society, the needs of individuals in attendance, and contemporary influences (legislative, technological, societal).

Faculty and Staff

Faculty refers to full-time or part-time teachers, assistant principals, librarians, teacher aides, paraprofessionals, etc. *Staff* refers to all other school personnel—secretary, custodian, cafeteria director, and the like.

Effectiveness and Efficiency

These words are used throughout the book to describe how well something is being done and at what cost in time, energy, money (effectiveness), and how it is being accomplished while perserving personnel worth (efficiency).[16]

Sampling

Many of the instruments in this book are designed for specific audiences. Time, energy, and cost may prohibit you from polling, studying, and testing everyone in your school or in the community. For this and other reasons, it is important to know about sampling techniques.

In certain chapters in this book, the term *random sampling* is used; that is, each individual in your population has an equal chance of being selected for your study. In addition, it is important that you know about two methods of random sampling: stratified random sampling and proportional sampling.

For example, you wish to find out how the public feels about your school. A questionnaire has been designed and you wish to send it to a random sample of the population. An analysis of your population suggests that there are several subpopulations (parents, graduates, citizens who live in the school's attendance area but have no children attending the school, etc.). Using the stratified random sampling technique you would take a random sample from each of the subpopulations.

Proportional sampling is a technique whereby you select samples that are in proportion to the population. For example, you wish to sample your graduates concerning the value they place on the education received at your school. In studying the population you note that 75 percent of the graduates were female, 25 percent male. The proportional sampling technique would require that you randomly select 75 percent female graduates for your study and 25 percent male graduates. These and other techniques are worthy of further study.[17]

PRINCIPLES OF EVALUATION

Some basic principles of evaluation which may be considered guidelines for the discussion of topics throughout this book follows:

1. Evaluation should help clarify the school's goals and objectives and the extent to which these are being accomplished.
2. Evaluation is a cooperative, team function and should be seen in a positive, optimistic way.
3. Evaluation should be an ongoing, continuous process.
4. Performance evaluation should be required of all school personnel.
5. Performance evaluation should be honest, open, and free from threats.
6. Evaluation should contribute to the improvement of attitudes, relationships, and morale.
7. Program and performance improvement should be the major purpose of a school's plans for evaluation.
8. Time, assistance, training, and an appropriate budget should be provided to each school for evaluation purposes.
9. Evaluation should help school personnel develop short- and long-range plans.
10. Evaluation should contribute to program and behavior changes.
11. Self-evaluation strategies should be an integral part of any school evaluation plan.
12. External evaluation plans (accrediting agencies) should contribute to and help with internal evaluation plans.
13. Evaluation should be a humane process designed to determine the strengths and weaknesses of programs and personnel.
14. Through the evaluation process teachers, parents, students, and citizens should be able to clarify and understand the objectives and programs of the school.
15. The evaluation process should promote a positive attitude toward self-appraisal and self-improvement.
16. The evaluation program should provide opportunities for school personnel to diagnose difficulties, strengthen existing programs, and establish pilot programs or projects to test new approaches.
17. Evaluation should be a process that will help teachers and learners determine the extent to which each has been successful in the teaching-learning process.
18. Evaluation should encourage a team effort, a cooperative spirit, and a feeling by the community that we are all accountable for the education of our young people.

These principles serve as a overall guide to those engaged in the evaluation process. School principals, because of the nature of their position as educational leaders, have additional responsibilities.

THE PRINCIPAL AS EVALUATOR

Informal evaluation is taking place in and out of school everyday. The building principal has the major responsibility for formalizing the evaluation process. Legally the building principal is the chief administrative officer, the supervisor, and the decision-maker. A principal's attitudes and procedures can make the evaluation program an enlightening, interesting, exciting venture or one that is frustrating, based on fear, and viewed negatively by those involved. What the principal does and how it is done determines, to a large extent, the effectiveness of the school district's and an individual school's evaluation program. Therefore, the following guidelines are suggested as you carry out your role in the evaluation process:

1. A principal must be knowledgeable about the school district's goals and objectives
2. A principal has to assist the superintendent in effectively carrying out the policies and procedures resulting from the school district's goals and objectives.
3. A principal should demonstrate leadership in formulating plans and procedures for the evaluation of these goals and objectives.
4. A principal must provide the students, parents, and teachers with the necessary information about the district's and school's evaluation program.
5. A principal must capitalize on the talents of the faculty, parents, students, and community personnel in helping formulate plans and procedures for carrying out the evaluation program at the individual level.
6. A principal has to provide a plan and secure resources for helping personnel get the job done.

In order to help you in your role as evaluator you might try the following suggestions:

1. Assess your current knowledge about evaluation.
2. Improve your knowledge and attitude about evaluation.
3. Find out how other principals plan for evaluation.
4. Determine what skills you have and what you will need for evaluating your school's programs and personnel.
5. Determine how your faculty and staff feel about evaluation.
6. Find out what knowledge and skill your faculty and staff have about evaluation.
7. Compare your current evaluation procedures with those suggested in this chapter and other chapters.
8. Promote a positive view of evaluation in the school and community.
9. Encourage self-evaluation techniques among school personnel including students.

There are, of course, areas that should be avoided, as in the following:

1. Evaluation should not be used as a threat to faculty and staff.
2. Do not assume that you are the only evaluator in the school.
3. Too much evaluation should not occur at any one time.
4. Evaluation should not be done without specific objectives and plans of action.
5. Do not use evaluation plans that do not involve the entire faculty and staff.
6. Do not allow someone outside the school to prepare evaluation plans that do not include you and your faculty and staff in the process.
7. People who want to evaluate for the purpose of finding scapegoats or cutting the budget should not gain your support.

8. Do not become discouraged if, as a result of your self-evaluation, you judge yourself too critically. You're only human.

CHECKING YOUR ATTITUDES ABOUT EVALUATION

How do you feel about evaluation? What are your attitudes about being evaluated? Included here are some statements about evaluation that will help you determine how you feel about it. This attitude inventory should be used for discussion purposes at faculty or in-service meetings. There is no intent here to have you try to obtain a numerical score as a measure of your attitudes. If used as a means of initiating discussion and debate, it will help you and your teachers work out the problems and concerns regarding evaluation.

Item 11 is an example of a *semantic differential scale*. If you wish, you may assign a numerical value to each score. A value of 5 is given to the space nearest the positive adjectives, and a value of 1 to the score nearest to the negative adjectives; values of 4, 3, and 2 are assigned to the remaining spaces. A total score can be obtained by adding the numerical values. The value of 3 is a neutral score and should not be included in the summation. A score of 40 reveals a very positive attitude toward evaluation or self-evaluation, while a score of 8 would indicate a very negative attitude toward those two concepts. You might then use the entire inventory a second time to determine if there were changes in attitudes after you and your faculty discussed the topic or tried out some of the evaluation suggestions in this book.

1. Evaluation will help the public determine who is accountable to whom and for what.
   ____ Agree   ____ Disagree   ____ Not Sure

2. The emphasis on accountability will detract from the affective influences the school promotes.
   ____ Agree   ____ Disagree   ____ Not Sure

3. Evaluation will help me understand what others expect of me as the principal (the teacher).
   ____ Agree   ____ Disagree   ____ Not Sure

4. If it cannot be measured, then we teachers and principals shouldn't be held responsible for it.
   ____ Agree   ____ Disagree   ____ Not Sure

5. Evaluation should help me determine my strong points.
   ____ Agree   ____ Disagree   ____ Not Sure

6. Evaluation will let everyone know my weaknesses as the school principal (the teacher).
   ____ Agree   ____ Disagree   ____ Not Sure

7. Evaluation will help improve faculty and staff morale.
   ____ Agree   ____ Disagree   ____ Not Sure

8. Evaluation may enhance the concept of team effort.
   ____ Agree   ____ Disagree   ____ Not Sure

9. Administrative evaluation should serve as a model for the evaluation of school personnel.
   ____ Agree   ____ Disagree   ____ Not Sure

10. The purpose of evaluation is to improve not to prove something.
　　____ Agree　　　　　　　　____ Disagree　　　　　　　____ Not Sure
11. Place a check mark near the word that best reflects how you feel about evaluation; repeat the process by substituting "evaluation" with "self-evaluation."

Good	____	____	____	____	____	Bad
Pleasant	____	____	____	____	____	Unpleasant
Free	____	____	____	____	____	Constrained
Valuable	____	____	____	____	____	Worthless
Simple	____	____	____	____	____	Complex
Successful	____	____	____	____	____	Unsuccessful
Progressive	____	____	____	____	____	Regressive
Fair	____	____	____	____	____	Unfair

In summary, if administrators do not value evaluation it would be foolhardy to think that other school personnel will take the lead. If administrators demonstrate negative attitudes, so will others. Today, principals must have a positive attitude about evaluation. As Howsam and Franco state the case:

1. It does little good to protest the limitations of evaluation. The fact is that given present circumstances at least, evaluation is both necessary and inevitable, regardless of its desirability, effectiveness, or consequences.
2. No matter how sound the research evidence, expert opinions, or other knowledge may be, quality is what the evaluator thinks it to be and behavior is what the beholder perceives it to be. Progress in evaluation depends largely upon the development of people.
3. While efforts at better formal evaluation probably should not cease, at this time most school systems would gain more from strong in-service efforts at developing mutual understanding of administrative and supervisory processes and behavior.[18]

ORGANIZING A SCHOOL EVALUATION COMMITTEE

Evaluation at the school district level should be an ongoing process that can be a part of or incorporated into an individual school's evaluation plans.

The patterns that follow can be utilized for either the entire school district or an individual school. However, the aim of this book is to provide principals and teachers with ideas for evaluating their programs, in their school, involving their own personnel. To do this, the principal should consider establishing a school evaluation committee initially by appointment or by requesting volunteers and eventually by election or some combination of election and volunteer methods.

Membership on the evaluation committee will depend on the size of the school. For example, if a school has a faculty of thirty or more members, then the committee probably should consist of nine to twelve members. About one-third of these should be department heads (if a high school) or other administrative personnel, one-third teachers, and one-third representatives from other areas (such as custodian, nurse, secretary, parents, students, and selected community leaders). In small schools, the committee should have a membership of about six to nine people with about one-third of that number representing teachers, support personnel (custodian, nurse, secretary, etc.), and parents and selected community leaders.

The principal and teachers can also consider the use of subcommittees so that the evaluation committee is not overburdened with work. If a subcommittee pattern is used at the individual school level, then one member of the evaluation committee should serve as chairperson of each subcommittee. This procedure insures feedback and continuity between the subcommittees and the evaluation committee. This pattern also requires the involvement of most school personnel, a strength if the evaluation process is to accomplish many of the eighteen principles. Subcommittee membership should consist of about four people including the chairperson.

Here is an example of the subcommittee pattern for a large school. Each subcommittee reports directly to the evaluation committee.

- Subcommittee on goals and objectives
- Subcommittee on teacher evaluation
- Subcommittee to evaluate supportive personnel
- Subcommittee to evaluate the learner
- Subcommittee to evaluate the administration
- Subcommittee to evaluate the curriculum
- Subcommittee to evaluate extracurricular activities
- Subcommittee to evaluate school-community relations.

Many schools are not large enough to follow this subcommittee pattern, therefore, the school's evaluation committee either assumes the tasks implied for each of the subcommittees, or an alternative pattern which reduces the number of subcommittees is used. For example, in small schools, a subcommittee pattern like the following could be established:

- Subcommittee to evaluate teacher effectiveness and the instructional program (including the student activities program)
- Subcommittee to evaluate administrative and support personnel
- Subcommittee to evaluate school-community relations.

There is one other pattern that may be of interest. After gathering information from faculty and staff about what should be evaluated, the principal can appoint or ask for volunteers to serve on

ad hoc evaluation committees. These committees would be discharged once their work is accomplished.

ORGANIZING THE WORK OF EVALUATION COMMITTEES

Once you and your faculty select a method of organizing for evaluation, be it a single evaluation committee, several subcommittees, or *ad hoc* committees, the work to be done should be organized in some way. There are many ways to plan. Other chapters will include plans for evaluating specific things, i.e., teacher effectiveness. A more general plan follows:

Step I—Purpose of evaluation. Early in the process, evaluation committees should take the opportunity to decide the purpose for which they have organized. Answering the following questions will help:

- Why has our committee organized?
- What are our immediate objectives?
- What might be our long-range objectives?

Step II—Evaluation needs. After answering the questions about the purposes of evaluation, the committees should decide what needs to be evaluated and when. To do this, information should be solicited from school personnel and others in the community (if you wish) regarding what and when something should be evaluated. Figure 1–1 shows an evaluation inventory that has been used successfully to identify evaluation needs.

Part II of Figure 1–1 enables the committee to determine priorities as viewed by those surveyed. It also assists the committee in planning for the current school year as well as at least three years ahead. Long-range planning is tentative, however. You may find that what is listed as items to be evaluated two years from now do not carry a high priority at that time. It is best to go back to those surveyed people and tell them what the priorities were two

Figure 1–1
Evaluation Needs Inventory

Directions: The school evaluation committee requests your help in deciding what areas of schooling should be evaluated and when it is best to evaluate that area. Please complete each item by checking the appropriate blank.

Part I

Items to Be Evaluated	Definitely Evaluate	Could Be Evaluated	No Need to Evaluate
1. School goals and objectives	___	___	___
2. School rules, regulations, and policies	___	___	___
3. School-community relations	___	___	___
4. Parent-teacher conferences	___	___	___
5. Grading and reporting practices	___	___	___
6. Report cards	___	___	___
7. Student needs and interests	___	___	___
8. Instructional objectives	___	___	___
9. Extracurricular activities	___	___	___
10. Faculty meetings and other school meetings	___	___	___
11. In-service programs	___	___	___
12. PTA meetings	___	___	___
13. School assemblies	___	___	___
14. Field trips	___	___	___
15. School fairs	___	___	___
16. Student council	___	___	___
17. School clubs and organizations	___	___	___
18. Secretaries, custodians, etc.	___	___	___
19. Paraprofessionals and teacher aides	___	___	___
20. Reading program	___	___	___
21. Substitute teachers	___	___	___
22. Math program	___	___	___
23. Science program	___	___	___
24. Social studies program	___	___	___
25. English-Language Arts program	___	___	___
26. Physical education program	___	___	___
27. Vocational program	___	___	___
28. Guidance program	___	___	___
29. Foreign language program	___	___	___
30. Instructional materials and equipment	___	___	___
31. Teacher effectiveness	___	___	___
32. Teacher evaluation techniques	___	___	___
33. Student learning	___	___	___
34. Student values and attitudes	___	___	___
35. School administration	___	___	___

(cont.)

Items to Be Evaluated	Definitely Evaluate	Could Be Evaluated	No Need to Evaluate
36. Attendance policies	____	____	____
37. Teaching strategies	____	____	____
38. Student-teacher relationships	____	____	____
39. Discipline	____	____	____
40. Instructional materials center, library, etc.	____	____	____
41. Study halls	____	____	____
42. School plant and facilities	____	____	____
43. Audio-visual materials	____	____	____
44. School organization (grouping, graded, nongraded, etc.)	____	____	____
45. Others_____	____	____	____

Part II

Please list five items that you identified in Part I as *Definitely Evaluate* and check the appropriate space in the column at the right.

	Sometime During the Next Three School Years	Sometime During the Next School Year	Sometime During This School Year
1. _____	_____	_____	_____
2. _____	_____	_____	_____
3. _____	_____	_____	_____
4. _____	_____	_____	_____
5. _____	_____	_____	_____

years ago and ask if these items continue to carry a high priority and should be evaluated. In any case, the idea does generate results useful in establishing immediate evaluation priorities. However, it would be foolhardy for the committee to attempt to evaluate all facets of education taking place in their school at one time. Some items that receive a high priority can be evaluated in less time than other items. For example, it takes less of the principal's or evaluation committee's time to evaluate field trips, attendance policies, study halls, meetings, etc., than it does to evaluate school goals and objectives, policies and procedures, or school-commu-

nity relations. Time is a factor that is worthy of consideration. It is important at this stage to determine the evaluation design.[19] It will also be helpful to consider the answers to these questions:

- What kinds of in-service programs will be needed to help personnel acquire some skills, competencies, and ideas in the evaluation process?
- What kinds of professional assistance will be needed? (For example, it would be wise for the committee to seek professional assistance from a computer programmer who could ad-

vise the committee on ways to use a computer and its programs for recording, summarizing, and analyzing the data.)
- What kinds of facilities, equipment, and materials will be required?

Step III—Data gathering. By using the results of the evaluation schedule, the committee determines what needs to be evaluated. To prepare the implementation phases of this evaluation plan, the committee should:

- Specify objectives.
- Decide what information to collect.
- Decide how to gather the information.
- Decide when to collect the information.
- Decide who will collect the information.

Step IV—Organizing and analyzing data. The people responsible for the previous steps should also be active in organizing and analyzing data. The subcommittee, if this is the procedure selected, would review what data have been collected and be responsible for categorizing and summarizing it. The method of analysis will depend upon the objective and the evaluation design.

Step V—Reporting the data. The committee needs to plan a method for reporting the data. The contents should include the *objectives* (why this item/program/procedure was evaluated), the *procedure* (how was it evaluated), the *results* (what was found as a result of the evaluation), and the *implications* (what one does with the results). The implication section of the report should include strengths and weaknesses found as a result of the study, as well as how to improve weaknesses while maintaining strengths. Questions such as the following will be helpful:

- What does the study reveal about strengths and weaknesses?
- What are the suggestions for further study?
- What program alternatives might be necessary?

- What appears to be the best solution (the best way to proceed)?
- What personnel resources are required?
- What additional information is needed?
- What financial commitments should be made?

The evaluation committee should involve others in deciding what should be done about the evaluation report. In other words, now that you have all of this information, what are you and your faculty going to do about it? All factors—programs, alternatives, suggestions, cost, time, effort—should be considered. This is a crucial step for the school principal because it is here that leadership and cooperative decision making can be demonstrated.

DEVELOPING AN EVALUATION PLAN

Be prepared! Plan carefully! These two warnings imply that you not launch into a self-evaluation or the evaluation of programs or personnel without some preparation and a plan of action. The idea presented here is one of many that a principal could use. This plan is merely illustrative. It does require you to think about what is to be evaluated and why.

Purpose. You should have an objective or two in mind about something or someone you wish to evaluate, including self-evaluation. Objectives should be carefully written and as specific as possible. Questions that are of value at this beginning stage include:

- What is the purpose of this evaluation?
- What are my objectives?
- Why do I want to evaluate this?

Orientation. You should prepare yourself as well as those who will be involved in the evaluation plan. Anyone who will be evaluated or asks to contribute to the plan should have an understanding of the purposes and objectives. In addition, participants should know what will be expected of them. There should be no surprises nor any hidden agendas.

Instruments. You will have to determine what methods and instruments will be used to assess those factors you wish to evaluate. The instruments must be selected on the basis of which ones will do the best job of assessment based on the statement of objectives. This should be done cooperatively with your faculty and staff. It could be of value to get some feedback from selected faculty and staff about some of the self-evaluation instruments you may wish to use.

Schedule. An evaluation schedule is important and useful, but it must be flexible. You should estimate the amount of time it will take you and others to carry out the evaluation program or self-evaluation ideas. The schedule should include target dates for orienting participants; for designing, preparing, or purchasing instruments; for collecting data; for collating, summarizing, and analyzing the data; and for preparing the final report.

Results. When you reach this stage, you should ask yourself the following questions:

- What am I going to do with the results?
- What do the results confirm, reveal, or suggest?
- Do these results help me determine the extent to which the objectives have been accomplished?
- With whom will I share the results of this evaluation?

Follow-up. Data collection and analysis are futile exercises unless something is done with the results. You might ask yourself the following questions:

- What procedures are suggested as a result of my analysis of the results?
- Should I change some or all of our procedures or practices?

- Have I shared the results with those concerned and given them an opportunity to suggest ways to improve?
- Should I plan additional evaluative procedures to determine progress in correcting weaknesses and maintaining strengths?
- Do these results suggest other areas that should be evaluated?

An example. John Smith, principal of a secondary school wants to evaluate himself as an administrator. To do this he designs the following plan:

Purpose. The objective of this evaluation is to determine how teachers view me as an administrator of this school in relation to how I see myself. I want to identify my strengths and weaknesses as teachers see them.

Orientation. At the next faculty meeting I will ask the teachers to help me with this evaluation on the premise that I want to improve as the principal of this school. I will provide them with a reprint of two articles—one on why teachers should evaluate principals, and the other on the value of self-evaluation. I will review with them the instrument I plan to use. I will encourage honesty and insure anonymity. I will tell them that the results will be shared with them. I will ask them for suggestions for improvement.

Instruments. I will use the *Administrator Image Questionnaire* (see Evaluation Instruments listed in Chapter 6).

Schedule. I will complete the instrument by March 1. This evaluation instrument will then be given to the teachers one week after the March faculty meeting. Results will be tabulated and summarized by the end of April. At least one meeting with the teachers will be held in May to review results. Implementation will be scheduled for the next school year.

Results. The data from this questionnaire will be tabulated, summarized, and analyzed in a report that I will give to the teachers (and superintendent) for their review. It will compare my self-evaluation with their evaluation.

Follow-up. After discussing the results with the teachers, I will prepare a plan for correcting any identified weaknesses and for maintaining strengths. This plan will include some or all of my own ideas and those of the faculty. A new plan will be developed for the next school year and will follow the same pattern so that the changes I make can be evaluated.

To summarize this evaluating plan in question form, and to serve as a guide to principals, you must decide:

1. What is to be evaluated?
2. Why is it to be evaluated?
3. How is it to be evaluated?
4. When is it to be evaluated?
5. By whom is it to be evaluated?
6. How are the data to be collected?
7. How are the data to be analyzed?
8. How are the data to be reported?
9. To whom will the reports be presented?
10. What will be done with the results in the report?

These questions apply to self-evaluation techniques the principal uses as well as to the evaluation of any phase of the school operation and the evaluation of personnel. They are questions that you should refer to every time you wish to conduct an evaluation.

As mentioned earlier, this plan is an illustration of one plan of action. Others have suggested different formats worthy of your or the committee's consideration. For example, Morphet, Johns, and Reller[20] describe a six-phase plan that principals and teachers will find useful when organizing themselves for program or personnel evaluation.

Phase I: Goal Setting

1. School personnel agree on what is to be evaluated.
2. Specific objectives are identified.

Phase II: Data-Identification

1. Agreement is reached on types of data to be collected.
2. Agreement is reached on procedures to be followed.
3. Evaluation criteria are to be used to assess the degree of achievement.
4. Conditions, constraints, and limitations should be identified.

Phase III: Instrumentation

1. Data collection instruments are examined.
2. New instruments to be devised are agreed upon.
3. Agreement is reached on what instruments will be used.

Phase IV: Procedural

1. A ''review calendar'' is developed.
2. Place and time of administering instruments is established.
3. Methods to be used in data analysis are determined.

Phase V: Implementation

1. Procedures in the review calendar are implemented.
2. Deviations from review calendar are identified and agreed upon by the group.

Phase VI: Reporting

1. Results of the evaluation are reported in an impartial manner.
2. Report should include an accounting for deviations from the review calendar.
3. Proposals for improvement-change should be included.

Brieve, Johnston, and Young[21] provide another scheme in an interesting workbook on educational planning that includes:

1. Establish goals.
2. Assess needs.
3. Identify resources and restraints.

4. Formulate performance objectives and priorities.
5. Generate alternatives.
6. Analyze alternatives.
7. Select alternatives.
8. Develop and implement process objectives.
9. Evaluate process and performance objectives.
10. Modify the system.
11. Establish goals.

Each of the plans suggested in this and other chapters are presented to help you organize your plans for evaluation and are based upon the assumption that you value planning for change as much as you may value change itself.

A FINAL COMMENT

With the advent of team management, it may be best to view the words *principal-administrator-supervisor* to connote all school personnel who have administrative duties—assistant principals, department chairpersons, and unit leaders. Without a doubt, these people along with the principal will have to take the initiative and assume major responsibilities for the formulation and evaluation of school programs and personnel. Such a change will probably raise questions about time, priorities, and resources; and rightfully so. The job of the principal, your job, is to see to it that those engaged in this do-it-yourself evaluation scheme have the time and resources to do the job efficiently and effectively.

EVALUATION INSTRUMENTS

In addition to the books and periodicals recommended in the reference sections of each chapter, there are some specific books that are valuable resources for program and personnel evaluation that should be part of your school or school district's professional library:

Mental Measurement Yearbook Series. Gryphon Press, Highland Park, N.J.

The volumes in this series include descriptions of tests, critical reviews, publishers' directions, and bibliographical references. Included in the series are (1) *Mental Measurement Yearbooks*, (2) *Tests in Print*, (3) *Reading Tests and Reviews*, and (4) *Personality Tests and Reviews*.

Scales for the Measurement of Attitudes. Jack M. Wright and Marvin E. Shaw. McGraw-Hill Book Co., New York, 1967.

This book contains information on 176 attitude tests useful in assessing a person's attitudes and belief system regarding social practices, significant others, social institutions, political attitudes, and the like.

Taxonomy of Educational Objectives: Handbook I: Cognitive Domain. Benjamin S. Bloom, ed. Longmans, Green Co., New York, 1956.

This text is the standard reference for classifying educational objectives in the cognitive area.

Taxonomy of Educational Objectives: Handbook II: Affective Domain. David L. Drathwohl; Benjamin S. Bloom; and B. B. Macia. David McKay Co., New York, 1964.

This text is the standard reference for classifying educational objectives in the affective area.

Handbook on Formative and Summative Evaluation of Student Learning. B. S. Bloom, J. T. Hastings, G. F. Madaus, eds. McGraw-Hill Book Co., New York, 1971.

This handbook is a useful teacher and administrator resource to help in the use of evaluation techniques to improve teaching and learning, in general, and major disciplines, in particular. Part One of this book is informative to administrators for its discussion of education and evaluation, using evaluation for instructional decisions and evaluation models and techniques.

Handbook of Research on Teaching. N. L. Gage, ed. Rand McNally and Co., Chicago, 1963.

This first handbook reports the research regarding teaching methods, teaching instruments and media, and teachers' characteristics and personality. Equally informative is the section on research methodology. A second handbook has also been published (Robert Traver, ed., 1975).

Evaluating Classroom Instruction: A Sourcebook of Instruments. George D. Borick and Susan K. Madden. Addison-Wesley Publishing Co., Reading, Mass., 1977.

The authors provide a comprehensive review of currently available instruments for evaluating classroom instruction including evaluation of the teacher, the student, their attitudes, their interests, their self-concepts, their performances, the classroom climate, and the like.

CSE-ECRC Preschool/Kindergarten Test Evaluation (1971) and *CSE Elementary School Test Evaluations* (1970). Ralph Hoepfner et al., eds. Los Angeles: University of California, Center For the Study of Education.

Each volume has over one hundred instruments for assessing affective, cognitive, psychomotor, and subject matter domains/objectives.

CSE Secondary School Test Evaluations: Grades 7 and 8 (1974); *CSE Secondary School Test Evaluations: Grades 9 and 10* (1975); and *CSE Secondary School Test Evaluations: Grades 11 and 12* (1976). Ralph Hoepfner et al., eds. Los Angeles: University of California, Center For the Study of Education.

These volumes provide over 3,000 instruments for assessing objectives at each of the identified grade levels and for each of the subject matter areas in most junior-senior high schools.

Encyclopedia of Educational Evaluation. Scarvia B. Anderson; Samuel Ball; and Richard T. Murphy. San Francisco: Jossey-Bass Publishing Co., 1975.

A useful resource for administrators, teachers, and others who want to update their knowledge of evaluation, planning, designs, systems, applications, and techniques.

Handbook of Organization Development in Schools. Richard A. Schmuck; Philip J. Runkel; Steven L. Saturen; Ronald T. Martell; C. Brooklyn Dern. Palo Alto, Calif.: Mayfield Publishing Co., 1972.

This handbook is a "tool kit" for administrators and others who want to diagnose, develop, and implement change. The text contains a variety of strategies, exercises, procedures, ideas, and instruments for improving organizational patterns, communication, conflict, meetings, problem solving and decision making, training, and evaluation.

Educational Evaluation and Decision Making. Daniel I. Stufflebeam et al. Phi Delta Kappa, Bloomington, Ind. 1971.

The authors of this book, PDK's National Study Committee on Education, offer an invaluable aid to district level administrators and others involved in evaluation for decision making.

Using Evaluations: Does Evaluation Make A Difference? Marvin C. Allsin and Richard Daillak. Peter White Center for The Study of Evaluation, UCLA Sage Publications, Beverly Hills, Calif.

This book describes, through a case study approach, the reality of evaluation as it actually occurs in schools, asking the reader to discover "a theory of evaluative utilization."

School Administrator's Accountability Manual: Tested Programs to Improve Your School's Effectiveness. Jerry J. Herman. Parker Publishing Co., West Nyack, N.Y., 1979.

This book is filled with suggestions, techniques, and guidelines for ways to increase and improve management efficiency, accountability, and decision making. Case studies and school accountability techniques used in related school districts provide usable, tested ideas and procedures for practicing administrators.

School Principal's Handbook of Evaluation Guidelines. John Frank, Jr. Parker Publishing Co., West Nyack, N.Y., 1979.

This handbook contains descriptions of the "best practices of twenty-five carefully selected school districts and dozens of individuals who are actively involved with various phases of school evaluation." This book provides specific guidelines and a variety of evaluation forms for assessing school programs and personnel.

ENDNOTES

1. See, for example, James B. Macdonald, "The Quality of Everyday Life in School," in *Schools in Search of Meaning,* ed. James B. Macdonald and Esther Zaret (Washington, D.C.: Association for Supervision and Curriculum Development, 1975), Chapter 4.

2. Theodore M. Black, "The Political Role of Educators," *Educational Leadership* 34 (November 1976): 122.

3. John E. Goodlad, *Accountability: An Alternative Perspective* (DeGamo Lecture, Society of Professors of Education, 1978), pp. 13, 15.

4. Francis Roberts, "School Principal: Minor Bureaucrat or Educational Leader?" *Urban Review* 8 (October 1975): 243.

5. Paul Woodring, "A Second Open Letter to Teachers," *Phi Delta Kappan* 59 (April 1978): 516.

6. Allan C. Ornstein, "Administrative Decentralization and Community Control," *Educational Forum* 39 (May 1975): 449–463.

7. Ray Cross, "The Administrative Team or Decentralization?" *National Elementary Principal* 54 (November/December 1974): 82.

8. Ernest R. House et al., "No Simple Answer: Critique of the 'Follow Through' Evaluation," *Educational Leadership* 35 (March 1978): 462.

9. John I. Goodlad and M. Frances Klein, *Looking Behind the Classroom Door* (Worthington, Ohio: Charles A. Jones Publishing Co., 1974).

10. Roberts, "School Principal," pp. 243, 247.

11. Michael Aiken and Jerald Hage, "Organizational Alienation: A Comparative Analysis," *American Sociological Review* 31 (August 1966): 497–507.

12. Ronald Brandt, "On Evaluation: An Interview with Daniel L. Stufflebeam," *Educational Leadership* 35 (January 1978): 253.

13. Elliot W. Eisner, "Some Alternatives To Quantitative Forms of Educational Evaluation." *Thrust For Educational Leadership* 5 (November 1975): 13–15.

14. Robert E. Stake and Gordon A. Hoke, "Evaluating An Arts Program: Movement and Dance In a Downstate District," *National Elementary School Principal* 55 (January/February 1976): 52–59.

15. Ibid., p. 54.

16. Howard J. Demeke, "Theory in Educational Administration: A Systems Approach," in *A Systems Approach to Educational Administration,* ed. Robert C. Maxson and Walter E. Sistrunk (Dubuque, Iowa: W. C. Brown Co., 1973), p. 33.

17. For an excellent discussion or sampling technique, see Clifford J. Drew, *Introduction to Designing Research and Evaluation* (St. Louis: C. V. Mosby, 1976), Chapter 5.

18. Robert B. Howsam and John M. Franco, "New Emphases in Evaluation of Administrations," *National Elementary Principal* 64 (April 1975): 40.

19. See, for example, Fred P. Barnes, *Research for the Practitioner in Education* (Washington, D.C.: Department of Elementary School Principals, NEA, 1964); and Paul R. Leedy, *Practical Research Planning and Design* (New York: Macmillan Publishing Co., 1974).

20. Edgar L. Morphet, Roe L. Johns, and Theodore L. Reller, *Educational Organization and Administration* (Englewood Cliffs, N.J.: Prentice-Hall, Inc., 1974), pp. 550–552.

21. Fred J. Brieve, A. P. Johnston, and Ken Young, *Educational Planning* (Worthington, Ohio: Charles A. Jones Publishing Co., 1973), p. 16.

SELECTED REFERENCES

Bell, Terrel H. *A Performance Accountability System for School Administrators.* West Nyack, N.Y.: Parker Publishing Co., 1974.

Bushnell, David S., and Rappaport, Donald, eds. *Planned Change in Education: A Systems Approach.* New York: Harcourt Brace Jovanovich, 1971.

De Novellis, Richard L., and Lewis, Arthur J. *Schools Become Accountable: A PACT Approach.* Washington, D.C.: Association for Supervision and Curriculum Development, 1974.

Ewing, David W. *The Human Side of Planning.* New York: Macmillan Co., 1969.

Gephart, William J. *Evaluation: Past, Present, and Future.* Bloomington, Ind.: Phi Delta Kappa, 1975.

Goodlad, John I. "A Perspective on Accountability." *Phi Delta Kappan* 57 (October 1975): 108–112.

Hartley, Harry J. "PPBS In Local Schools: A Short Report." *Bulletin of the National Association of Secondary School Principals* 56 (October 1972): 1–16.

Lessinger, Leon M. *Every Kid A Winner: Accountability in Education.* New York: Simon and Schuster, 1970.

Matthews, Maxin R. "Educational Accountability: To Whom—For What?" *Thrust For Educational Leadership* 2 (October 1972): 5–10.

Performance Based Management Systems: A Method for Accomplishment. Harrisburg, Penn.: Department of Education, ESEA Title III, 1976.

Rothman, Jack; English, John L.; and Theresa, Joseph G. *Promoting Innovation and Change in Organizations and Communities: A Planning Manual.* New York: John Wiley and Sons, 1976.

Schmuck, Richard A., and Runkel, Philip J. *Organizational Training for a School Faculty.* Eugene, Ore.: The Center for the Advanced Study of Educational Administration, 1970.

Wick, John W., and Beggs, Donald L. *Evaluation for Decision-Making in the Schools.* Boston: Houghton Mifflin, 1971.

2

EVALUATING SCHOOL AND CLASSROOM CLIMATE

The primary basis for evaluating a school should be whether the students and teachers find it a satisfying place to be.

Christopher Jencks

Even casual observers of schools are aware of the climate, the atmosphere, that intangible that one feels when one walks into a school. How many times have you heard school visitors reflect on the atmosphere and reputation of their local school?

"You walk into that school and you get a feeling that they know what school is all about."

"That school is a very pleasant place to be."

"It's a zoo!"

"They are so disorganized; I don't know how people can work there everyday."

"Don't go there when they're changing classes. You'll get trampled."

"I'm afraid to go into that school alone!"

Regardless of the reliability of these remarks, they reflect people's perceptions of school, and unfortunately for principals, many of the negative perceptions are expressed publically. School climate, then, is an important concern for school principals. Principals directly affect the climate within their school by their leadership style, the opportunities they provide for school personnel to grow professionally and personally, and the atmosphere of trust, openness, and humaneness they attempt to create. These are not just words for the printed page for we do know that the school climate influences the behavior of school personnel. We do know that maximum productivity is attained in a threat-free climate. We do know that school climate influences innovation and change. We do know that administrative behavior and style

21

affects the climate of a school. We also know that classroom climate is influenced by the general climate of the school and a teacher's style and performance.

ORGANIZATIONAL/SCHOOL CLIMATE: SOME GENERALIZATIONS

The principal plays a crucial role in creating a psychologically and physically healthful school climate. In order to effectively accomplish the leadership tasks required in creating a school climate free from fears, threats, coersion, physical violence, and vandalism, it would seem best to summarize the research in this area. Here, then, are some generalizations regarding an organization's climate:

1. Climate is significantly associated with the accuracy of communications in that a hostile, more closed, formal climate tends to block communications while a supportive, relatively open, informal climate with high levels of trust facilitates accuracy in communications.
2. An open and supportive climate produces greater spontaneity and initiative and tends to improve decision making and problem-solving ability of those affected.
3. An open and supportive climate tends to promote greater production and improved quality on both voluntary and required tasks.
4. An open and supportive climate tends to build greater commitment to and enthusiasm for the philosophy and mission of the organization.
5. A closed and hostile climate, on the other hand, tends to produce greater dependence upon the formal leaders and less upon group member initiative.
6. A closed and hostile climate tends to promote self-interest, lack of creativity, and lack of enthusiasm for the work of the organization.
7. A closed and hostile climate produces greater anxiety and passiveness toward the organization and its mission.
8. A closed and hostile climate often produces defensiveness and a resistance to ideas and suggestions, whereas a supportive climate tends to produce outgoing, open, tolerant employees and clientele.[1]

These generalizations suggest that a school principal would want to examine the school climate to determine the extent to which (1) there is effective communication; (2) school personnel view the climate to be "open" or "closed"; (3) the existing climate contributes to creativity, experimentation, and the expression of individual skill and talent; and (4) the principal's behavior contributes to a positive, productive, and pleasing environment. It is for these reasons that a school principal evaluates people's perceptions of the climate of the school. It is necessary to know how people view the school climate in order to implement ideas for improving that climate. The positive and negative factors existing in the school environment should be explored because many of these may have a direct bearing on effective teaching and learning. There is a need to know because "the climate of an organization is the first and most important concern in initiating and sustaining change."[2] There is also a need to know because of the relationship between the principles of organizational structure and theories of leadership. This relationship has been summarized as follows:

1. Organizational structure is designed as an instrument by which members of an organization together with their clients outside of the organization arrive at mutual goals and ways of achieving them.
2. Organizational structure is invented to carry policy agreement into action. . . . Rules and regulations agreed upon by members should become formal procedures of the organization. They should be written and constantly tested for their effectiveness as a means of achieving the goals intended.
3. The operational procedures must provide for a division of labor with a definite set of job expectations for each of the members. . . .

Team effort can be accomplished only by diligent effort to arrive at agreement about their functions and the relationships that must exist among them.

4. The authority for the activity carried on by members of the organization is derived from three sources: the legal limitations placed upon the institution, the institutional policy, and the agreement on job expectations indicated above.

5. Adequate provision is made for the emergence of leadership with the organization. . . . The organization places great reliance on emergent leadership.

6. Status in an organization is earned through group acceptance and demonstration of competence and not by virtue of assignment.

7. Organizational structure makes provision for catalytic, coordinating, expediting, consulting, helping, appraising, and controlling functions.

8. Organizational structure encourages both formal and informal communication.

9. Organizational structure provides resource people who work toward organizational betterment through small groups.

10. Innovation, creativity, experimentation are encouraged as means of improving the achievement of institutional purposes.

11. Appraising the effectiveness of the school is of vital importance.[3]

These two summaries should encourage you to use the references at the end of this chapter for further study of the concepts of organizational structure, climate, and leadership.

COMPETENCY RATING SCALE

Klopf et al. have developed a taxonomy of leadership competencies, one of which is the development of a humanistic climate.[4] The authors believe that certain tasks are required if a principal hopes to attain this leadership competency. Each question in the following rating scale contains a competency that implies something you should be doing in your school. For example, the question, "Is the team concept one that you should try to develop among school personnel?" suggests that you, as the principal, should try to create a team effort among school personnel since this may be a factor contributing to a more humanistic climate.

The questions for competency enable you to compare your self-evaluation response (P) with those of the faculty (T) and others (O) you select to complete the scale. Following the scale is a suggestion for scoring and comparing the results.*

Question	*Definitely/ Always*		*Occasionally/ Sometimes*		*Seldom/ Never*
(1) P: Is the team concept one that you try to develop among school personnel?	5	4	3	2	1
T: Has your principal developed or tried to implement a team concept in your school?	5	4	3	2	1

*Permission to reprint the specific tasks has been granted. Copyright 1975, National Association of Elementary School Principals. All rights reserved.

Question	Definitely/ Always		Occasionally/ Sometimes		Seldom/ Never
O: Do you feel that teachers and administrator(s) work together as a team?	5	4	3	2	1
(2) P: Do you delegate leadership responsibility among members of your staff when appropriate?	5	4	3	2	1
T: Has your principal delegated leadership responsibility to teachers and others when appropriate?	5	4	3	2	1
(3) P: Do you make yourself accessible to teachers?	5	4	3	2	1
T: Is your principal accessible to the teachers in this school?	5	4	3	2	1
O: Do you feel that the principal is accessible to the teachers of this school?	5	4	3	2	1
(4) P: Do you encourage teachers to share their problems, needs, feelings, and frustrations with you?	5	4	3	2	1

Question	Definitely/ Always		Occasionally/ Sometimes		Seldom/ Never
T: Can teachers share their problems, needs, feelings, and frustrations with the principal?	5	4	3	2	1
O: Do you feel that teachers are encouraged to share their problems, needs, feelings, and frustrations with the principal?	5	4	3	2	1
(5) P: Have you worked cooperatively with school personnel and its clientele to develop goals and objectives for this school?	5	4	3	2	1
T: Have teachers worked with the principal and others to develop goals and objectives for this school?	5	4	3	2	1
O: Do you feel that the principal, teachers, parents, and others have worked cooperatively to develop goals and objectives for this school?	5	4	3	2	1

Question	Definitely/ Always		Occasionally/ Sometimes		Seldom/ Never
(6) P: Do you encourage teachers and other school personnel to implement strategies for carrying out school objectives?	5	4	3	2	1
T: Have teachers been encouraged to implement strategies that will carry out school objectives?	5	4	3	2	1
O: Do you feel that the principal encourages teachers and others to implement strategies that carry out school objectives?	5	4	3	2	1
(7) P: Have you developed with others in the school an assessment program that will determine the school's effectiveness?	5	4	3	2	1
T: Have teachers and others been involved in developing an assessment program to determine the school's effectiveness?	5	4	3	2	1

Question	Definitely/ Always		Occasionally/ Sometimes		Seldom/ Never
O: Do you feel that the teachers, principal, and others have an assessment program that determines the effectiveness of this school?	5	4	3	2	1
(8) P: Do you include classroom teachers, personnel staff, special teachers (art, music, p.e., etc.), and others to share their ideas and perceptions about each child in the school?	5	4	3	2	1
T: Are you involved in sharing your ideas and perceptions about each child in your classroom with pupil personnel staff, special teachers, and others?	5	4	3	2	1
O: Does the school staff (special teachers, guidance counselors, psychologist, aides, and others) share their ideas about each child with the classroom teacher and vice versa?	5	4	3	2	1

Question	Definitely/ Always		Occasionally/ Sometimes		Seldom/ Never
(9) P: Do you help teachers and parents share their ideas and perceptions of a child's strengths, weaknesses, and potential and plan accordingly?	5	4	3	2	1
T: Are you encouraged by the administration to discuss with parents their child's strengths, weaknesses, and potential and cooperatively develop plans to help the child?	5	4	3	2	1
O: Do you feel that teachers are encouraged by the administration to share information with parents and to cooperatively plan ideas that will meet the child's learning needs?	5	4	3	2	1
(10) P: Do you involve school staff to personally recruit parent volunteers?	5	4	3	2	1
T: Are you personally involved in recruiting parent volunteers?	5	4	3	2	1

Question	Definitely/ Always		Occasionally/ Sometimes		Seldom/ Never
O: Do you feel that the school staff is encouraged to personally recruit parent volunteers?	5	4	3	2	1
(11) P: Do you plan and implement parent workshops that will help them work with children in school or at home?	5	4	3	2	1
T: Are workshops for parents planned and implemented by teachers and the principal?	5	4	3	2	1
O: Does this school offer parent workshops that will help them help their child at home and at school?	5	4	3	2	1
(12) P: Do you solicit and use ideas and suggestions from teachers and others when planning the school program?	5	4	3	2	1
T: Are teachers encouraged to share ideas and suggestions with the principal when planning the school program?	5	4	3	2	1

Question	Definitely/ Always		Occasionally/ Sometimes		Seldom/ Never
O: Do you feel that the ideas and suggestions of teachers and others are considered when the school's programs are being planned?	5	4	3	2	1
(13) P: Do you encourage (by some action) a stronger relation-ship between teachers and instructional aides?	5	4	3	2	1
T: Does your princi-pal implement plans that encourage you and other teachers to develop a positive relationship with instructional aides?	5	4	3	2	1
O: Does the principal encourage a posi-tive relationship between teachers and instructional aides?	5	4	3	2	1
(14) P: Do you meet formally and/or informally with students and encourage them to share ideas, prob-lems, needs, and feelings with you?	5	4	3	2	1

Question	Definitely/ Always		Occasionally/ Sometimes		Seldom/ Never
T: Are the students in the school encouraged to share their ideas, problems, needs, and feelings with the principal?	5	4	3	2	1
O: Do you feel that the students are encouraged to share their ideas, problems, needs, and feelings with the principal?	5	4	3	2	1

Humanistic Climate Summary:

1. Add your score and place it on the line:____
2. Find the mean of the teachers' scores (add their scores and divide by the number of teachers). Place the mean score on the line:____
3. Find the mean score of the "others" (add their scores and divide by the number who completed the scale). Place the mean score on the line:____

Do teachers and others perceive you differently on this competency than you see yourself? What items showed the greater discrepancy between your self-perception and those of teachers and others? What can you do about this? What specific plans can you make that might change their perceptions? Were there items on which you were rated high (5–4) by teachers and yet you rated yourself lower (3-2-1)? What do you feel caused this discrepancy?

A school's climate is the direct result of attitudes, behavior, and interactions among teachers, administrators, parents, students, and staff. If a study of a school's climate reveals that there is a lack of trust, a lack of openness, a feeling that the school is not moving toward its goals, that members are not satisfied, and that it is less than a humane place to be, then it would seem that school personnel and parents should be confronted with evidence. Maybe an objective analysis of the evidence will help some people change their behavior and create plans for trying to improve the school's climate. The evidence of a positive, open, trustful, supportive climate of a school should also be shared with others. This evidence can be gathered from the instruments recommended at the end of this chapter and those described in this chapter.

ASSESSING CLIMATE: A CHECKLIST

The role of a philanthropic foundation in assessing and improving the climate of schools is exemplary. The CFK Ltd., a philanthropic foundation founded by the late Charles F. Kettering II in 1967, exists to be of service to public education by assisting school systems in "developing individualized continuing education programs for their school administrators, developing learning programs for principals and other administrators so that they might serve as climate leaders within their schools and/or school systems and using the results of the above endeavors on a non-grant basis."[5]

CFK Ltd. has published two booklets related to school climate. The first is titled *The Principal as the School's Climate Leader: A New Role for the Principalship.* The second, and the one reviewed in this section, is titled *School Climate Improvement: A Challenge to the School Administrator.*

The authors identify two major goals of a humane school climate. One is *productivity;* that is, a wholesome, stimulating, and productive learning environment conducive to academic achievement and personal growth of youth at different levels of development. The other is *satisfaction;* that is, a pleasant and satisfying school situation within which many people can live and work.

The authors list eight factors that affect the climate of a school, all of which are essential to establishing a humane school climate. The authors encourage readers to delete or add items; each factor has broad descriptions summarized as follows:

1. Respect—for students, teachers, administrators, others; a place for self-respecting individuals; no put-downs.
2. Trust—confidence that behavior will be honest, straightforward; belief that others will not let you down.
3. High Morale—school personnel feel good about what is happening.
4. Opportunities for Input—opportunities to share ideas, know that they are considered; self-esteem; part of the decision-making process; use of personnel resources.
5. Continuous Academic and Social Growth—opportunities for students and school personnel to improve their skills, knowledge, attitudes academically and socially.
6. Cohesiveness—a person's feeling toward the school; have a chance to exert their influence in collaboration with others.
7. School Renewal—develop improvement projects; self-renewing; value pluralism, diversity; "new" not seen as threatening; school is organized to approve improvement projects rapidly, effectively without stress, conflict, frustration.
8. Caring—school personnel feel that others care for them; each knows it will make a difference to someone else if he is happy or sad, healthy or ill.[6]

These qualities, coupled with the basic human needs of school personnel, are essential to a productive and satisfying environment. The basic human needs include physiological needs, safety needs, acceptance and friendship needs, achievement and recognition needs, and needs that maximize one's potential.[7]

The School Problems Checklist shown in Figure 2–1 is a quick way for a school principal to examine the existing school climate. While many of the problems on the checklist require a good deal of administrative time and energy, they are only symptomatic of deeper climate concerns. Any administrator who checks the first two columns regularly should study the problem in greater detail. The evaluation instruments described at the end of this chapter will help the school principal accomplish this task.

ASSESSING THE SCHOOL'S ORGANIZATIONAL HEALTH

A healthy school climate is a prelude to change. Organizational health has long been considered an important factor to change, innovation, and individual and group productivity. As part of this dis-

Figure 2–1
School Problems Checklist*

	Extent of Problems		
Problems	Great	Moderate	Little/None
1. Vandalism	——	——	——
2. Truancy	——	——	——
3. Student behavior	——	——	——
4. School spirit	——	——	——
5. Student dropout rate	——	——	——
6. Student absentee rate	——	——	——
7. Student attitude toward school	——	——	——
8. Student feelings about teachers	——	——	——
9. Student verbal/physical abuse	——	——	——
10. Student apathy toward school events	——	——	——
11. Students carrying weapons	——	——	——
12. Problems on playground/parking lot	——	——	——
13. Student harassment of local merchants	——	——	——
14. Student feelings that they are merely a "number" because of the size of the school	——	——	——
15. Crowded conditions	——	——	——
16. Weak student government	——	——	——
17. Incidences of suspensions	——	——	——
18. Incidences of expulsions	——	——	——
19. Thefts of student property	——	——	——
20. Thefts of teacher/staff property	——	——	——
21. Thefts of school property	——	——	——
22. Teacher/staff apathy	——	——	——
23. Teacher/staff cliques	——	——	——
24. Teacher/staff absentee rate	——	——	——
25. Unavailability of supplies/equipment	——	——	——
26. School image in the community	——	——	——
27. Negative newspaper articles about school	——	——	——
28. Number and kind of complaints from school neighbors	——	——	——
29. Other_____	——	——	——
30. Other_____	——	——	——

*Adapted from Robert H. Fox et al., *School Climate Improvement: A Challenge to the School Administrator* (Bloomington, Indiana: Phi Delta Kappa, n.d.), p. 3.

cussion about school climate, it is imperative that you, the principal, recognize the conditions that promote organizational health because organizational health influences the school's climate and potential for change and innovation. Suggestions have been provided for evaluating the climate of the school. What can a principal do to determine the "health" of the school?

Kimpston and Sonnabend[8] completed a study designed to determine whether there is a relationship between a school's organizational health and innovation in schools. Specifically, they ask whether faculty members view their school's organizational health more positively when the school is engaged in some innovative practices. Twenty junior or senior high schools were identified as least innovative, and twenty were identified as most innovative. Using an instrument that they developed (see Figure 2–2) and administered to the faculty (1134) in these forty schools, these researchers found that faculty members in innovative schools viewed school's organizational health more positively particularly on factors of decision making (the extent to which a building administration involves staff in the decision-making process for solving problems); innovativeness (how the staff members feel about trying new methods, new designs, and new programs); and community relations (how well the school staff act and react with their surrounding environment).

Figure 2–2
Organizational Health Description Questionnaire*

Directions: The purpose of this questionnaire is to secure a description of (1) the organizational behaviors of public school faculty, and (2) the organizational conditions under which faculty members work. The items in the questionnaire describe typical behaviors or conditions that exist within a secondary school. Please indicate to what extent each of these descriptions characterize *your school*. Do not evaluate the items in terms of "good" or "bad" behaviors or conditions. Respond in terms of how well the statement describes the conditions in your school. Read each item carefully and mark your answers by placing a check mark on the appropriate line. Your response will remain anonymous. Be as candid as possible.

	Strongly Agree (A)	Mildly Agree (B)	Mildly Disagree (C)	Strongly Disagree (D)
1. Teachers willingly spend time after school with students who seek their help.	___	___	___	___
2. There is a feeling of togetherness within the faculty.	___	___	___	___
3. Teachers are willing to try innovations in this school.	___	___	___	___
4. The school administration provides needed information to the staff.	___	___	___	___
5. Decision making in this school could best be described as democratic.	___	___	___	___
6. Students are involved in decision making in this school.	___	___	___	___
7. Efforts are made by the faculty to discuss this school's goals.	___	___	___	___
8. Problems are solved in this school and not just ignored.	___	___	___	___

(cont.)

*Richard D. Kimpston and Leslie C. Sonnabend, Mimeograph. Reprinted by permission from the authors.

	Strongly Agree (A)	Mildly Agree (B)	Mildly Disagree (C)	Strongly Disagree (D)
9. A deterrent to change in this school is the stress which accompanies that change.	___	___	___	___
10. Feedback information is secured and utilized in conducting and sustaining change in our school.	___	___	___	___
11. Teachers value their professional association with this faculty.	___	___	___	___
12. In our school there is willingness to respond to community requests but the action taken is based upon professional knowledge.	___	___	___	___
13. Teachers feel threatened by community pressures.	___	___	___	___
14. Faculty members are aware of instructional resources available to them within their community.	___	___	___	___
15. Many school problems are solved by individual faculty members because the organization in generally unresponsive.	___	___	___	___
16. There is generally a pessimistic atmosphere in this school.	___	___	___	___
17. Teachers in this school present new ideas for improvement.	___	___	___	___
18. The goals of this school are seen as achievable by faculty members.	___	___	___	___
19. Teachers feel that communication lines are open with the school administration.	___	___	___	___
20. In general, teachers' opinions are valued in decision making.	___	___	___	___
21. Faculty opinions are solicited but seldom used in our school.	___	___	___	___
22. Educational changes are generally made in our school without sufficient study and preparation.	___	___	___	___
23. Our school has procedures for identifying school problems.	___	___	___	___
24. Many school problems are solved by group action.	___	___	___	___
25. The right person is doing the right job in this school.	___	___	___	___

(cont.)

	Strongly Agree (A)	Mildly Agree (B)	Mildly Disagree (C)	Strongly Disagree (D)
26. Innovativeness is uncharacteristic of this school.	____	____	____	____
27. Community requests receive scant attention in this school.	____	____	____	____
28. Resource personnel available within this school district are utilized in this school.	____	____	____	____
29. Faculty members view school goals as appropriate.	____	____	____	____
30. The public is made aware of our school's activities.	____	____	____	____
31. Any faculty member in this school may assume leadership responsibilities.	____	____	____	____
32. Solutions to problems are actively sought from the staff.	____	____	____	____
33. This school has an ongoing plan for facilitating change.	____	____	____	____
34. The strengths of faculty members are utilized in this school.	____	____	____	____
35. Teachers enjoy getting together informally with other faculty members.	____	____	____	____
36. Ideas for improvement generally receive support in this school.	____	____	____	____
37. Teachers in this school are given considerable latitude in carrying out instruction.	____	____	____	____
38. Faculty members are generally unaware that goals exist for this school.	____	____	____	____
39. Procedures for communication with the community have been established.	____	____	____	____
40. Decision making in this school could best be described as undemocratic.	____	____	____	____
41. It is difficult to change anything in this school.	____	____	____	____
42. In our school, procedures have been established to evaluate our effectiveness in resolving school problems.	____	____	____	____

(cont.)

	Strongly Agree (A)	Mildly Agree (B)	Mildly Disagree (C)	Strongly Disagree (D)
43. There is general agreement by faculty members as to the appropriateness of the school goals.	——	——	——	——
44. Most teachers make an effort to communicate with the administration.	——	——	——	——
45. There is no opportunity for faculty to grow and develop professionally in this school.	——	——	——	——
46. Many teachers attend school social functions.	——	——	——	——
47. Most teachers would rather teach in this school than someplace else.	——	——	——	——
48. A climate of experimentation pervades this school.	——	——	——	——
49. Teachers are protected from unreasonable community and parental demands.	——	——	——	——
50. The teachers in this building enjoy their work.	——	——	——	——

You might find the results of the questionnaire interesting and informative. Rather than obtaining a total score it may be best that you examine the teachers' rating for each characteristic so that you can plan for change—improvement if it is needed. It is easiest to give each teacher a score sheet, as shown in Figure 2–3, for this purpose.

An item analysis is also possible and informative. For example, have the teachers rate each of the five statements regarding "innovativeness." How many of your teachers willingly innovate by trying new ideas for improvement? Is there an atmosphere and support for change and for trying new ideas? How many of your teachers feel that change, innovativeness, and trying new ideas is not a priority?

Is it possible for a principal to administer a school with an unhealthy climate? Probably so—at least for a short period of time. I have seen situations where school principals, resulting from their own insecurities and distrust of people, contributed to a school climate that warped faculty attitudes. These principals encouraged only responses that they wanted to hear, promoted superficial change, were master manipulators of individuals and groups, and controlled communication flowing in and out of school. They are among those who resist change and look for excuses such as, "You guys at the college level don't know what it's like to be a principal in the real world!" One can easily lose count of the number of excuses some teachers and principals provide for not solving their problems, for not wanting to change, innovate, or try new things. The most frequent excuse is to blame it on the "system." In city school districts the "system" is usually identified as the central office. "We can't change; we can't do that because it won't sell with the people at central office." In smaller school districts, the "system" is usually the superintendent or sometimes the board of education. For the board of education, the "system" is the public or the

Figure 2–3
Organizational Health Description Questionnaire Score Sheet

Directions: Your name is not necessary. Please take the Organizational Health Description Questionnaire that you just completed and *circle* the number that corresponds to the letter you circled for each item. Add your circled numbers for each characteristic and place it on the line.

Characteristic	Items	A	B	C	D	
Goal	7	4	3	2	1	
Focus	18	4	3	2	1	
	29	4	3	2	1	
	38	1	2	3	4	
	43	4	3	2	1	——
Communication	4	4	3	2	1	
Adequacy	19	4	3	2	1	
	30	4	3	2	1	
	39	4	3	2	1	
	44	4	3	2	1	——
Optimal Power	5	4	3	2	1	
Equalization	20	4	3	2	1	
	6	4	3	2	1	
	31	4	3	2	1	
	40	1	2	3	4	——
Resource	14	4	3	2	1	
Utilization	25	4	3	2	1	
	28	4	3	2	1	
	34	4	3	2	1	
	45	1	2	3	4	——
Cohesiveness	2	4	3	2	1	
	11	4	3	2	1	
	15	1	2	3	4	
	24	4	3	2	1	
	47	4	3	2	1	——
Morale	1	4	3	2	1	
	16	1	2	3	4	
	35	4	3	2	1	
	46	4	3	2	1	
	50	4	3	2	1	——

(cont.)

Characteristic	Items	Score			
		A	B	C	D
Innovativeness	3	4	3	2	1
	17	4	3	2	1
	26	1	2	3	4
	36	4	3	2	1
	38	4	3	2	1 |_____
Autonomy	12	4	3	2	1
	13	1	2	3	4
	27	1	2	3	4
	37	4	3	2	1
	49	4	3	2	1 |_____
Adaptation	9	1	2	3	4
	10	4	3	2	1
	22	1	2	3	4
	33	4	3	2	1
	41	1	2	3	4 |_____
Problem-Solving Adequacy	8	4	3	2	1
	21	1	2	3	4
	23	4	3	2	1
	32	4	3	2	1
	42	4	3	2	1 |_____

community. And so it goes. The "system," that barrier to change, varies according to the people you talk to and their position in the school's organizational structure.

But there are many principals who are leaders, who want their schools to be the best possible, and who encourage and get faculty, parent, and student loyalty, input, work. There are principals who take educational risks because they believe it will benefit students. There are principals who want to know how they and their staff and their school are doing. There are principals, armed with information, who plan carefully to change those things that need to be changed. There are principals who

would not fit Charles Silberman's major criticism of educators, namely, their "mindlessness"; that is, "the failure or refusal to think seriously about educational purpose and the reluctance to question established practices."[9]

There are several instruments suggested in Chapter 5 that will help teachers and principals/supervisors assess the climate of the classroom. For example, the Tuckman Teacher Feedback Form (Figure 5–11) has been described and recommended by Ronald Hyman as one way to observe and improve classroom climate.[10] In this section the emphasis will be on finding out how students feel about the climate of their classroom.

Assessing Student Perceptions

The scale in Figure 2–4 is an easy way for teachers and students to assess their views and perceptions of the class. As you can see, the student or teacher merely checks the space near the adjective that best describes personal feelings about the class. This attitude scale takes only two or three minutes to complete. To obtain a total score, assign the value of 5, 4, 3, 2, and 1 to each of the spaces for all odd-numbered items. Reverse the numbering (1, 2, 3, 4, and 5) for all even-numbered items. Then add the numbers where a check mark has been placed. It is best not to include the third space (3) in the tabulation. The scores will range from 15 (very poor attitude) to 75 (very positive attitude). You could arbitrarily decide that students with a score ranging from 60 to 75 are those with positive attitudes and those with scores between 15 to 30 have negative attitudes.

Once these data are available, a teacher then knows how many students have negative attitudes. For example, suppose a teacher finds that twelve out of thirty students have negative attitudes. The task then is to determine why these twelve students have this kind of attitude. What might be causing this feeling? These and other questions may be answered by individual consultation with each student (if names were placed on the scale) or by conducting a class discussion.

Rating Our Class

Another way teachers can gain insight into the perceptions students have about their class is shown below. In this case students are asked to estimate how many students in their class reflect the characteristics listed. Students must place a check mark on the appropriate line. (Teachers may also use this scale by changing the question stem to, "How many students in your class . . . ?").

How many students in class:	*All* *100%*	*Half* *50%*	*Some* *25%*	*None* *0%*
1. don't care about what's going on in class?	___	___	___	___
2. seem bored and uninterested?	___	___	___	___
3. leave their seats without permission?	___	___	___	___
4. don't do as the teacher requests?	___	___	___	___
5. are enjoyable to work with?	___	___	___	___
6. copy from others?	___	___	___	___
7. ask questions about the subject?	___	___	___	___
8. ask the teacher for help when they need it?	___	___	___	___
9. pay attention when the teacher is talking?	___	___	___	___
10. willingly participate in class activities?	___	___	___	___
11. are courteous and cooperative?	___	___	___	___
12. willingly assume responsibility?	___	___	___	___
13. complete assignments without complaining?	___	___	___	___
14. are prepared to discuss the topic or subject being taught?	___	___	___	___
15. enjoy coming to class?	___	___	___	___

Figure 2–4
Our Class

Directions: Place a check mark on the line nearest each word that describes our class in your opinion. If you have no strong feeling about the item, place the check mark on the third line.

Our Class

1. Active	___	___	___	___	___	Passive
2. Bored	___	___	___	___	___	Interested
3. Prepared	___	___	___	___	___	Unprepared
4. Restless	___	___	___	___	___	Attentive
5. Responsible	___	___	___	___	___	Obstructive
6. Uncertain	___	___	___	___	___	Confident
7. Alert	___	___	___	___	___	Apathetic
8. Thoughtless	___	___	___	___	___	Thoughtful
9. Good	___	___	___	___	___	Bad
10. Ignorant	___	___	___	___	___	Intelligent
11. Foolish	___	___	___	___	___	Wise
12. Sociable	___	___	___	___	___	Unsociable
13. Happy	___	___	___	___	___	Sad
14. Tense	___	___	___	___	___	Relaxed
15. Cheerful	___	___	___	___	___	Depressed

Class Opinionnaire

Some teachers may wish to assess student feelings about the climate of the class by having them answer questions about it. Figure 2–5 is an example of an opinionnaire.

Classroom Climate Checklist

The following checklist can provide some useful data to teachers about the climate of the classroom in relation to teacher behavior, student behavior, interrelationships, and physical conditions. In the checklist, all of the odd-numbered items are negative factors; that is, factors that may contribute to a poor classroom climate. Students should merely check those items that tell about "life" in their classroom:

1. ____ students seldom study or do their work
2. ____ teacher praises us
3. ____ teacher seems to have favorite students
4. ____ students are encouraged to ask questions
5. ____ teacher calls on the same students all the time
6. ____ a lot of instructional materials are used
7. ____ teacher uses worksheets too much
8. ____ teacher has a good sense of humor
9. ____ students need to participate more in class
10. ____ teacher makes subject(s) interesting
11. ____ teacher is sarcastic
12. ____ students are not afraid to answer questions
13. ____ more students should be allowed to participate in discussions
14. ____ students are not afraid of being smart
15. ____ teacher needs to know us better
16. ____ teacher apologizes for personal mistakes
17. ____ teacher's tests are difficult to understand
18. ____ students take care of bulletin boards
19. ____ teacher doesn't let us make many decisions
20. ____ students have a feeling of accomplishment

21. _____ assignments are generally boring
22. _____ students help each other to do a good job
23. _____ teacher doesn't give us interesting things to do
24. _____ students can work on things they like to do
25. _____ teacher has little or no control over students
26. _____ teacher lets us plan class activities
27. _____ teacher doesn't smile much; seems grouchy
28. _____ students can work together to solve problems
29. _____ teacher lectures too much
30. _____ teacher lets us plan some of the assignments
31. _____ more group activities are needed
32. _____ teacher makes us work hard
33. _____ too many students disrupt class
34. _____ teacher helps us to know each other better
35. _____ teacher talks too much
36. _____ teacher and students are well-organized
37. _____ teacher never calls on nonvolunteers
38. _____ classroom is cheerful and bright
39. _____ teacher's directions are seldom clear
40. _____ students have a good feeling about being in this class
41. _____ students don't have much respect for the teacher
42. _____ students are proud of this class
43. _____ students need to take things more seriously
44. _____ students are not afraid to ask for help
45. _____ more individual assignments are needed
46. _____ classroom is neat, clean and attractive
47. _____ students are jealous of each other's talents
48. _____ students can move about class quietly without permission
49. _____ students can leave their seats without permission
50. _____ teacher shows students are understood
51. _____ students and teacher waste a lot of time

52. _____ students can arrange their own seating plan
53. _____ teacher doesn't allow us to discuss things
54. _____ teacher doesn't shout at us
55. _____ our lessons are not very well-planned
56. _____ students brag about the class outside of school
57. _____ students are seldom courteous or friendly to one another
58. _____ students are free to suggest ways to improve the class
59. _____ students do little to prevent problems in class
60. _____ teacher encourages us to discuss things in small groups

ASSESSING RULES, REGULATIONS, AND DISCIPLINE

There is little need to repeat the litany of statistics documenting the increase in school vandalism, assaults, behavior problems, truancy, and other acts that are adversely affecting the climate of schools and classrooms. The major purpose here is to help you determine whether or not these problems exist in your school to the degree that they interfere with instruction and detract from the positive school climate you and your teachers are working to maintain (note the assumption). In addition, it would be informational to assess the perceptions of teachers, students, and parents regarding school discipline, safety, and control. In this regard, evaluating rules, regulations, and discipline problems seems to be an appropriate extension of the discussion in Chapter 4 regarding the evaluation of school safety. Limitations should be noted. There is no attempt to diagnose and prescribe approaches to behavior problems that teachers encounter in their classrooms.

Rules and Regulations Evaluation

There are several questions that you and the faculty should consider regarding school rules, regulations, policies, and procedures. Each question can be rewritten as a criterion for guiding actions.

Figure 2-5
Opinionnaire

Directions: In order to voice your opinions about what makes for a good class, an enjoyable classroom, and better teaching and learning, write down your answers to the following questions. Remember there are no right or wrong answers. I want your opinion.

1. What are the good things about our class? List five.
   a. _____
   b. _____
   c. _____
   d. _____
   e. _____

2. What are some things you don't like about this class? List five.
   a. _____
   b. _____
   c. _____
   d. _____
   e. _____

3. What do you like best about our classroom? List at least three things.
   a. _____
   b. _____
   c. _____

4. What do you like least about our classroom? List at least three.
   a. _____
   b. _____
   c. _____

5. What bothers you most about the way I teach?

6. What bothers you most about your classmates?

7. What bothers you most about yourself?

8. Would you recommend a friend to become a member of this class? Tell me why you answered yes or no.

9. If you were the teacher in this classroom, what would you do to make it a better place for your students?

10. How do you feel about:
    a. Your relationship with me?

    b. Your relationship with your classmates?

1. Are the school rules and regulations based upon board of education policies?
   a. How do you know?
   b. When was the last time you checked?
   c. Might you have one or more rules, etc., that deviate from board of education policies?
2. Are the school rules and regulations available to school personnel?
   a. Does each teacher have a written copy?
   b. Does each student have a copy in a student handbook?
   c. Does each parent have a copy?
3 Is there general agreement on the rules and regulations established for the school?
   a. How do you know?
   b. Have you checked on this lately?
4. Are the rules and regulations stated in a positive manner?
5. Do the rules emphasize responsibility rather than restrictions?

These and other questions can serve as the basis for discussions with faculty and students regarding school rules and regulations. It may be of value to have a committee composed of teachers, students, parents, and an administrator (yourself or an assistant if you have one) to evaluate existing school rules and regulations. If you decide to do this, this committee should initially obtain copies of all school rules, regulations, policies, and procedures. These materials can be judged on the basis of the five previous questions. In addition, the committee may find it valuable to evaluate these materials by asking teachers, students, and parents to judge them. Figures 2–6, 2–7, and 2–8 are examples of such questionnaires.

In Figure 2–6, a sample teacher questionnaire is provided. One of the basic questions that may come out of a discussion of the items on this questionnaire is whether or not there are rules and regulations in your school that may violate a student's civil rights. Rules governing dress codes, search and seizure, student discipline, and the like, are particularly sensitive to laws and legal rulings about the violation of a student's civil rights.

Figure 2–7 is an example of a student questionnaire regarding rules and regulations. It should be obvious that students should have an opportunity, either in classes or through their student council, to discuss the rationale and necessity for school rules and regulations. Periodic review of rules and regulations is helpful to all parties. It may be best to begin each school year with a review of the school rules in each classroom (homeroom) to clear up misunderstandings and to generate discussion about the need for rules, the need for people to have rights, and the need to exercise responsibilities that will insure that these rights are applicable to all.

Figure 2–8 is an example of a parent questionnaire designed to obtain parent opinion. There is an interesting paradox now occurring. Many parents and citizens want the schools to "crack down" on students. They are pressuring for law and order almost to the point where they are willing to deny the students their civil rights. Yet many of these same parents will threaten the school with a lawsuit the moment disciplinary action is taken against their son or daughter. In any event, it is important to involve parents in a review of school rules and regulations.

Regardless of the extent of agreement or disagreement about school rules and regulations, and regardless of the amount of involvement teachers, students, and parents have in creating and deciding about school rules and regulations, student misbehavior will not disappear.

Evaluating Discipline Practices

You cannot have learning without discipline. Teachers cannot teach, and learners cannot learn in an environment that is disruptive, distractive, and bound with fear for personal safety. Learning, by its very nature, requires self-discipline. Only indi-

Figure 2-6
Teacher Questionnaire Concerning School Rules

Grade or Subject Taught_____

1. Do you have a copy of all school rules and regulations?
   ____Yes   ____No
2. Are there any rules and regulations that you feel should be changed?
   ____Yes   ____No
   (If yes, please identify.)

3. Do you feel that parents and students have an understanding of the rules and regulations of this school?
   ____Yes   ____No
   (If no, please explain.)

4. In your opinion, do teachers carry out the rules and regulations as stated?
   ____Yes   ____No
   (If no, please explain.)

5. In your opinion, does the administration carry out the rules and regulations as stated?
   ____Yes   ____No
   (If no, please explain.)

6. Does this school have a good reputation concerning student behavior?
   ____ Definitely   ____ Not sure   ____ I think so
   ____ It depends who you talk to   ____ Not at all
7. Do teachers seem satisfied with the present school rules and regulations?
   ____ Definitely   ____ Not sure   ____ I think so
   ____ Some are, some aren't   ____ Many are not
8. Do teachers feel that rules and regulations promote student self-dignity, self-worth, and responsibility?
   ____ All or most do   ____ Some or a few do   ____ Many do not
9. Do teachers feel that most parents support the rules and regulations?
   ____Yes, they do   ____ Some do, some don't   ____ Many do not
10. Please list the rules and regulations that you feel should be revised or discussed at faculty meetings.

Figure 2–7
Student Questionnaire Concerning School Rules

Directions: This questionnaire is designed to find out how you feel about school rules and regulations. Please circle the number that represents how you feel.

School_____Grade_____Room_____

	No Opinion	Definitely	Sometimes	Not at All
1. This school has rules and regulations everyone must follow.	1	2	3	4
2. This school has rules and regulations most students should follow.	1	2	3	4
3. Students have very little to say about the rules and regulations established for this school.	1	2	3	4
4. Rules and regulations are well understood by the students.	1	2	3	4
5. Parents generally support the rules and regulations of this school.	1	2	3	4
6. Teachers are understanding in carrying out the rules and regulations of this school.	1	2	3	4
7. Students should be punished or disciplined for breaking the school's rules and regulations.	1	2	3	4
8. The rules and regulations are applied to all students fairly and consistently.	1	2	3	4
9. There should be class discussions on the rationale for rules and regulations.	1	2	3	4

10. Please indicate below which rules and regulations you feel should be revised or discussed.

Figure 2–8
Parent Questionnaire Concerning School Rules

Directions: The subcommittee is studying school rules and regulations. Reactions and feelings of parents are most important. Please share your opinion by circling the number that best describes your feeling. Thank you for your time and cooperation.

	No Opinion	Definitely	Sometimes	Not at All
1. Most parents support the rules and regulations at this school.	1	2	3	4
2. Parents generally agree with the school's methods of maintaining order and discipline.	1	2	3	4
3. This school has a good reputation concerning student behavior.	1	2	3	4
4. Parents understand the rationale for specific school rules and regulations.	1	2	3	4
5. Most parents feel that students comply with existing school rules and regulations.	1	2	3	4
6. Many parents feel that the administration and teachers are too lenient in carrying out school rules and regulations.	1	2	3	4
7. Many parents feel that the administration and teachers are too harsh in carrying out school rules and regulations.	1	2	3	4
8. It would be beneficial if more parents were involved in developing policies concerning school rules and regulations.	1	2	3	4
9. Most parents agree that the student who disobeys a school rule or regulation should be punished or disciplined.	1	2	3	4

10. Please state below your comments or questions concerning existing school rules and regulations.

viduals can learn, and to do so those individuals must have an environment that encourages and instructs them how to learn and gives them the opportunity to do so. Disruptive and distractive student behavior reduces teaching-learning opportunities. It violates the rights of teachers and students who come to school for this purpose. Yet the school and its personnel have to exhaust every possibility and all existing services to help disruptive and nondisruptive students find success in school.

In relation to the general school climate it may be helpful for you and your teachers to discuss the answers to the following questions:

1. Do teachers enforce school rules and regulations consistently?
2. Do the same groups of teachers complain about student behavior?
3. Do teachers ask for help in training to deal with student behavior problems?
4. Do teachers send behavior problems to the office rather than handle the problem themselves?
5. Does this school need a security officer?
6. Does this school need monitors to keep order?
7. Are teachers and students fearful about coming to school each day?
8. Do students complain that they didn't know they were breaking a school rule when they are caught?
9. Do the penalties students receive fit the misbehavior or rule that was broken?
10. Do parents criticize the school for its lack of discipline?
11. Do students fear using school facilities (halls, toilets, etc.)?
12. Do students criticize the school for its lack of discipline?
13. Do discipline problems have ethnic or racial overtones or implications?
14. Does the administration spend an excessive amount of time handling discipline problems?

Many times there is a tendency among teachers and others to overstate the case about discipline. I remember a faculty suggesting that if we could "get rid of five percent of the students in this school, we would have a really good school." However, I am convinced that teachers would find another five percent in a year or two. It would be informative for the teachers to analyze school offenses (student misbehaviors) with the hope that the data will serve as a springboard to corrective action. The inventory (Figure 2–9) can be used to find out how parents, teachers, or students feel about the frequency of offenses occurring at school, or in a particular class, or with a particular group, and the probable cause for the offense. In addition, it can also be used to obtain information about a particular student's behavior as seen by that student's teacher(s). If used for this purpose, the student's name or a code is used at the top of the inventory. The results are confidential and used to plan ways to help the student.

A FINAL COMMENT

Ways for evaluating and improving the health and climate of your school has been the major focus of this chapter. A final perspective on this discussion encompasses a thought about two important factors relating to school health and climate: the environment (in and out of school) and the student peer groups. These two factors seem to influence student academic and personal-social behavior.[11]

If schooling is to contribute to productive learning and the development of self-understanding, openness, trust, and sincerity (humanness), then it seems that principals and teachers have to employ strategies that maximize potential for students to teach one another facts, concepts, ideas, opinions, attitudes, and values that reflect the best in our cultural heritage, our democratic ideals, and our humanness. In addition, principals and teachers must "compensate or remedy environmental or peer influences which are detrimental to student development."[12]

You, the faculty, staff, students, and parents must expose students to a productive learning envi-

Figure 2-9
Students' Misbehaviors/Offenses Inventory

Directions: This inventory attempts to find out how you feel about the frequency of student misbehaviors/offenses in this school (class, group) and the probable causes. Place a check mark on one of the lines under *Frequency* and circle those numbers that reflect your view of the causes for the misbehavior/offense using the following guide:

1—home environment	5—school or teacher caused
2—parent attitude	6—students have personal problems
3—lack of parent control	7—students have learning problems
4—peer group influence	8—all of the causes

Frequency

Offenses	Excessive	Moderate	Rare	Causes
1. Habitual tardiness	____	____	____	1 2 3 4 5 6 7 8
2. Regularly skipping class	____	____	____	1 2 3 4 5 6 7 8
3. Truancy, poor attendance	____	____	____	1 2 3 4 5 6 7 8
4. Cheating	____	____	____	1 2 3 4 5 6 7 8
5. Disruptive behavior	____	____	____	1 2 3 4 5 6 7 8
6. Continual inattention in class	____	____	____	1 2 3 4 5 6 7 8
7. Rowdiness	____	____	____	1 2 3 4 5 6 7 8
8. Persistent silent contempt	____	____	____	1 2 3 4 5 6 7 8
9. Sneering, muttering	____	____	____	1 2 3 4 5 6 7 8
10. Swearing	____	____	____	1 2 3 4 5 6 7 8
11. Carries weapons	____	____	____	1 2 3 4 5 6 7 8
12. Unacceptable sexual behavior	____	____	____	1 2 3 4 5 6 7 8
13. Physical assaults on students	____	____	____	1 2 3 4 5 6 7 8
14. Physical assaults on teachers, other adults	____	____	____	1 2 3 4 5 6 7 8
15. Excessive talking	____	____	____	1 2 3 4 5 6 7 8
16. Lack of interest	____	____	____	1 2 3 4 5 6 7 8
17. Not listening	____	____	____	1 2 3 4 5 6 7 8
18. Destructive of school property	____	____	____	1 2 3 4 5 6 7 8
19. Destructive of student property	____	____	____	1 2 3 4 5 6 7 8
20. Drug/alcohol use	____	____	____	1 2 3 4 5 6 7 8
21. Disrespect, not courteous	____	____	____	1 2 3 4 5 6 7 8
22. Failure to complete school work	____	____	____	1 2 3 4 5 6 7 8
23. Smoking	____	____	____	1 2 3 4 5 6 7 8
24. Other (list)				

ronment and minimize factors which interfere with productive learning and positive human relationships.

EVALUATION INSTRUMENTS

Hopefully, a case has been made that will cause you and your faculty to attend to the climate of the school and each classroom. A selected list of additional instruments are described for possible use in your school.

Leader Behavior Description Questionnaire. Bureau of Business Research, Ohio State University, Columbus, Ohio 43210.

The LBDQ is a self-administering rating scale representing two aspects of leadership: initiating structure (establishing administrative procedures, channels of communication, ways to get the job done) and consideration (mutual trust, respect, warmth between leader and group). It has been found that high "leader behavior" scores are associated with high teacher morale scores, and that "consideration" is more clearly correlated with teacher morale than "initiating structure."

Barclay Classroom Climate Inventory. Educational Skills Development, Inc., 179 East Maxwell Street, Lexington, Ky. 40508.

The BCCI consists of thirty-two independent scales. It uses self-report judgments, peer nominations, and teacher expectations to measure affective and social needs of students in grades 3 to 6. The BCCI takes about seventy-five minutes to administer and is scored by computer. The computer printout on each child includes an overall summary, special characteristics summary, problem analysis, intervention direction, and prescription.

Organizational Climate Description Questionnaire. Midwest Administration Center, University of Chicago, 5835 South Kimbark Avenue, Chicago.

This instrument, developed by Halpin and Croft, is self-administering and may be completed by the principal, teachers, and other school personnel in about twenty minutes using a four-point rating scale. The sixty-four-item test yields six climate profiles described in the test booklet: open, autonomous, controlled, familiar, paternal, and closed.

QUESTA. Educational Testing Service, Princeton, N.J. 08540.

The Questionnaire for Students, Teachers, Administrators, and Parents is a program designed to help secondary school principals and others gather useful data on students, teachers, administrators, and parents relative to the school environment. The package contains:

1. Questionnaire for New Students (twenty-one questions).
2. Questionnaire on Students' Views of Personal Relations, Communications, Counseling and Other Pupil Concerns (twenty questions).
3. Questionnaire on Teachers' and Administrators' Views of Personal Relations, Communication, Counseling and Other Pupil Concerns (nineteen questions).
4. Questionnaire on Students' Views of the School's Purposes, Programs and Teaching (seventeen questions).
5. Questionnaire on Teachers' and Administrators' Views of the School's Purposes, Programs and Teaching (seventeen questions).

Each questionnaire provides for fifteen local option questions. Scoring is done by ETS.

High School Characteristics Index. George C. Stern. *People in Context* (New York: John Wiley, 1970). Stern and Associates, Syracuse, N.Y.

This 300-item true and false test is in booklet form with clear directions to students. The index can be completed in about sixty minutes and will yield information on how students perceive the school environment. There are thirty scales of ten items each assessing a variety of factors such as student organizations, interests, and activities; rules and regulations; teaching and classroom activities; the curriculum; policies and procedures; and so on.

B. Elliott describes his use of the instrument in an article titled, "Assessing the Environment of the Secondary School," *Bulletin of the National Secondary School Principals Association* 56 (November 1972): 75–78.

Assessment of Student Attitudes Toward Learning Environment. Research for Better Schools, Inc. 1976, Philadelphia.

This twenty-six item instrument is useful in secondary schools in assessing students' attitudes toward education in general, school curriculum, school resources, and learning environments. This attitude scale can be completed in about fifteen minutes and yields an overall score and four sub-scale scores.

Classroom Climate Questionnaire. H. J. Walberg, Harvard University, Cambridge, Mass.

This questionnaire contains eighty items that describe the characteristics of classes, such as friction, intimacy, deviation, control, alienation, formality, democracy, etc. Students respond to a four-point agreement-disagreement scale.

School Climate Profile. Phi Delta Kappa, Bloomington, Ind.

This profile should be used in conjunction with the comprehensive treatment of school climate provided in Robert S. Fox et al., *School Climate Improvement: A Challenge to the School Administrator* (Bloomington, Indiana: Phi Delta Kappa, n.d.). The profile is presented in four parts—general climate factors, program determinants, process determinants, and material determinants. The entire instrument takes twenty to twenty-five minutes to complete, but school administrators may administer it in several short sessions. Principals should complete the instrument as well as teachers, students, parents, and other school personnel. The compilation of perceptions from a wide range of people will give the principal a much better "picture" of the climate of the school he or she administrates.

ENDNOTES

1. Dale Alam, "Summary of Seminar Proceedings in Education 700," in *A Systems Approach to Educational Administration,* ed. Robert Maxson and Walter E. Sistrunk (Dubuque, Iowa: W. C. Brown Co., 1973), pp. 83–84.

2. E. Dale Doak, "Organizational Climate: Prelude to Change," *Educational Leadership* 27 (1970): 367.

3. Glen Hass et al., *Leadership for Improving Instruction* (Washington, D.C.: Association for Supervision and Curriculum Development, 1960), pp. 58–61.

4. Gordon J. Klopf et al., "A Taxonomy of Educational Leadership," *National Elementary Principal* 53 (July/August 1974): 54–56.

5. Robert S. Fox et al., *School Climate Improvement: A Challenge to the School Administrator* (Bloomington, Ind.: Phi Delta Kappa, n.d.), p. iv.

6. Ibid., pp. 7–9, 51.

7. Ibid., p. 9.

8. Richard D. Kimpston and Leslie C. Sonnabend, "Organizational Health: A Requisite for Innovation?" *Educational Leadership* (March 1973): 543–547.

9. Charles Silberman, *Crisis in the Classroom* (New York: Random House, 1970), p. 11.

10. See Ronald T. Hyman, *School Administrator's Handbook of Teacher Supervision and Evaluation Methods* (Englewood Cliffs, N.J.: Prentice-Hall, 1975), Chapter 4.

11. Raphael O. Nystrand and Luvern L. Cunningham, "Organizing Schools to Develop Humane Capabilities," in *To Nurture Humaneness: Commitment for the '70s,* ed. Mary-Margaret Scobey and Grace Graham. (Washington, D.C.: Association for Supervision and Curriculum Development, 1970), pp. 132–133.

12. Ibid., p. 133.

SELECTED REFERENCES

Breckenridge, Eileen. "Improving School Climate." *Phi Delta Kappan* 57 (December 1976): 314–318.

Dale, Edgar. *Building a Learning Environment.* Bloomington, Ind.: Phi Delta Kappa, 1972.

Ellenburg, F. C. "Factors Affecting Teacher Morale: Meaning for Principals." *Bulletin of the National Association of Secondary School Principals* 56 (December 1972): 37–45.

English, Fenwick W. *School Organization and Management.* Worthington, Ohio: Charles A. Jones Publishing Co., 1975.

Goldmeier, Harold. "Vandalism: The Effects of Unmanageable Confrontations." *Adolescence* 9 (Spring 1974): 49–56.

Milgram, Stanley. *Obedience to Authority.* New York: Harper & Row, 1974.

Phi Delta Kappan 59 (January 1978). (The theme of this issue is violence and discipline problems.)

Refexes, Frederick L. "Factors That Affect Teacher Morale." *Nation's Schools* 63 (February 1959): 59–63.

Thompson, Marion; Brassell, William R.; Persons, Scott; Tucker, Richard; and Rollins, Howard. "Contingency Management in the Schools: How Often and How Well Does It Work?" *American Education Research Journal* 11 (Winter 1974): 19–28.

Walden, John C; Taylor, Thomas N.; and Watkins, J. Foster. "Organizational Climate Changes Over Time." *Educational Forum* 40 (November 1975): 87–93.

Wells, Elmer. *Vandalism and Violence: Innovative Strategies to Reduce Cost to Schools.* Washington, D.C.: National School Public Relations Association, 1971.

Wiggins, Thomas W. "A Comparative Investigation of Principal Behavior and School Climate." *The Journal of Educational Research* 66 (November 1972): 103–105.

Wise, Arthur E., and Monley-Casimir, Michael E. "Law, Freedom, Equality—and Schooling." In *Freedom, Bureaucracy, and Schooling,* ed. Vernon F. Haubrick. Washington, D.C.: Association for Supervision and Curriculum Development, 1971.

3

EVALUATING AND IMPROVING OFFICE, FOOD, AND TRANSPORTATION SERVICES

We think in generalities, but we live in details.

Alfred North Whitehead

A school principal is many things to many people. The varying perceptions people have about the role and expectations of the school principal is testimony to this point. The job, however perceived, requires melding the manager-administrative tasks with the instructional-leadership tasks. One of the major problems the school principal copes with each day is how to maintain a balance between these two roles. Most principals appreciate the time and energy required to manage the school plant and its operations as well as the several noninstructional services provided students. Many principals feel guilty when they find that they are not giving enough of their time to the instructional-leadership role. However, it is impossible for today's school principal to abandon either role. Both roles are essential to first-rate quality education at the building level; both require time and energy; and both require periodic review and renewal.

In this chapter, the focus will be centered on three services requiring managerial skill and leadership: school office services, food services, and transportation services. Volumes have been written on each of these three school services. For this reason, this one chapter cannot delve into the details for organizing and administering these services.

SCHOOL OFFICE SERVICES

There is general agreement among school principals that the school office is the school's service center and that the principal is the person responsible for operating it efficiently and effectively.

In order for the varied school services to be managed and delivered when needed, there are certain tasks that each principal must do to insure that the school office is an effective service center. Some of these major tasks are outlined here for your review:

1. You must continually and effectively supervise and evaluate secretarial-clerical personnel.
2. You must promote good human relations between yourself and secretarial-clerical personnel and between secretarial-clerical personnel and other school personnel.
3. You must convince secretarial-clerical personnel that their work is important toward accomplishing the school's objectives.
4. You must insure that secretarial-clerical personnel have physical facilities that (a) provide adequate space to get the work done; (b) are pleasant and provide privacy when needed; and (c) do not interfere with the traffic flow in and out of the office.
5. You must provide secretarial-clerical personnel with the necessary equipment to get the job done.
6. You must create a filing system that is efficient and up-to-date.
7. You must require the use of standardized forms that save time and energy.
8. You should encourage the use of electronic data processing and help secretarial-clerical personnel acquire the skills to operate these machines.
9. You must provide each secretarial-clerical staff member an office manual that includes a job description, policies, procedures, and specific instructions.

This last task is particularly important and can lead to a better understanding by secretaries and clerical staff of their jobs, responsibilities, and how, when, and why they will be supervised and evaluated. Job descriptions for a principal's secretary should include, among other things, a description or listing of the tasks under (1) qualifications, (2) salary and working conditions, (3) receptionist, (4) office procedures, (5) records, (6) reports, and (7) other duties peculiar to a particular school.

Evaluating Office Services and Management

With these tasks in mind, there might be a need to find out from teachers and others who use the services of the school office how they perceive or rate this service. The evaluation form shown in Figure 3–1 is designed to help you do this.

Results from this kind of questionnaire may provide you with several ideas that you may wish to consider in order to help make the school office the communication and production center it is intended to be. After an evaluation of what is, you could generate ideas for what ought to be. Obviously, not all the ideas will be implemented because of district restrictions, budget, and/or certain school factors that make the implementation of the idea impractical or impossible. However, you should list the ideas and evaluate the chances of implementation later. Today's idea may be tomorrow's practice. Here are a few ideas:

- Add additional secretarial-clerical help, if needed; even part-time assistance will help.
- Use student clerks; particularly at the high school level a program may be worked out with the business department to provide actual work experience for youngsters.
- Take a course or design your own independent study guide for learning effective office management techniques.
- Create a small committee of people to develop an office procedures manual.
- Find parents in the community who are managers of large business offices and ask them to do a study of the effectiveness and efficiency of the school office.
- Post a master calendar that identifies important "due-dates," activities, reporting dates, etc.
- Consider the use of additional part-time secretarial-clerical help during peak-load periods such as the opening and closing of school.
- Try a POW squad (a group of parent-office workers who would be willing to volunteer their services when called upon to do so).

Figure 3–1
Evaluating Office Services

Directions: The purpose of this questionnaire is to obtain your rating of office services. The rating of the office staff is designed to determine ways to improve services to teachers, not to collect data about faults and weaknesses. Please answer each question carefully and as completely as time will allow. Your answers will be held in confidence.

Name:_____

1. Are you satisfied with the services provided by this office? ____Yes   ____At times   ____No
   Suggestions for improvement:

2. Are you satisfied with the secretarial services provided? ____Yes   ____At times   ____No
   Suggestions for improvement:

3. Are you satisfied with the support services provided? ____Yes   ____At times   ____No
   Suggestions for improvement:

4. Are you aware of any major problems and/or complaints about the following services:
   a. Supplies: ____Yes   ____No (If yes, please specify.)

   b. Secretarial: ____Yes   ____No (If yes, please specify.)

   c. Clerks: ____Yes   ____No (If yes, please specify.)

   d. Duplicating: ____Yes   ____No (If yes, please specify.)

   e. Equipment: ____Yes   ____No (If yes, please specify.)

   f. Other categories:

5. What office services are you *not* receiving that should be considered?

- Plan a year's program of inservice activities-training for your office staff. Don't forget to include the office staff in the planning.
- Have your office staff do an analysis of their job by logging the tasks and activities over a week or two; tabulate and summarize by the day or week, and/or type of task. You can use the results to help the staff plan for a more efficient operation of the office, if needed.
- Design a daily task analysis chart for the office staff to complete. Use the results as the focal point for a conference with each one and obtain their opinion of how time may be better utilized.

Add your own ideas to this list, then try a few and find out what happens. The implementation of these and other ideas described in the remainder of this chapter may help create a more effective and efficient school office. However, to provide means for checking on your office managerial skills, I have found eighteen basic recommendations in the literature regarding the school office. To help you evaluate the extent to which some or all of these recommendations are implemented in your school office, a self-evaluation checklist has been prepared (Figure 3–2).

With modifications in the wording of this checklist, it may be used by teachers and staff to assess their perceptions of how well the school office functions. In any event, the purpose is to find out if improvements are necessary.

Two major school office services require special analysis by today's practicing administrators: student records and reports and the school budget.

Figure 3–2
Office Management Self-Evaluation Checklist

1. How would you rate the organization and administration of the school office?
   ____Excellent   ____Good   ____Fair   ____Poor

2. Does the office run efficiently in the principal's absence?
   ____Definitely   ____Somewhat   ____Not at all

3. Do the office functions seem to be properly delegated to appropriate office personnel?
   ____Yes   ____No   ____For some, but not all

4. Is there a procedural manual for each member of the office staff?
   ____Yes   ____No   ____We don't need one

5. Is the office organized in such a way that it provides a direct service to the school's educational program?
   ____Definitely   ____Somewhat   ____Not at all

6. Are in-service training opportunities provided members of the office staff?
   ____Regularly   ____Sometimes   ____Never/Seldom

7. Is the filing system effective and efficient?
   ____Yes   ____No

8. Does each member of the office staff know the daily tasks they are expected to perform?
   ____Yes   ____No

9. Is there a job description for each member of the office staff?
   ____Yes   ____No

10. Are appropriate time-saving machines and equipment available to the office staff?
    ____Yes   ____No   ____A few are, but we need more

11. Is there an office schedule (routine but flexible) for each member of the office staff?
    ____Yes   ____No   ____We really don't need one

12. Is there a procedure for faculty and staff to follow should they wish to use school office services?
    ____Yes   ____No

13. Is there a cooperative system for the supervising and evaluating of office staff?
    ____Yes   ____No

(cont.)

14. Does the layout of the office (color, work space, ventilation, light, etc.) contribute to efficiency and favorable working conditions?
____Definitely ____Somewhat ____Not at all
15. Is there an office work-climate that is friendly, cooperative, and one of high morale?
____Definitely ____Somewhat ____Not at all
16. Is the procedure for obtaining school supplies and equipment efficient enough so that it requires a minimum amount of time and effort?
____Yes ____No
17. Does the office staff respond politely and courteously to the inquiries and/or visitations by faculty, students, parents, and others?
____Most do ____Some do, some don't ____Few do
18. Is the office staff encouraged to share their ideas and suggestions for more effective management with the principal or his or her representative?
____Yes ____No ____Yes, but few do

EVALUATING RECORDS AND REPORTS

It should be the intent of all school principals, faculty, pupil personnel staff, and other school employees who have responsibilities regarding student records and reports to know and carry out school district policies regarding student records. The established practices in an individual school regarding the collection, maintenance, and dissemination of information about students should assure a balance between a student's right to privacy and the need to use information for designed educational purposes.

The management of school records and reports is time-consuming but necessary. There are many more records and reports to be monitored at the secondary level than at the elementary level. Most of the records maintained in individual schools are those about students, thus the principal must assure that necessary skills are developed to manage not only student personnel records, but also the plethora of other records and reports.

The "paper chase" is a burden faced by all administrators. A rule-of-thumb principle should be that each record, each report, each form used in school should be justified by its function. The use of machines, computerizing as much as possible, helps reduce the workload.

There are, however, several questions that you, teachers, and pupil personnel staff should ask about school records and reports as a means for self-evaluation:

1. How efficiently and effectively do we organize and administer the use of records and reports in this school?
2. Do we try to eliminate multiple and duplicate records, reports, forms, etc., wherever possible?
3. How much time do teachers use in completing school forms, slips, records, and reports?
4. Have we tried to computerize records when and where possible?
5. What is our policy relative to the confidentiality of student/faculty records and reports?
6. How have we helped each other learn to interpret material that appears in our school's records and reports?
7. What guidelines have we prepared for teachers and staff relative to the collection, maintenance, and use of information in student reports?
8. Have we evaluated our management of records and reports including existing policies and practices?

9. What information should be collected about each student in our school?
10. How should this information be categorized? For example, will we have separate files on each student such as a cumulative record file, behavior file, teacher professional file, with each file containing different kinds of information?
11. Who has access to student records and reports? Are there policies and procedures for identifying who examined a student's file? Are policies available regarding access by students and parents, by authorized school personnel, by third parties?
12. How is confidentiality assured?
13. When should some records be destroyed?
14. How may student records be amended?
15. What strategies are necessary to carry out the functions implied in these questions?

These questions and others focus on the issues of confidentiality, invasion of privacy, and the right to know. The principal has a responsibility to obtain information that will be of value for the interpretation of and planning for the educational progress of each student. It is also the responsibility of the principal to have this information used discreetly and professionally. If the axiom "what you don't know can hurt you," is applicable to anything dealing with school, it is in this area that it takes on validity. Because of social circumstances, legal uses, and specific laws, it is imperative that each school and school district have a specific set of policies and procedures, in writing, that should be required reading by all school personnel handling student records and reports. To help focus on this problem, the following questions should be considered:

1. Does your school district have written policies regarding pupil personnel records?
2. If your school district does have a policy, do you and your faculty/staff know what it says? (Suggestion: Is it time for a review?)

3. If your district does not have a policy, do you feel that you and the faculty/staff could work out a procedure that would include the following:
   a. Identify the minimum pupil data necessary for meeting the needs of the school district?
   b. Establish behavioral records helpful toward meeting the educational needs of each child?
   c. Create temporary teacher files with information helpful to teachers for instructing that child?
   d. Develop procedures under which each of the above are to be retained, for how long, and where they are to be filed?
   e. Develop a list of procedures that insure the confidentiality of information released?
4. Are you and your faculty/staff aware of the various forms used by the district regarding the requests and release of pupil personnel records? (Suggestion: If you currently do not have such forms, consider using forms modeled from other schools who have had success with them. Ask your administrative colleagues for suggestions.)
5. How would you and the faculty/staff rate knowledge about the issues, state statutes, and laws governing pupil personnel records and reports?

Each state has laws regulating student records. Each state requires the local school board to adopt policies and procedures to carry out these regulations. Each school, under the direction of the principal, must establish procedures and practices that implement school board policies. To carry out the functions implied and described previously, the principal, faculty, pupil personnel staff, and clerks must know these policies, and the practices required for each function. In summary, a school principal should have forms available for a student or parent who requests to inspect the records; for informing graduating students (and those leaving school) about the destruction of records; for notifying students and parents of the destruction of material in a student's temporary file; for obtaining consent for the release of a student's record to a third party; for notification that a student's record has been provided to a third party who does not need student consent; for releasing certain information to a student's new school; for the possible publication of certain student information during the school year; and for maintaining a log of persons who have obtained access to a student's records.

The second major school-office-responsibility faced by building principals relates to establishing and administering the school budget.

BUDGET AND ACCOUNTING PROCEDURES

There are four basic steps for establishing a school budget: preparing the budget; presenting it to the board of education and eventually to the public; administering the approved budget; and evaluating the plan to determine how the money appropriated was used and for what purpose.

There are a multitude of management systems designed to facilitate (and in some cases complicate) the process of budget planning. General practice has the school principal active in each phase, particularly in the preparation, administration, and evaluation of the school budget. It seems apparent, then, that a school principal be able to demonstrate knowledge and skill in:

- Understanding budget-making procedures
- Developing a school budget which results from consultation with faculty and staff
- Preparing a school budget that supports the school's educational program
- Keeping accurate financial records of receipts and expenditures
- Preparing and delivering sound financial reports to the superintendent (or the superin-

tendent's designee-school business manager), the board, and the school's public
- Effectively managing and evaluating budget allocations made to the school.

No pretense is made here to provide a short course on school budget and finance. Experienced principals have probably had a course called school business management and have learned from on-the-job-training. Aspiring principals will probably have to take a school business management course that may or may not answer all of their questions. What is presented here is an overview designed to help you evaluate how to go about the task of budgeting, and if you are a practicing administrator, how skillfully you administer and account for budget allocations. Information, then, will be presented (for your self-evaluation) relative to three primary responsibilities: the preparation of the school budget; the administration of that budget; and the managing and accounting procedures you use in your school.

Preparing the Budget

The first step to budget preparation is to know about the classification system used in the school district. Principals should ask themselves these questions:

1. Do I know the basic budget categories used by my school district?
2. Do I use these categories in the preparation of my school budget?
3. Do I know how the total school budget is put together?
4. Is the school district's classification system of value to me as I prepare and evaluate my school budget?

Recommended procedures for preparing a school budget are identified in the evaluation scale in Figure 3–3. You might begin by determining which of the ten procedures you actually used last year.

Figure 3-3
Evaluation of Budget Preparation Procedures

Evaluate the extent to which your budget preparation procedures:

	Great	Moderate	Little
1. Assess the educational needs of:			
a. students.	___	___	___
b. teachers.	___	___	___
c. staff.	___	___	___
d. professional service personnel.	___	___	___
2. Involve careful thought on your part.	___	___	___
3. Reflect the objectives of the instructional program.	___	___	___
4. Reflect the objectives of student activities and services.	___	___	___
5. Reflect the priorities established by you and others.	___	___	___
6. Reflect cost-estimates.	___	___	___
7. Include alternatives should budget not be approved or be reduced.	___	___	___
8. Reflect evaluation of monies spent during the past year.	___	___	___
9. Require teachers and others to provide rationales for requests.	___	___	___
10. Reflect your consultation with superintendent and/or central office staff.	___	___	___

Following your evaluation of the extent to which you use these procedures in preparing your school budget, it is important that you and your staff consider each school program and service. Use the following outline in evaluating and preparing a budget for these programs and services:

- Purpose of the program and/or service
- Specific activities and procedures required in providing this program and/or service
- Personnel needs and costs for each program and/or service
- Support personnel needed (example: part-time secretary for speech pathologist) and cost

- Supplies and equipment needed for each program and/or service
- Building space needs for each program and/or service
- Last year's evaluation of program and service activities, costs, benefits, and personnel.

This review procedure requires that you and your faculty/staff give some serious thought to the programs and services provided to the young people in attendance. Not only does it provide an overall view of programs and services, but it encourages a yearly examination of program success and failures, personnel performance, and use of funds.

In review, the principal, with the cooperation of the personnel in the school, prepares the budget after examining school programs and services in relation to the:

- Purpose (objectives) of each
- Activities and procedures
- Personnel needed
- Support personnel needed
- Supplies and equipment needed
- Building space needed
- Evaluation results from previous and current year
- Projected cost estimates for next two or three years.

Administering the Budget

My experience as a school board member convinces me that school principals can be a valuable asset in the preparation and administration of the school budget. Public response to school budget meetings is not impressive, yet there is widespread concern about the budget—the cost of educating young people. Minimal attendance at annual budget meetings places a greater burden on board members and school administrators to get the budget message to the people. The usual school district activities of holding public hearings, publishing budget information in newspapers, bulletins, and newsletters, and meeting with community groups can be supplemented by a school principal who is probably closer to the school's public than is the central office staff, the superintendent, and/or any particular board of education member. In preparing and administering the budget, the principal can use a variety of methods for informing the school's clientele about it. Some ideas will be presented in the chapter on school-community relationships. The point here is that the principal should not underestimate his or her influence in this area.

Once the school budget has been approved, the monies are to be put to use for the purposes intended. Most school districts employ automated accounting procedures that save time and effort. Most systems now have procedures that centralize purchasing; require competitive bids for supplies, equipment, and repairs; include methods for the requisitioning of supplies and equipment; and provide guidelines for school principals for the management of individual school accounts.

The tasks of the school principal in this area will vary according to the size and level of the school. Junior-senior high school principals will have many more accounting tasks to perform than will middle-elementary school principals. Some of the tasks may be common to both, in kind, but certainly vary in degree. For example, an elementary principal may have responsibility for book fees, as will the high school principal, but the high school principal's tasks are increased because of the number of students, the variety of programs, and the procedures used. Nevertheless, each and every principal has a responsibility for accounting for the revenue and expenditures for their individual school.

Evaluating Accounting Procedures

Almost every textbook on school administration has a chapter on school financial accounting. Few provide a method that principals can use to evaluate current practices. Adequte, effective financial procedures are essential. The major question is how can school principals evaluate the effectiveness of their current accounting practices? To answer this question an evaluation form was designed and is recommended for use by principals (Figure 3-4).

It should be noted that each "procedure" item is based upon recommendations from the literature and/or actual administrative practices. A principal who rates a particular item "sometimes" or "seldom" should take the time to examine the reasons for the rating, his or her current procedures, and ways these procedures can be changed.

Figure 3–4
Evaluating Procedures for School Fund Accounting

Write the appropriate number in the box using the following scale: 1—Definitely; 2—Sometimes; 3—Seldom or Never; 4—Not Applicable	Bookstore	Student sales	Athletic funds	Luncheon sales	Petty cash	School fees	Tickets for school events	Special programs	School supplies	School equipment	Book rentals	Comments
My Procedure: is efficient												
requires receipts												
requires vouchers												
is subject to audit												
requires monthly reports												
requires an annual report												
requires all persons handling money to be bonded												
includes the use of forms that are clear and accurate												
includes banking all money received												
includes a method for authorizing expenditures												
requires that expenditures be paid only by check												
in general, provides an effective accounting system												

Evaluating Budget Management

If a school principal has prepared the individual school budget carefully and with proper justifications, the use of monies should be able to be evaluated with the same care and concern. No doubt the school district will have some specific method for evaluating the school budget. As suggested earlier, most school districts are required to submit to an annual audit. For a school principal, the evaluation of the budget centers around how the monies were spent, what accounting procedures were used, how the supplies and equipment were purchased and used, and how the principal managed school funds. The

form provided in Figure 3–5 illustrates an idea for evaluating how effectively and efficiently the principal manages the budget.

As the figure shows, the principal can obtain a rating from his or her superiors (the superintendent, business manager) and from faculty and staff. Comparisons may be made. Additional items may be added to assess varying school policies and procedures.

In review, this discussion has focused on several major administrative responsibilities regarding office services including the evaluation of office service and management, the evaluation of school records and reports, and the evaluation of budget and accounting procedures.

Figure 3–5
Form for Evaluating School Principal's Management of School Budget

Directions: This form is designed to help me determine how effectively and efficiently I manage the school budget. Please circle the number that best reflects your perception of that item. Thank you for your time and cooperation.

Respondent: ___Administrator ___Teacher ___Staff

Item	Excellent		Good		Poor
1. Preparation of the school budget	1	2	3	4	5
2. Management of school funds	1	2	3	4	5
3. Management of school supplies and equipment	1	2	3	4	5
4. Involves faculty and staff in budget preparation	1	2	3	4	5
5. Involves faculty and staff in budget evaluation	1	2	3	4	5
6. Keeps school personnel informed about budget throughout the school year	1	2	3	4	5
7. Demonstrates leadership in attaining program and service objectives within budget limitations	1	2	3	4	5
8. Demonstrates leadership in identifying needs and resources to meet these needs	1	2	3	4	5
9. Other	1	2	3	4	5

There are two additional services worthy of discussion and evaluation—food and transportation. The remainder of this chapter will examine ways to evaluate these services and the personnel who provide them.

MANAGING FOOD SERVICES

Here is a scenario regarding the food service program in the typical elementary or secondary school. Let's assume it is your school. There is a lunch program operating daily, serving a "Type A" lunch supplemented by other food options (sandwiches, snacks, etc.). Many students bring a sack lunch and purchase only milk and dessert. The food is either prepared in your school building or it is delivered to the school from a centralized food preparation area in the school district. You have limited or no responsibilities regarding the selection, preparation, or portioning of the daily lunches (and breakfast in some school districts). You administer the lunch program following policies established by the school board and rules and regulations established by the district's food director.

You notice and can expect over the next decade an increase in student participation in the school's food service programs. You have come to realize that there are a variety of reasons for this current or expected increase in the number of students remaining at school for lunch. One reason may be that the school board has established a "closed" lunch period (students are not allowed to leave school grounds during the lunch period). Other reasons, all obvious to you, include the fact that more of the students in your school are coming from single-parent homes; there is a significant increase in families in which both parents work; there are many more students qualifying for a governmentally-subsidized lunch (and breakfast); and for many of your students the breakfast and/or lunch they receive at school may be their most nutritious meal of the day.

With this scene in mind, an examination of ways you can evaluate and improve the food services in your school may be worthwhile. An outline of a principal's specific responsibilities will help set the stage for the recommended evaluation techniques.

Principal's Responsibilities

This section includes an outline of specific responsibilities each school principal should follow in order to operate an effective and efficient food service program. You might use these responsibilities as a guide for self-evaluation and/or as a means for improving what you currently do regarding this school service. Therefore, to insure a sound and productive food service program, you should:

1. Use school board policies as guidelines for developing program rules and regulations.
2. Insure that teachers, students, and food service personnel understand and implement ways that the food service program contributes to and is incorporated into the school's educational program.
3. Create a representative committee to establish food service program goals and objectives, if these are not currently available.
4. Clearly establish "line" responsibilities regarding the evaluation and supervision of food service programs and personnel.
5. Create an environment in the lunchroom/cafeteria that contributes to healthy eating habits, manners, behavior, and decorum.
6. Provide adequate and attractive space and facilities for food service personnel and participants.
7. Continually assess administrative methods of operating the food service programs; i.e., scheduling, food selection, preparation, delivery, distribution, traffic flow, etc.
8. Inspect and evaluate the equipment and supplies and the need for repair and/or replacement.

9. Establish simple, reliable accounting procedures for budgeting and handling cash receipts.
10. Encourage and promote cooperation and communication between food service personnel and the faculty and staff.
11. Periodically solicit participants' attitudes and opinions regarding the school's food service program.
12. Work with the food service director (dietician) in providing in-service training opportunities for food service personnel.
13. Find out and then disseminate to others the different and interesting things other school districts are doing regarding food service programs.[1]

EVALUATING FOOD SERVICES

Since there is no uniform food service program operating in all school districts and since each school food service operation is conditioned by a variety of on-site factors (availability of a lunch room, conversion of gym to lunch facility, preparation of food in or out of the school, etc.), school principals should develop their own plans and procedures to insure effective and efficient operating of the food service program. As suggested in Chapter 1, establishing a school committee may be the best approach in assessing the food service program, its procedures, and its personnel. The following items may be worthy of evaluation. Reasons for evaluating the particular items are described with some suggestions for how and when the item should be assessed.

Philosophy

Why? Increasingly, school teachers are examining and using the food service program as part of the educational outcomes of the curriculum. "However, the primary role of the food services operation is that of providing tasty, tempting, balanced meals of reasonable costs to the students."[2]

How? Have teachers discuss, illustrate, and assess how the food service program could be incorporated into such courses as chemistry, biology, health, consumer economics, and sociology. Teachers may also be encouraged to show how they use the food service program to provide student opportunities for learning:

- To select the right foods (nutrition)
- To maintain a proper diet
- Career education possibilities in the service occupations
- Socialization skills, manners, decorum, and proper behavior
- About cleaniness, waste, and sanitation
- About foods of various cultures and nationalities.

When? If the curriculum possibilities of the food service program have not been examined in your school, it may be a good idea to ask the teachers to consider this opportunity at the next curriculum meeting. If your school does incorporate some of these ideas, an evaluation of the worth and progress to date may be warranted.

Problems/Issues

Why? Principals should be aware of national and state issues because knowledge and understanding of these may be helpful in decision making at the local level. For example, there has been much debate and discussion of such topics as open and closed lunch periods, waste of food in school lunch programs, junk foods from school vending machines, use of student help in the cafeteria, the need for schools to serve breakfast, mass feeding psychology, student behavior, and alternate ways of providing food services to students.[3]

How? A great deal of information can be obtained by reading appropriate educational journals, using the resources at the end of this chapter, and by attending educational conferences with programs on these topics.

When? Spend fifteen to twenty minutes each day reading about these topics. Seek out conferences and, if you have time, start educating yourself now.

Personnel

Why? Like other school personnel, food service personnel need to be supervised and evaluated so that strengths and limitations of each member and the entire group are identified and defined.

How? In cooperation with the district's food service director, the union representative (if your food service employees belong to a union) and the school principal should establish a supervisory and evaluation plan. There must be agreement on who is going to do what; that is, in the supervision and evaluation of food service personnel what will be the responsibilities of the food service director vis-à-vis the school principal? In most school districts, the school principal assumes supervisory responsibilities of personnel working in that school. (An example of the type of rating scales that can be used for evaluating food service and other personnel is shown later in this chapter.)

When? Food service personnel should be evaluated yearly, as should all faculty and staff in your school, with the purposes, criteria, and procedures understood and accepted by those involved.

Accounting

Why? Since the principal is primarily responsible for the security of cash, checks, and the accounting procedures used in the school, an evaluation of the procedures used in carrying out this responsibility is paramount.

How? A school principal could benefit from observing how lunch monies are collected and transported either to the school office or the bank each day. Careful observation may suggest that better ways of collecting and transporting these monies is necessary. Recall the discussion regarding ways to evaluate accounting procedures (Figure 3–5). In addition, the checklist in Figure 3–6 may provide ideas and serve as a check on what you are currently doing in your school regarding school lunch accounts.

When? A few minutes to observe your procedures over the next two or three days may save you hours of explanations later on. After completing the observation and the checklist, take a few more minutes to decide if there is, indeed, a better, safer, more responsible way of accounting for school food service monies.

Operation

Why? The school principal carries the primary responsibility for the management of the school's food service operation. This responsibility includes, among other things, the preparation and delivery of food; the quality and quantity of food served per lunch; the number of students and others participating in the lunch program; the scheduling and supervising of students; the traffic flow to and from the cafeteria; the equipment and supplies in the kitchen and cafeteria; the physical facilities and atmosphere in the cafeteria; the collection and handling of monies; an adherence to the school district's policies and procedures; the school's compliance with state and local health and sanitation laws; the attitude of students and others toward the food service program and its personnel; and the working relationship among food service personnel, district office staff, and the school's faculty and staff.

How? There are a number of ways principals can assess the extent to which they are successfully managing each of the responsibilities listed above. A few examples will illustrate this point:

1. *Rating scales* can be effective in soliciting lunch participants' attitudes about the program.
2. *Observing and recording* aspects of the daily operation such as student behavior, length of time it takes to get lunch and pay for it, handling of trays and cash registers, food waste, and quantity of food per lunch can provide useful information to solve potential or current problems.

Figure 3-6
Lunch Fees Accounting Checklist

	We Do This Now	Good Idea; We Should Do This	No Need To Do This In Our School
1. A cash register, with printed tape recording each cash transaction, is used for lunch payments.	____	____	____
2. Each teacher collects monies for snacks and lunches, then files a daily accounting report with the school secretary.	____	____	____
3. Students/others buy food tickets daily or weekly from the homeroom teacher or the school office (store).	____	____	____
4. A ledger is used for keeping lunch records of expenditures and receipts.	____	____	____
5. Money is placed in a safe area, preferably in the school safe.	____	____	____
6. Daily cash vouchers are transported to the district's business office or bank in locked moneybags each day.	____	____	____
7. All persons handling school food service monies are bonded.	____	____	____
8. Receipts are obtained for all monies deposited each day/week.	____	____	____
9. A monthly financial accounting statement should be filed with the business manager.			

3. *Opinionnaires* can be used to find out about users' opinions for improving the school lunch program.

4. *Interviews* with students, teachers, and food service personnel may provide helpful information for better management of this program.

5. *Conferences* with groups of students, teachers, and food service personnel may reveal concerns, problems, issues, strengths, and weaknesses in the way the program is operating and managed.

When? Principals should use at least one method of assessing the food service operation in their school each school year.

Student Participation and Behavior

Why? It is well known, at least among students, that participation in the lunch programs is directly related to a variety of factors, some of which are the behavior of students, the attractiveness and decor of the cafeteria, the quality and variety of foods, the time it takes to get and eat lunch, and so on.

In some schools, the cafeteria, like the restrooms, is the last place most students wish to visit. In other schools, students can hardly wait for the lunch period so that they can rest, relax, and enjoy a delicious lunch while socializing with their friends.

Student participation is essential if the school food service program is to be an educational and financial success. It is estimated that at least one-third to one-half of the student body must participate. For this reason, principals should rely on student judgment regarding participation, quantity and quality of foods served, the atmosphere of the cafeteria, and other factors that will influence their willingness to participate. Many times the perceptions and judgments of the principal and teachers regarding the school's lunch program will differ from those of the student body. Principals and teachers may want a quiet, restful, atmosphere and shorter lunch period while students prefer a longer time for eating lunch in an atmosphere of noise, talk, and opportunity for socializing. It is important to underscore the point that student participation is dependent upon their attitudes and desires to eat in the school cafeteria.[4]

There are several factors that tend to increase student participation in the school lunch program. Some of the major factors include teachers and students eating together, an increase in the number of students bussed to school, a history of cafeteria service in the school, sufficient seating capacity, publishing the menu in advance, a variety of food choices, food quality and quantity, shorter lines and an adequate eating time, closed lunch periods, and a lack of nearby restaurants.[5]

How? The evaluation techniques recommended under the discussion of the "Operation" of the food service program would be appropriate here. In addition, it may be helpful to have an example of a student rating scale that you can use or adapt to evaluate the lunch program in your school. Figure 3–7 is an example of such a student rating scale.

When? One is tempted to suggest that this evaluation be done yearly, but time and other tasks suggest that a principal should assess student opinions when participation decreases, when there are more lunchroom problems than usual, and when and if an assessment has not been done for two or three years.

Figure 3–7
Student Rating Scale for Lunch Program

Directions: We want your opinion and your rating of this school's lunch program. The information you provide will help us improve and do a better job. "Grade" each of the items below by circling the letter that best describes your rating of that item.

Item	Excellent	Good	Fair	Poor
1. Time for lunch	A	B	C	D
2. Lunchroom atmosphere	A	B	C	D
3. Quality of lunch	A	B	C	D
4. Quantity of lunch	A	B	C	D
5. Behavior of students	A	B	C	D
6. Variety of lunches	A	B	C	D
7. Cost of lunch	A	B	C	D
8. Cafeteria workers	A	B	C	D
9. Student workers	A	B	C	D
10. Length of lunch times	A	B	C	D
11. Condition of trays and utensils	A	B	C	D
12. Attractiveness of lunchroom	A	B	C	D
13. Traffic flow to and from lunch	A	B	C	D
14. Waste disposal procedures	A	B	C	D
15. Teacher/aide supervision	A	B	C	D

(cont.)

16. What *improvements* do you suggest regarding:
    a. physical facilities?

    b. food offerings?

    c. student conduct?

    d. lunch period (time)?

    e. other (specify)?

17. If you were in charge of this school's lunch program, what would you change and/or improve?

18. Name two or three major things that "bug" you about this school's lunch program.
    a. _____
    b. _____
    c. _____

MANAGING TRANSPORTATION SERVICES

What was once a rural phenomenon has become an important service for over 40 percent of the school children in this country. From the concept of transportation to get children to their local schools and for transportation to school-sponsored events, school districts now provide transportation services for handicapped and other special students, for students attending special "magnet" schools, and for helping the community racially balance the schools.

The managerial responsibilities of the school principal are carried out within the parameters of the school board's transportation service policies. In reality, the principal has administrative and supervisory responsibilities for services provided only to the students at the school level. However, these responsibilities must be discharged with knowledge and understanding of federal, state, and local laws and regulations and the school district's policies and procedures. For example, the school principal administers and supervises transportation services on the basis of decisions others have made regarding:

- Who will receive transportation services
- What other transportation services will be provided students in the school district; i.e., athletics, field trips, etc.
- How federal, state, and local regulations offset the district's transportation plans
- How students qualify for these services
- What rules and regulations guide student behavior, pick-up and delivery, safety measures, etc.
- What the district can and cannot afford
- The best way to provide transportation services, i.e., contract for the service or have a district-owned service

- The best routing and scheduling methods to serve all qualified students in all schools
- The standards, specifications, inspection, and maintenance of transportation vehicles
- The methods for recruiting, selecting, and training of transportation personnel
- The plans and procedures for evaluating transportation services and personnel.

Evaluating Administration Responsibilities

It may be best to provide you with a list of responsibilities you, as principal, should be doing about transportation services for the students in your school. As you read each item on this list, decide whether (1) this item is something you are currently doing; (2) if so, how well are you doing it?; and (3) if not, why aren't you doing it? This procedure offers a means for self-evaluation. So, as principal you should:

- Know and implement school board policies
- Know and implement the transportation and director's rules and regulations
- Keep school personnel informed of policies, rules, and regulations
- Inform parents, students, and teachers about local school rules, regulations, and procedures
- Provide for the supervision of students while loading and unloading buses
- Solve problems relating to bus services as quickly as possible
- Attend to the needs of special students (see next section)
- Maintain adequate accident records and reports
- Maintain adequate misbehavior records and reports
- Establish simple, easy-to-use forms for teachers, coaches, and others requesting special transportation services
- Publish bus routes and schedules periodically throughout the school year
- Evaluate bus services for your school annually (see Evaluation Instruments section at the end of this chapter)

- Develop notification procedures for students who ride the buses should they become ill during the school day
- Develop procedures that will provide for children who miss the school bus
- Develop an after-school bus schedule and procedure if your school has after-school activities programs
- Encourage teachers to incorporate safety program content into their curriculum
- Establish standards of bus conduct that students must follow
- Develop procedures for handling cases of misconduct
- Encourage teachers and others to develop transportation (bus/bike) safety programs
- Check on the district procedures for vehicle maintenance and repairs
- Ride the buses at least once a year
- Follow a school bus in your car to check on driving and student behavior
- Report concerns and compliments to the district's transportation director
- Establish and publish emergency procedures should the school close for some reason
- Respond immediately to parent concerns and requests
- Work with teachers to develop constructive activities students can do on the bus while riding to and from school.[6]

In addition to these responsibilities, building principals must attend to the transportation needs of special students. Although each school district is responsible for providing safe, reliable transportation for handicapped students, it is the building principal's tasks to:

- Identify students in the school who need special transportation
- Arrange with the district's transportation director the kind of transportation needed; i.e., taxicab, private automobile, minibuses, buses with wheelchair lifts, regular school bus
- Notify the parents and teachers of the kind of transportation that will be provided

- Insure that adequate procedures are implemented for vehicle loading and unloading at the school and the home or shop
- Promote pre-service and in-service training opportunities for drivers servicing handicapped students
- Periodically supervise and evaluate transportation services for handicapped students in the school.

EVALUATING AND SUPERVISING STAFF PERSONNEL

In most school districts, there is a five-step process regarding the employment of staff personnel. The details of this process are usually negotiated in advance with union representatives. Three of the five steps—recruitment, selection, and training—are usually done at the district level. The school principal, while having some input into these three tasks, is required to attend to the remaining two steps —supervision and evaluation.

The recruitment process in any school district should involve personnel from individual schools as well as from the district office. A representative committee of administrators, teachers, staff, parents, union representatives, and, in some cases, students should be involved in some manner. All applicants should be required to file a written application with references, and any other information necessary to help the selection process.

The selection of personnel should be based on the evidence at hand and on the regulations required by the equal employment opportunity mandates. The selection should be made only after the finalists in the recruitment process have completed required tests—written, oral, or performance—and after they have been interviewed by the committee at the school level.

The training of personnel should coincide with a probationary period during which time the new employees are carefully supervised and trained to accomplish the tasks required for the job. Orientation programs, procedure books, hand-

books, and in-service programs should be made available to all new employees.

Procedures for supervising employees should be detailed, in advance, so that the supervisor and the employees know the criteria for supervision, i.e., based on job description, use of an observation instrument, a required conference, etc. Supervisory practices should be viewed as a positive process focusing on ways to help employees improve skills, attitudes, and performance.

The evaluation process, in conjunction with the supervision tasks, is a major responsibility of the school principal. The school principal is, and should be, responsible for providing periodic supervisory and evaluation reports. The evaluation should be based on the job description, the employee's performance, and the purpose of the evaluation (whether it be for retention/dismissal or promotion/compensation).

Evaluating Performance

Most school districts have standard employee performance review forms for the secretarial-clerical staff, food service personnel, and transportation personnel. Many of these evaluation forms have similar characteristics. For example, the forms will include such items as:

- Name of employee, job title, department
- Name of supervisor/evaluator, review period
- Job description (major responsibilities, duties, and goals of job)
- Rating scale (from poor to outstanding)
- Criteria (quality, quantity, and knowledge of work; initiative; reliability; attitude; attendance; punctuality; interpersonal relations; credibility; adaptability; judgment; overall performance)
- A section for supervisor's comments
- A section for performance improvement goals
- A section for employee's comments
- Spaces for signatures, dates, and conferences.

The form shown in Figure 3–8 is a composite of several forms used to evaluate staff personnel.

Figure 3-8
Staff Personnel Evaluation/Observation Form

School:_____

Name:_____ Job Title:_____

Length of Service:_____ Date:_____

Performance Items I   *Performance Rating*

	Acceptable	Needs Improving	Unacceptable
1. Job knowledge	____	____	____
2. Accuracy	____	____	____
3. Alertness	____	____	____
4. Dependability	____	____	____
5. Thoroughness	____	____	____
6. Attendance	____	____	____
7. Effort	____	____	____
8. Orderliness	____	____	____
9. Quality of work	____	____	____
10. Quantity of work	____	____	____
11. Neatness	____	____	____
12. Punctuality	____	____	____
13. Appearance	____	____	____

Evidence/Comments for Needs Improving or Unacceptable ratings:

Performance Items II   *Performance Rating*

	Excellent	Good	Fair	Unsatisfactory
14. Relationship with co-workers	____	____	____	____
15. Relationship with administrator(s)	____	____	____	____
16. Relationship with teachers	____	____	____	____
17. Relationship with students	____	____	____	____
18. Relationship with parents	____	____	____	____
19. Relationship with public	____	____	____	____

Evidence/Comments for Fair or Unsatisfactory ratings:

Performance Items III   *Performance Rating*

Demonstrates this quality:	Always	Usually	Sometimes	Never
20. Courteous	____	____	____	____
21. Creative	____	____	____	____
22. Ambitious	____	____	____	____

(cont.)

| | Performance Rating | | | |
Demonstrates this quality:	Always	Usually	Sometimes	Never
23. Communicative	___	___	___	___
24. Adaptive	___	___	___	___
25. Resourceful	___	___	___	___
26. Personable	___	___	___	___
27. Cooperative	___	___	___	___
28. Initiates	___	___	___	___
29. Evaluates	___	___	___	___

Evidence/Comments for None rating:

Overall Rating

___Very Acceptable   ___Acceptable   ___Unacceptable
    (Excellent)   (Good)   (Poor)

Recommendation

___Merit consideration   ___Work on performance   ___Dismissal
                            areas* during next
                            evaluation period

*Performance areas to be improved:

*Evaluation procedures to be used:

In addition to the evaluation of staff personnel working in your school (bus drivers are viewed as members of the school staff), it is essential that you and the faculty be concerned about attitudes and morale. Job satisfaction is related to job performance. For this reason, it is important that you attempt to solicit, via interviews or questionnaires, the staff's concerns, suggestions, and perhaps their gripes. Some principals use a questionnaire like the one shown in Figure 3–9.

The content for this kind of questionnaire helps the principal when meeting with the staff because it serves as an agenda, as a focal point for interviews and conferences, and as a record for tracking change and improvements. The purpose of these meetings should be a desire on the principal's part to solicit suggestions for improving services to students; to obtain recommendations for a more effective operation of each of the services (office, food transportation); to determine where areas of conflict may exist between faculty and staff; to get help in evaluating school services, policies, and procedures; and to maintain and promote satisfaction and morale among staff personnel.

While the suggestions are applicable to all staff personnel, evaluating custodial services and

Figure 3-9
Questionnaire for Staff Personnel

Directions: Your evaluation of the school's activities and personnel will be most helpful in maintaining efficiency and morale. Your cooperation is most appreciated. Please answer each question carefully and as completely as time will allow. The information will be confidential.

Name:_____ Position:_____

1. Do you feel you are treated by the professional staff as a member of the school team?
   ____Yes   ____At times   ____No
   Describe specific incidents if you wish:

2. Do you feel the principal gives you the support you need to carry out your duties efficiently and effectively?
   ____Yes   ____At times   ____No
   Comment:

3. In general, are you satisfied with your work and surroundings?
   ____Yes   ____At times   ____No
   Comment:

4. What improvement(s) in your work and surroundings would you suggest?

5. When problems arise, do you feel that the principal gives them the attention they deserve?
   ____Yes   ____At times   ____No
   Explain:

performance will be included in the next chapter as part of the discussion on plant and facilities management.

A FINAL COMMENT

All school principals continue to try to balance their administrative-manager role with their instructional-leadership role. The success of this attempt is dependent upon a variety of factors, one of which is the managerial skills principals bring to the job. Effective management of school offices and services should allow you time for demonstrat-

ing an interest and skill in instructional leadership. Therefore, you should try to perform the following skills:

1. Arrange your personal schedule so that you spend at least two hours each week in a classroom.
2. Assess the time and tasks you spend in doing office work.
3. Organize the school office and services so that they are an example of efficiency and effectiveness.
4. Seek additional help if you really feel you need it.

5. Keep the office open to communication from all sources.
6. Periodically assess office, food, and transportation services.
7. Assess accounting and budgeting procedures that hold people who handle money responsible for what they do with it.
8. Involve faculty and staff in the preparation and evaluation of the school budget and the evaluation of school services.
9. Keep yourself, the faculty, and the staff up-to-date on current issues and trends in school funding and accounting procedures, as well as food and transportation services.
10. Automate records, files, budget, and accounting procedures as much as possible.

EVALUATION INSTRUMENTS

Much of the content for evaluating and improving office and budget management will be found in resources dealing with school business management practices and program-personnel evaluation. Some examples follow.

"Evaluative Checklist—An Instrument for Self-Evaluating an Educational Media Program in School Systems." Ross L. Neagley, N. Dean Evans, and Clarence A. Lynn, Jr. *The School Administrator and Learning Resources* (Englewood Cliffs, New Jersey: Prentice-Hall, 1969).

Although this checklist is designed for school systems, it can be adapted for evaluating the educational media program in a school. Criteria are identified regarding commitment to an educational media program, services, the center, physical facilities, and staff. Also included is a profile sheet so one can plot a profile of their educational media program.

"Checklist on School Insurance Program Administration" and "Self-Inspection Blank." *School Business Management Handbook No. 2: Insurance* (Albany, New York: The State Education Department, 1963).

The first checklist is a twenty-four-item questionnaire with a "yes-no" response useful to principals interested in obtaining proper and adequate insurance coverage. The Self-Inspection Blank is useful for on-site inspections of safety factors in a school building, although some items are not applicable to schools.

"Evaluation Review Instrument." Lesley H. Brower, Jr., William A. Atkins, Jr., and Esin Kaya. *Developing an Educationally Accountable Program* (Berkeley, California: McCutchan Publishing Corp., 1973).

This four-part instrument uses a rating scale to help school administrators evaluate evaluation reports that you or others may have completed. Part One includes a section for obtaining general information; Part Two provides a critique of the evaluation design; Part Three is a scale for assessing the project evaluation process; and Part Four enables you to evaluate the evaluator's (your) recommendations.

Project 4-E: Evaluating Elementary Education Effectively. James W. Altschuld and Dale Baker (Columbus, Ohio: Columbus City School District, 1971).

This twenty-one-page evaluation checklist uses a variety of rating scales (yes-no, short answer, multiple choice, and questions) to evaluate elementary school organization and administration, curriculum and instruction, pupil services, staff personnel, instructional materials and equipment, physical facilities, and school-community relations.

Checklist for the Evaluation of Transportation Services

Emery Stoops, Max Rafferty, and Russell E. Johnson. *Handbook of Educational Administration: A Guide for the Practitioner* (Boston: Allyn and Bacon, Inc., 1975), pp. 414–417.

This evaluation checklist was developed by Irving R. Melbo et al. for the Taft City School District. It consists of thirty-seven statements, each with a possible rating of superior, average, or poor.

It may be used to help develop transportation policies and administration of these policies.

Bus Service Evaluation Form

Edward F. DeRoche and Jeffrey S. Kaiser. *Administering School Support Services* (West Nyack, N.Y.: Parker Publishing Co. 1980), pp. 255–257.

This form is a rating scale that principals can use to rate bus service to the school in four areas: administration, personnel, equipment, and programs.

ENDNOTES

1. Edward F. DeRoche and Jeffrey S. Kaiser, *Administering School Support Services* (West Nyack, N.Y.: Parker Publishing, 1980), pp. 226–227.

2. I. Carl Candoli et al., *School Business Administration: A Planning Approach* (Boston: Allyn and Bacon, 1978), p. 228.

3. DeRoche and Kaiser, *Administering School Support Services*, pp. 225–229.

4. Emery Stoops; Max Rafferty; and Russell E. Johnson, *Handbook of Educational Administration: A Guide for the Practitioners* (Boston: Allyn and Bacon, 1975), pp. 463–464.

5. DeRoche and Kaiser, *Administering School Support Services*, pp. 216–217.

6. Ibid., pp. 248–249.

SELECTED REFERENCES

Berk, Laura E., and Benson, Minnie P. "Riding Easy." *Childhood Education* (October 1975): 20–24.

Bragin, Jeanette. *Guiding Principles and Practices in Office Management.* Chicago: Association of School Business Officials, 1966.

Bulletin of the National Association of Secondary School Principals 56 (October 1972). (The theme of this issue is PPBS—Planning, Programming, Budgeting Systems.)

Candoli, Carl; Hack, Walter G.; Ray, John R.; and Stollar, Dewey H. *School Business Administration: A Planning Approach.* Boston: Allyn and Bacon, 1978.

Delahanty, Joseph F. *Pupil Transportation Safety Program Plan.* Washington, D.C.: Department of Transportation, May 1973.

Greenhalgh, John. *Practitioner's Guide to School Business Management.* Boston: Allyn and Bacon, 1978.

Grossman, Alvin, and Howe, Robert L. *Data Processing for Educators.* Chicago: Educational Methods, 1965.

Jones, Florence G., and Wilson, Harold M. *How to Plan a More Efficient School Office.* Englewood Cliffs, N.J.: Prentice-Hall, 1966.

Knezevich, Stephen J. *Management by Objectives and Results.* Arlington, Va.: American Association of School Administrators, 1973.

Nelson, D. Lloyd, and Purdy, William M. *School Business Administration.* Lexington, Mass.: D. C. Heath and Co., 1971.

Perryman, John N. *The School Administrator and the Food Service Program.* Washington, D.C.: National Association of Elementary School Principals, 1972.

School Planning—Safe Transportation. Trenton, N.J.: Bureau of Pupil Transportation, New Jersey Department of Education, 1969.

School Transportation: A Guide for Supervisors. Chicago: National Safety Council, 1967.

Schrieber, Ernest. *400+ Ways to Save Money in Your Schools.* Blackwood, N.J.: Educational Impact, 1978.

Watson, Olive B. *School and Institutional Lunchroom Management.* West Nyack, N.Y.: Parker Publishing Co., 1968.

Weiss, Edmond H., and Sison, Roger L. "The Student as Planning and Cost Center: An Administrative System for the 1980's." *Phi Delta Kappan* 54 (December 1974): 272–274.

Whitlock, James W. *Automatic Data Processing in Education.* New York: The Macmillan Co., 1964.

4

EVALUATING AND IMPROVING PLANT AND FACILITIES MANAGEMENT

The virtue of a man ought to be measured, not by his extraordinary exertions, but by his every-day conduct.

Blaise Pascal

How times have changed. Few, if any, texts on educational administration published during the last three decades addressed themselves to the closing of schools because of declining enrollment, or for new use of school buildings that are no longer needed for traditional classrooms. Today's educational administrators will have to make do with the plant and facilities for which they are responsible. Some principals will have schools that are relatively new, reflecting current educational trends with open classrooms, pod-arrangements, schools without walls, flexible room designs, and other modern aspects of construction, design, and facilities. Other principals will continue to manage two- or three-story schools, and old, functional, traditional buildings with solid walls, large corridors, and crate-like construction.

Regardless of the kind of building—old, new, flexible, inflexible, single- or multiple-story construction—the principal has the responsibility to supervise, manage, evaluate, and improve the school plant and its facilities. The responsibility takes on greater significance in this current era since the public has "pressured" school boards and administrators to make do with what they have.

As principal, you should obtain evaluative data regarding four major factors: the efficient use of the school building; the operation and care of the school building and grounds; the management of school supplies and equipment; and the safety, security, and insurance of school plant and its facilities. Information resulting from an evaluation of each of these four factors should help you manage the school plant more efficiently and creatively.

PRINCIPLES AND PRACTICES

Recognizing the changes that take place educationally and socially, the school principal should reflect upon the following principles and practices before evaluation plans are implemented:

1. Theoretically, the school plant and its facilities should be influenced by the education programs and school services. In practice, and in many instances this is not the case, the school plant sometimes influences the school programs. The principal and others should be aware of the extent to which this exists.
2. Plans should be developed to use all of the space within the school. Space should not be wasted.
3. The school plant and its facilities should be modified to meet the needs and changes required by the educational program and/or school services (including special education students).[1]
4. Safety, security, comfort, and adaptability should be essential factors in plant and facilities management.
5. The proper care of school plant and facilities requires the involvement of faculty, staff, and students.
6. Plans should be developed for the proper supervision and management of the plant and its facilities, supplies, and equipment.
7. Wherever possible, the principal should delegate responsibility for plant management to an assistant principal and/or custodian.
8. The principal should continuously evaluate educational needs and services and determine the extent to which the physical facilities, supplies, and equipment are meeting these needs.
9. School grounds and its equipment should reflect educational, recreational, and community needs.
10. Purchasing of school supplies and equipment should, wherever possible, be centralized and result from bids.

HOW TO EVALUATE
UTILIZATION OF SCHOOL SPACE

Evaluating and planning for the efficient use of the school building requires the cooperation of teachers and staff. They are in a central position to inform the principal about the use of space in the building regarding the educational program. In planning for evaluation, you, as principal, should consider two factors: one is the efficient use of the school plant during the day, when the usual educational program is in session, and the other is the use of school plant and facilities when school is not in session.

Determining Building Use

One method for determining the use of the school building is the utilization of a building-use chart. The purpose of such a chart is to determine how, when, and why specific space is used in the school building. The information gleaned from a chart of this kind may help principals, teachers, and staff plan for a more creative use of school space for programs and services provided. Figure 4–1 shows a daily building-use chart that may be useful in determining room utilization except for classrooms. The chart provides a way to examine specific room use for each hour. However, you may find it more effective to include the school's time schedule rather than an hourly schedule.

When using this chart, you should write in the room capacity for each room in the building and the number of students using the room during each time frame. This could also be accomplished by asking each person in charge of a particular room to indicate the room capacity and the number of students in the room each hour (or each scheduled period), each day for one week. For example, you might ask the librarian to provide you with the preceding information. You could duplicate the chart and, using the above procedure, have the band director, music teacher(s), art teacher(s), and others gather the needed information. It should be noted that the chart provides two spaces per time frame. The space at the top is used to record student

Figure 4-1
Daily Building-Use Chart

Day:_____ Date:_____	Room Capacity	8:00	9:00	10:00	11:00	12:00	1:00	2:00	3:00	4:00	5:00	Utilization Percent Average
Library	50	10 20%	15 30%	40 80%	25 50%	20 40%	45 90%	40 80%	30 60%	10 20%	5 10%	48%
Band room												
Auditorium												
Multipurpose room												
Science laboratory												
Cafeteria												
Art room												
Business Education room												
Home Economics room												
Industrial Arts room												
Gymnasium												
Special Education room												
Guidance Center												
Health Care Services												
Speech Service area												
Bookstore												
Study Hall												
Other												
Building Utilization Summary												

use. The space at the bottom of the block is the utilization percentage averaged for the day. An example is shown under the Library section. Note that the room capacity is fifty people and that on this particular day ten used the library room at 8:00 A.M., fifteen at 9:00 A.M., and so on. Also note the percentage of utilization for each hour. This figure is obtained by dividing the number of students using the room by the room capacity. The utilization percent average is computed by adding the percentages and dividing by the number of scores. Thus, on a particular day this library is used every hour, with certain low and peak periods, and an average utilization rate (in relation to room capacity) of a little less than 50 percent.

The principal can obtain some idea of building use by examining the percentages found in the Building Utilization Summary column. Again, this figure is derived by adding the percentages for the time frame and dividing by the number of rooms on the chart.

Determining Class Use

Figure 4–2 is an example of a classroom-use chart. The chart can be duplicated and given to classroom teachers and others if the principal decides to use

Figure 4–2
Classroom Utilization Chart

Teacher: John Jones   Room Capacity: 30
Room Number: 101   Date:_____

Period	M	T	W	Th	F	Room Available	Used Less Than 70 Percent of Capacity
Before School	0	0	0	0	0	M–F	M–F
Home Room	26	26	26	26	26	0	None
1	28	24	29	18	22	0	Th
2	19	0	22	28	30	I	M
3							
4							
5							
6							
7							
8							
After School							

this form to collect classroom-use data as well as use of other rooms in the building.

The example shown allows the teacher to identify room use for each day of the week. It also provides a quick summary of nonroom use that may be of value when a room is needed for a special reason. The variation in the figures shown is due to different class sizes resulting from grouping and/or the scheduling of sections in each subject matter area. The last two columns of the chart enable the principal to determine quickly when the room is available (unless used for other purposes not charted) and when the room is being used at less than 70 percent capacity (an arbitrary figure).

EVALUATING COMMUNITY USE OF SCHOOL FACILITIES

Many communities now offer a variety of programs in school buildings after regular school hours. Adult education programs, programs for young and old citizens, and recreational and cultural programs are all scheduled in existing school facilities. In many instances schools are open up to fifteen hours per day. The advantages are many and so are the problems.

Problems with Community Use

Extensive use of school plant and facilities does create several problems for school principals that require attention. Among the major concerns are the following:

1. There is a need for supervision of groups using the facilities.
2. There is also a need for supervision and care of the plant and its facilities during and after school hours. This requires additional custodial staff or paying extra fees to the existing custodial staff.
3. School use costs money for heating, lighting, ventilating, cleaning, and supplies and equipment.

4. A schedule must be made by the principal and/or the principal's designee. This may cause problems when a number of groups want to use the facilities at the same time.
5. Scheduling groups for use of school facilities requires that priority be provided in this fashion: school-concerned activities, extracurricular activities, local groups, and then other self-supported agencies, organizations, and associations. This procedure sometimes causes problems for the school principal.

Regardless of these disadvantages, it is important to remember that the school is a community facility and the advantages certainly outweigh the disadvantages. The disadvantages can be lessened somewhat by specific board of education policies on community use of school facilities.

Checklist for Developing Policies

In general, community use of school buildings is guided by policies and procedures of the board of education. The principal's job is to carry out the school board's policies, clarify these policies to community groups when necessary, and record and report the extent of community use and its effect on the school plant, facilities, supplies, and equipment. To assist principals with this task the following checklist is provided.

1. ____ Does your school board of education have a policy regarding community use of the school plant and its facilities?
2. ____ Do you know what the policies are or at least where to find them if needed?
3. ____ Does your school policy provide classifications of uses?
4. ____ Does the policy provide a rental fee for use of school facilities?
5. ____ Does the policy state what procedures should be followed by groups requesting the use of school facilities?
6. ____ Does the policy state the arrangements necessary for custodial services?

7. ____ Does the policy provide guidelines for safety and security during those times community groups are using school facilities?

8. ____ Does the policy provide guidelines for each school administrator?

9. ____ Do you file a report of community use of school facilities that includes:
   a. Calendar of events scheduled?
   b. Groups using facilities?
   c. Building condition after each event?
   d. Special concerns?
   e. Fees collected?

10. ____ Does the policy require the filing of an application? (Example: The application should require specific information, including a guarantee regarding damage and/or injuries.)

HOW TO EVALUATE MAINTENANCE OF PLANT AND FACILITIES

The principal is responsible for the proper maintenance of the school plant, its facilities, and its grounds. The primary goal should be to keep the building in good operating condition, including safety and security, for daily use. The resource for these tasks is the school's custodial staff.

Self-Evaluation Questions

A principal should have specific plans and procedures for the care and maintenance of the school plant and facilities. To insure this, you should consider each of the following questions:

1. Do you have a monthly or biannual plan for supervising/inspecting the school plant, its site, and its facilities?

2. Do you involve custodians and others in planning for the care and maintenance of the school and facilities?

3. Do you have procedures that require teachers and staff to determine the extent to which existing facilities meet the needs of the instructional program, extracurricular programs, and school services?

4. Do you have procedures that identify major alterations, expansion, or remodeling that should be made to better serve the school's programs and services?

5. Do you regularly evaluate any plans and procedures you implement to assess care and maintenance of the school and facilities?

The evaluation checklists that follow enable a principal, custodian, or both to rate the condition of each item. They provide a means for determining what action should be taken and when. The schedule column enables the principal to engage in short- and long-range planning. The forms provide an excellent way to plan courses of action and a schedule for budgeting for the actions to be taken. The items are by no means a complete listing but they are as comprehensive as will be found in the literature. The principal should add items that reflect factors peculiar to his or her own particular school and grounds.

Checklist for the Inspection of a School's Interior

The checklist shown in Figure 4–3 may be used monthly or biannually by the principal and/or custodian. The data from this checklist can be used for establishing priorities for alterations, remodeling, or additions to the interior of the school.

Checklist for the Inspection of Classrooms

Figure 4–4 illustrates a list of points that should be considered when inspecting classrooms. Periodic inspection of classrooms should be planned by the principal and custodian. However, the key to classroom conditions is the teacher. Each teacher should be required to complete the checklist at least once each year. This procedure, coupled with an inspection by the principal and the custodian, will contribute to safe and functional classrooms.

Figure 4-3
Checklist for Regular Inspection of Individual School—Interior (Excluding Classrooms)

School:_____ Date:_____

Inspected by:_____

Items	Condition			Action					Schedule			Comments/ Notations
	Good	Fair	Poor	Repair	Replace	Remodel	Paint	Clean	This Year	Next Year	Year After	
Plumbing												
Drinking fountains	—	—	—	—	—	—	—	—	—	—	—	___
Toilets	—	—	—	—	—	—	—	—	—	—	—	___
Sinks	—	—	—	—	—	—	—	—	—	—	—	___
Dryers	—	—	—	—	—	—	—	—	—	—	—	___
Showers	—	—	—	—	—	—	—	—	—	—	—	___
Water pipes	—	—	—	—	—	—	—	—	—	—	—	___
Drainage pipes	—	—	—	—	—	—	—	—	—	—	—	___
Electrical												
Fixtures	—	—	—	—	—	—	—	—	—	—	—	___
Lights	—	—	—	—	—	—	—	—	—	—	—	___
Bulletin boards	—	—	—	—	—	—	—	—	—	—	—	___
Ceilings	—	—	—	—	—	—	—	—	—	—	—	___
Wood/Metal trim	—	—	—	—	—	—	—	—	—	—	—	___
Hardware	—	—	—	—	—	—	—	—	—	—	—	___
Floors	—	—	—	—	—	—	—	—	—	—	—	___
Carpets	—	—	—	—	—	—	—	—	—	—	—	___
Safety Devices												
Firehose cabinet	—	—	—	—	—	—	—	—	—	—	—	___
Fire extinguishers	—	—	—	—	—	—	—	—	—	—	—	___
Water shutoff valve	—	—	—	—	—	—	—	—	—	—	—	___
Gas shutoff valve	—	—	—	—	—	—	—	—	—	—	—	___
Electrical master switches	—	—	—	—	—	—	—	—	—	—	—	___
Plates	—	—	—	—	—	—	—	—	—	—	—	___
Switches	—	—	—	—	—	—	—	—	—	—	—	___
Lights	—	—	—	—	—	—	—	—	—	—	—	___
Wiring	—	—	—	—	—	—	—	—	—	—	—	___
Heating/ Ventilation												
Boilers	—	—	—	—	—	—	—	—	—	—	—	___
Pumps	—	—	—	—	—	—	—	—	—	—	—	___
Radiators	—	—	—	—	—	—	—	—	—	—	—	___
Ducts	—	—	—	—	—	—	—	—	—	—	—	___

(cont.)

| Items | Condition | | | Action | | | | | Schedule | | | Comments/ Notations |
	Good	Fair	Poor	Repair	Replace	Remodel	Paint	Clean	This Year	Next Year	Year After	
Corridors/ Halls												
Walls	—	—	—	—	—	—	—	—	—	—	—	
Stairways	—	—	—	—	—	—	—	—	—	—	—	
Railings	—	—	—	—	—	—	—	—	—	—	—	
Door panic bolts	—	—	—	—	—	—	—	—	—	—	—	

Figure 4-4
Checklist for Regular Inspection of Classrooms

School:_____ Date:_____

Inspected by:_____

| Items | Condition | | | Action | | | | | Schedule | | | Comments/ Notations |
	Good	Fair	Poor	Repair	Replace	Remodel	Paint	Clean	This Year	Next Year	Year After	
Ceiling	—	—	—	—	—	—	—	—	—	—	—	
Walls	—	—	—	—	—	—	—	—	—	—	—	
Floor	—	—	—	—	—	—	—	—	—	—	—	
Trim	—	—	—	—	—	—	—	—	—	—	—	
Hardware	—	—	—	—	—	—	—	—	—	—	—	
Cabinets	—	—	—	—	—	—	—	—	—	—	—	
Bulletin boards	—	—	—	—	—	—	—	—	—	—	—	
Chalk boards	—	—	—	—	—	—	—	—	—	—	—	
Furniture	—	—	—	—	—	—	—	—	—	—	—	
Electrical fixtures	—	—	—	—	—	—	—	—	—	—	—	
Heating ducts	—	—	—	—	—	—	—	—	—	—	—	
Ventilation unit	—	—	—	—	—	—	—	—	—	—	—	
Shades/blinds	—	—	—	—	—	—	—	—	—	—	—	
Intercom system	—	—	—	—	—	—	—	—	—	—	—	
Plumbing	—	—	—	—	—	—	—	—	—	—	—	
Plumbing fixtures	—	—	—	—	—	—	—	—	—	—	—	
Bookcases	—	—	—	—	—	—	—	—	—	—	—	
Clock	—	—	—	—	—	—	—	—	—	—	—	
Lockers	—	—	—	—	—	—	—	—	—	—	—	

Checklist for the Inspection of a School's Exterior

One's first impression of a school is obtained by observing the exterior of the school plant. Old schools can be made just as attractive as new schools. Inspection of exterior items is essential because failure to repair items such as roofing, gutters, etc., can often lead to greater expense later on. Therefore, it is essential that the principal and custodians regularly inspect the exterior of the school building. Some of the major items that deserve special attention are identified in Figure 4-5.

Checklist for the Inspection of School Grounds

The school's grounds and its equipment cannot be supervised all the time. Community use of these facilities takes place after school hours. In most cases the use is recreational; sometimes it is destructive. These factors call for the school principal and custodians to insure that regular inspection takes place. It is best to document the inspection in case of liability suits regarding safety of grounds and equipment. Monthly inspections using the checklist in Figure 4-6 is recommended.

Figure 4-5
Checklist for Regular Inspection of Individual School—Exterior

School:_____ Date:_____
Inspected by:_____

Items	Condition			Action					Schedule			Comments/ Notations
	Good	Fair	Poor	Repair	Replace	Remodel	Paint	Clean	This Year	Next Year	Year After	
Roofing	—	—	—	—	—	—	—	—	—	—	—	_____
Skylights	—	—	—	—	—	—	—	—	—	—	—	_____
Roof vents	—	—	—	—	—	—	—	—	—	—	—	_____
Chimneys	—	—	—	—	—	—	—	—	—	—	—	_____
Walls	—	—	—	—	—	—	—	—	—	—	—	_____
Columns	—	—	—	—	—	—	—	—	—	—	—	_____
Windows	—	—	—	—	—	—	—	—	—	—	—	_____
Sashes	—	—	—	—	—	—	—	—	—	—	—	_____
Facia	—	—	—	—	—	—	—	—	—	—	—	_____
Soffits	—	—	—	—	—	—	—	—	—	—	—	_____
Doors	—	—	—	—	—	—	—	—	—	—	—	_____
Entrance/ Exit stairs	—	—	—	—	—	—	—	—	—	—	—	_____
Downspouts	—	—	—	—	—	—	—	—	—	—	—	_____
Gutters	—	—	—	—	—	—	—	—	—	—	—	_____
Louvers	—	—	—	—	—	—	—	—	—	—	—	_____
Screens	—	—	—	—	—	—	—	—	—	—	—	_____
Fire escapes	—	—	—	—	—	—	—	—	—	—	—	_____
Footing/ Foundation	—	—	—	—	—	—	—	—	—	—	—	_____
Masonry	—	—	—	—	—	—	—	—	—	—	—	_____

Figure 4–6
Checklist for Regular Inspection of School Grounds

School:_____ Date:_____
Inspected by:_____

Items	Condition			Action					Schedule			Comments/ Notations
	Good	Fair	Poor	Repair	Replace	Remodel	Paint	Clean	This Year	Next Year	Year After	
Curbs and gutters	—	—	—	—	—	—	—	—	—	—	—	_____
Driveways	—	—	—	—	—	—	—	—	—	—	—	_____
Sidewalks	—	—	—	—	—	—	—	—	—	—	—	_____
Parking lot	—	—	—	—	—	—	—	—	—	—	—	_____
Water meter	—	—	—	—	—	—	—	—	—	—	—	_____
Gas meter	—	—	—	—	—	—	—	—	—	—	—	_____
Electrical meter	—	—	—	—	—	—	—	—	—	—	—	_____
Fences	—	—	—	—	—	—	—	—	—	—	—	_____
Gates	—	—	—	—	—	—	—	—	—	—	—	_____
Bicycle racks	—	—	—	—	—	—	—	—	—	—	—	_____
Flag pole	—	—	—	—	—	—	—	—	—	—	—	_____
Turf	—	—	—	—	—	—	—	—	—	—	—	_____
Lawns	—	—	—	—	—	—	—	—	—	—	—	_____
Trees	—	—	—	—	—	—	—	—	—	—	—	_____
Shrubs	—	—	—	—	—	—	—	—	—	—	—	_____
Sprinkling system	—	—	—	—	—	—	—	—	—	—	—	_____
Fertilizer/ sand	—	—	—	—	—	—	—	—	—	—	—	_____
Top soil	—	—	—	—	—	—	—	—	—	—	—	_____
Benches/ bleachers	—	—	—	—	—	—	—	—	—	—	—	_____
Drainage	—	—	—	—	—	—	—	—	—	—	—	_____
Playground equipment	—	—	—	—	—	—	—	—	—	—	—	_____

Buildings and Grounds Committee

Many school districts have a buildings and grounds committee that studies and recommends to the school board of education things that should be done in this area. One principal created a school-grounds beautification committee. This committee prepared a slide presentation on things that needed to be done to improve the school grounds. They showed the slides to the board of education, the school PTA, and to other citizens, and then outlined what had to be done. Monies were donated and collected from an aluminum-can collection project and private donations. As a result, the committee implemented a "Save-a-Tree" project, mended school fences, planted shrubs, and other projects to beautify the school grounds are planned. The idea has merit; it works and it should be initiated by other principals.

ENERGY CONSERVATION EVALUATION

The value of establishing a buildings and grounds committee is simply that the committee can be a valuable resource both for beautification projects and for the ever necessary energy conservation programs.

Since the oil embargo of 1973, the per pupil energy cost has tripled, while money for educational programs has decreased. In addition, efforts to find new sources of energy to combat depleting resources and to control the rapidly escalating energy conservation costs have caused the government and the public to look to the principal to assume leadership in meeting the challenge and responsibilities of energy conservation.

Consider the fact that over half of today's schools were built between 1955 and 1965, when there was a need for rapid construction of school buildings at low cost and when energy was cheap and plentiful. This resulted in poorly designed buildings that are estimated to waste anywhere from one-fourth to one-half of the energy used.[2] For example, one state estimates that its schools waste more than nine million dollars of energy annually and that the average school could save over $4000 per year by reducing energy waste.[3]

Energy Management Checklist

The school principal has to take the lead in organizing and managing an energy conservation program. To help you carry out this responsibility, the following checklist is provided as a guide whether or not you currently have an energy conservation program.

1. ____ Do you currently have an energy conservation program?
2. ____ Do you plan to start a program within the next school year?
3. ____ Is energy conservation an established priority by the school board or superintendent?
4. ____ Does the program involve teachers, staff, and community experts?
5. ____ Do you provide school personnel, parents, and your public with information about energy conservation programs at the local, state, and national level?
6. ____ Do teachers implement units or discuss energy conservation topics with students in their classes?
7. ____ Have teachers and students explored ways to save energy at home and at school?
8. ____ Have you devoted at least one faculty meeting to the topic of energy conservation?
9. ____ Have you created a committee to help you implement an energy consevation program?
10. ____ Have you, with the committee, conducted energy surveys and audits of the school building?
11. ____ Has the committee helped you determine the opportunities present in your school for conserving energy?
12. ____ Has the committee estimated the cost of implementing energy conservation practices?
13. ____ Has the committee estimated the potential benefits (savings) if some or all of the energy conservation recommendations are implemented?
14. ____ Has the committee established a list of priorities for implementing recommended energy conservation practices?
15. ____ Have the energy conservation recommendations been implemented?
16. ____ Have you established, with the committee, ways to monitor the energy conservation measures?

17. ____ Have you and the committee constructed or purchased appropriate forms and checklists for recording the data to be collected?
18. ____ Have you and the committee documented the energy conservation results in a manner that is readable and understandable to the public?
19. ____ Have you considered ways you will share the results of the "audit" and program with the school personnel and the public?

The energy management process has been summarized in four key words: identify, quantify, modify, and verify.[4]

In summary, the principal is responsible for managing others in the efficient and effective use of the school plant and its facilities. The previous sections of this chapter have described ways to evaluate school-space utilization, community use of the building, maintenance of plant and facilities, and energy conservation.

The building principal also has responsibilities regarding the management of supplies and equipment, safety and security measures, and the evaluation of custodial personnel and services. These are discussed in the following sections of this chapter.

MANAGING SCHOOL SUPPLIES AND EQUIPMENT

There are seven functions that principals must implement to effectively manage the school's supplies and equipment:

- Requisitioning—What procedures do you use to find out supply and equipment needs of teachers, custodians, secretaries, librarians, and other school personnel?
- Purchasing—What procedures do you use to purchase needed supplies and equipment?
- Receiving—What procedures do you employ for receiving supplies and equipment?
- Storing—What procedures do you use to store school supplies and equipment?

- Distributing—What procedures are used in your school for distributing supplies and equipment?
- Inventorying—What procedures do you use to keep records and reports on school supplies and equipment?
- Evaluating—What evaluating methods do you use to determine how effectively and efficiently you manage school supplies and equipment?

Principles and Practices

When one considers the cost of school supplies and equipment and the contribution they make to the instructional program, the importance of proper management takes on added significance. For this reason, a school principal should consider these principles and practices.

1. The selection of school supplies and equipment should result from a team approach; that is, the principal should involve teachers, custodians, secretary, and others in the selection process.
2. Standardized procedures for requisitioning and purchasing supplies and equipment should be implemented.
3. Standardized supply and equipment lists should be utilized.
4. School personnel should consider cooperative (sharing) use of some supplies and equipment, particularly those that are very expensive.
5. The principal, teachers, and staff should decide whether to use an open or closed stockroom approach. Open stockroom means that personnel are allowed to take supplies as needed. Closed stockroom means that personnel requisition needed supplies and, if approved by the principal, the material is delivered to the classroom by the custodian.
6. The principal or the principal's designee should employ a method for receiving, storing, and inventorying all school supplies and equipment.

7 A team approach should be employed for evaluating the extent to which supplies and equipment ordered and received contributes to the purposes for which it was purchased.

8. The principal should establish the concept of commonality: "those who share, care."[5]

Selecting and Requisitioning

To answer the questions asked in the introduction to this section, examine your current procedures for selecting and requisitioning supplies and equipment with the suggestions that follow:

1. A school team or committee is appointed to obtain supply and equipment needs of all school personnel.
2. The committee uses standardized catalogs for the selection of supplies and equipment.
3. The committee recommendations go to the principal with priority ratings for each item.
4. The committee is given opportunities and responsibilities for the evaluation of supplies and equipment to be purchased (quality, economy) as well as matching supply and equipment requests with the needs of the school program and personnel.
5. The principal prepares a suggested supply and equipment budget establishing his or her own priority ratings.
6. All forms used should meet certain criteria: completed in triplicate, ordering date, priority rating, name of person ordering, school or department, vendor, item, price, etc.
7. Whenever possible use an electronic data processing system similar to the one that follows. In this system all school personnel receive a computer card and a set of directions (Figure 4–7). The school system employing this procedure uses three standardized catalogs. Both the person ordering and the school principal identify the items' priority rating. Although not all the information is provided here (location code, program code, etc.), what is presented is sufficient for comparison purposes and possible use by school principals.

Purchasing

The major question here is whether or not purchasing is done by the individual school principal or the school district. Centralizing the purchasing procedures has been found to be of benefit to school districts because buying material in bulk and obtaining bids saves money. The principal's main task is to be sure the purchase orders are ready (usually late spring or early summer) so that the materials are received when the school year opens. The procedure in most school districts requires the principal to submit purchase lists by a certain date, and then let the central office coordinate all requests, prepare orders and appropriate requisition and order forms for carrying out these procedures.

Receiving, Storing, and Distributing

Consider the following guidelines in your receiving, storing, and distributing procedures:

1. Check the item against the invoice.
2. Check the item against the requisition.
3. Check the item for damage.
4. Store supplies and equipment in safe, convenient places.
5. Require that storage facilities be neat, orderly, and uniform.
6. Allow some supplies and equipment to be stored in classrooms, media center, etc., on shelves, in closets, and the like for easier access for teachers and others.
7. Determine whether the open or closed stockroom approach will be used.

Inventories

The major purposes of maintaining inventories of supplies and equipment are:

1. It helps you determine what you have and what you'll need; therefore, it is a good method for budget preparation.
2. It helps you to know what you had in case of fire, theft, or loss through some other reason.

Figure 4–7
Computer Card for Ordering Supplies and Equipment

DIST.	FUND	LOC.	PROG.	PROJ.	OBJ.	TYPL	STAFF-CODE	P	VEN./MISC.	ITEM	UNITS	UNIT COST	TOTAL COST

BUDGET PREPARATION
EPL–SE   CESA # 16

FUND   LOC.   PROG.   PROJ.   OBJ.   TYPE   20=REC.   40=EXP.   OTHER INFORMATION

STAFF CODE   PRIORITY CODE   1   2   3   MISC.

ITEM DESCRIPTION

UNITS   UNIT COST   TOTAL COST

CAT. YR. _____   CAT. PAGE _____   ITEM NO _____   BID: YES ◯   NO ◯

COMPANY _____

ADDRESS _____   CITY _____   STATE _____   ZIP CODE _____

OVER: ◯   APPROVED: DEPT. HEAD _____   PRINCIPAL _____   CENT. OFF. _____

1 2 3 4 5 6 7 8 9 10 11 12 13 14 15 16 17 18 19 20 21 22 23 24 25 26 27 28 29 30 31 32 33 34 35 36 37 38 39 40 41 42 43 44 45 46 47 48 49 50 51 52 53 54 55 56 57 58 59 60 61 62 63 64 65 66 67 68 69 70 71 72 73 74 75 76 77 78 79 80
IBM W56179   ELP–SE 250–3

USE PENCIL ONLY

1. Enter Fund Code. This will be 10 except for Junior Kindergarten (4-year-olds) and Recreation, which is 80.
2. Enter Location Code.
3. Enter Program Code.
4. Enter zeroes as the Project Code.
5. Enter Object Code.
6. Enter Type Code 40 (Expenditure).
7. Staff Code. Enter first five letters of your last name.
8. Place an "X" indicating your priority.
9. Miscellaneous. Do not use unless your principal feels it is necessary.
10. Describe the item, leaving a space between words. You may continue your description on Line 14, "Other Information," if more space is needed. Print "See Attached Sheet" when an attached sheet is used.
11. Enter the quantity *and* units, i.e., 2 dozen, 1 box, 1 case, etc.
12. Enter the unit cost.
13. Enter the total cost (catalog price unless you have a firm quote valid for 180 days).
14. Continue the description given in No. 10 if more space is required, or print additional information.

Sizes, color, style, finish, etc., *must* be included. Note in *red* if item is not to be ordered by Business Office.

15. Enter the year of the catalog.
16. Enter the catalog page number.
17. Enter the catalog item number.
18. Print the name of the company.
19. Print the *complete* address.
20. Place a red "X" here if you have additional information on the back. Utilize Space 14, "Other Information," first.
21. Check carefully the number you place in the units position. Note the quantity per package listed in the catalog. Include units of measure such as doz., lbs., oz., boxes (bx.), cases (cs.), cartons (ctn.), pkg., etc.
22. Make sure to include all information necessary for ordering, i.e., model number, size, color, finish, style, etc.
23. Make sure you are using the correct code numbers. If you have a question, please contact your school principal.
24. Consider your budget requests carefully.

Courtesy of Cooperative Educational Service Agency #16, Waukesha, Wisconsin.

3. It helps school personnel appreciate what they have, and it enables them to plan what they need.

Inventories can be taken annually or continuously throughout the school year. It may be best to inventory equipment on an annual basis and supplies on a continuing basis. That is, teachers and staff should list supplies they have used three or four times throughout the school year rather than wait until the end of the year. When these are filed with the principal at the end of each school year, it serves as an overview of what is and is not available. The principal can use these inventories to prioritize the requisitions received from individual's or a committee.

A useful inventory form for annually itemizing school equipment is shown in Figure 4–8. One of the advantages of a form such as this is that it helps whoever does the inventorying to evaluate the condition of the equipment. This helps the principal establish priorities for repair or replacement and thus contributes to equipment budget preparation.

Figure 4–8
Equipment Inventory Form

Name:_____Date:_____
School:_____

Equipment Item	Date of Purchase	Number	Condition E—Excellent G—Good F—Fair P—Poor	Repair	Replace	Repair Priority	Replace Priority	Estimated Cost	Comment

Figure 4–9 illustrates a form that may be used by the teachers, secretaries, and others for implementing a procedure that continuously records the use of school supplies. Teachers can select certain students to help them complete the inventory in each of the three months. If a central, closed storeroom is used for the distribution of supplies, the secretary or custodian can use the inventory form as well. One of the advantages of this kind of form is that it informs the teachers and principal when crucial supplies are getting low.

Instructional Material Inventory

Inventories of instructional material such as textbooks, workbooks, reference books, and supplementary texts should be of special concern to principals and teachers for these reasons:

1. These materials are subject to theft, fire, and misplacement.
2. They are expensive items to repair or replace.
3. They usually last four to five years.
4. New textbook adoptions cost money and should be carefully budgeted in advance.
5. They are essential to the instructional program.

So, the inventorying of instructional materials will tell you what you have and what you'll need; two essential factors for instructional and budget planning.

Inventories of instruction materials should be an annual activity. Depending on the individual school situation, it can be done during the final days of school or, if the principal wishes to use the information for budget preparation, it can be com-

Figure 4–9
Continuous Supply Inventory Form

Name:_____Grade/Dept.:_____
School:_____

Items	No. at Start of Year	Number Left In			Amount to Replace	Est. Cost
		November	February	June		

pleted during the spring recess. Some students are more than willing to help teachers with tasks such as this. In fact, I believe that students should be given a much more active role in the housekeeping activities necessary in keeping the school lively, bright, and clean. It not only develops responsibility but it provides opportunities for teachers and students to interact in settings other than the classroom.

The inventorying of instructional materials should be complete. That is, it should include textbooks, supplementary texts, reference books, workbooks, trade books, programmed texts, special master packages, periodicals, games and puzzles, and all of the audio-visual material in the classroom or in the department resource center. There are numerous forms that can be used for keeping an inventory. One example is shown in Figure 4–10.

Figure 4–10
Textbook Inventory Form

Name:_____Grade/Dept:_____
School:_____

Title	C	No. B	No. E	YP	YU	Condition U Rb Rp	Recommendations

Code:
C   = Copyright Date
No. B = Number of book at start of this school year
No. E = Number of book at end of this school year (or at spring recess)
YP   = Year Purchased
YU   = Years in Use
U   = Usable for Another Year
Rb   = Needs Rebinding
Rp   = Needs Replacing

As you will note, this inventory has several features not found in traditional textbook inventory forms. It enables the teacher to determine how many texts have been lost, misplaced, or stolen within the year. It helps identify how many years the texts have been in use. It aids the teacher to judge the condition of the texts and to make recommendations. This information enables the principal and/or committee to plan accordingly. The same kind of form can be used for other instructional materials, i.e., workbooks, reference books, etc.

Evaluating Management of School Supplies and Equipment

Now that you have been introduced to several ideas, some old and some new, hopefully you are ready to grasp the opportunity to evaluate your current procedures for managing school supplies and equipment. Figure 4–11 provides a scale to help you do this.

Although all of the items may not be appropriate because of the nature of your situation, they may be changed to meet specific needs. This

Figure 4–11
Evaluation Scale for Managing School Supplies and Equipment

Directions: Circle one number in your column that best describes how you rate the procedure. Scale: 1—Every Time; 2—Most of the Time; 3—Some of the Time; 4—Little of the Time; 5—Never.

Procedures	Principal	Faculty/Staff	Central Office/Supt.
1. Selection is based on needs of program and personnel.	1 2 3 4 5	1 2 3 4 5	1 2 3 4 5
2. Selection procedures involve faculty and staff.	1 2 3 4 5	1 2 3 4 5	1 2 3 4 5
3. Standard catalogs are used for ordering.	1 2 3 4 5	1 2 3 4 5	1 2 3 4 5
4. Orders are placed promptly and accurately.	1 2 3 4 5	1 2 3 4 5	1 2 3 4 5
5. Faculty and staff are informed when requisitions are not approved.	1 2 3 4 5	1 2 3 4 5	1 2 3 4 5
6. Procedures for receiving items include invoice and order check, damage check, etc.	1 2 3 4 5	1 2 3 4 5	1 2 3 4 5
7. Storage facilities are adequate.	1 2 3 4 5	1 2 3 4 5	1 2 3 4 5
8. Distribution to faculty and staff is adequate.	1 2 3 4 5	1 2 3 4 5	1 2 3 4 5
9. Requisitioning classroom supplies and equipment is efficient and not time-consuming.	1 2 3 4 5	1 2 3 4 5	1 2 3 4 5
10. Annual inventory checklists and directions are required and provided.	1 2 3 4 5	1 2 3 4 5	1 2 3 4 5

(cont.)

Procedures	Principal	Faculty/Staff	Central Office/Supt.
11. Equipment is replaced and/or repaired promptly.	1 2 3 4 5	1 2 3 4 5	1 2 3 4 5
12. Instructions are provided for using equipment.	1 2 3 4 5	1 2 3 4 5	1 2 3 4 5
13. Conservation and nonwaste of supplies is promoted.	1 2 3 4 5	1 2 3 4 5	1 2 3 4 5
14. Care and protection of equipment is promoted.	1 2 3 4 5	1 2 3 4 5	1 2 3 4 5
15. Yearly evaluation of the value of certain supplies and equipment to the instructional program is encouraged.	1 2 3 4 5	1 2 3 4 5	1 2 3 4 5

evaluation scale allows you to evaluate yourself while obtaining evaluative information from your faculty-staff and from the central office/superintendent. As suggested in other sections of this book, discussion and decisions relative to discrepancies in the ratings is worth your time and effort.

EVALUATING AND IMPROVING SCHOOL SAFETY

This section focuses on a discussion of evaluation and improving school building safety related to fire and accident prevention.

A safe school results when the principal performs the following:

1. Establish a safety-conscious tone.
2. Implement a safety education program.
3. Provide in-service training for faculty and staff.
4. Promote special safety programs and assemblies.
5. Establish a school safety patrol.
6. Participate in safety campaigns.
7. Utilize community resource personnel.
8. Actively demonstrate concern about the safety of all people in the school.

Self-Evaluation Checklist

As a school principal you may wish to check yourself on the items in Figure 4–12. The checklist enables you to assess what you did during the past year and, if you think the item has merit, plan when you will implement the suggestion.

Fire Inspections

The importance of regular building inspections for potential fire hazards cannot be understated. Besides requesting that fire officials inspect the building regularly (usually once each year), the principal would benefit from a self-inspection plan that includes the involvement of the school custodian as well as other school personnel. A useful self-inspection checklist is available to schools from the American Fire Insurance Association (Figure 4–13).

Fire Drills and Evacuations

The principal has the responsibility to become acquainted with state laws and local ordinances regarding fire and accident regulations for school buildings. Most states require a monthly fire drill. Evacuation procedures have taken on greater importance because coupled with the potential for

Figure 4–12
Principal's Self-Evaluation Safety Checklist

	Yes	No	Good Idea! I'll Do This Next Year*
During the Past School Year:			
1. I invited fire officials to inspect the school.	___	___	___
2. I regularly inspected the school building for fire hazzards.	___	___	___
3. I regularly checked fire fighting equipment.	___	___	___
4. I prepared a checklist of things to be inspected regularly by the custodian.	___	___	___
5. I provided written safety procedures for school personnel.	___	___	___
6. I prepared a list of safety activities that teachers and students can use in the classroom.	___	___	___
7. I promoted the inclusion of topics on safety and accident prevention for in-service and faculty meetings.	___	___	___
8. I honestly tried to create a safety-conscious atmosphere.	___	___	___
9. I held regular fire drills and building evacuation activities.	___	___	___
10. I encouraged the use of safety topics in our curriculum.	___	___	___

*Write below the date, week, or month you plan to do something about this item.

fire has been the phenomenon of bomb threats. Managing procedures for the efficient and safe evacuation of the school building should not be taken lightly. To assist you in this task, the following questions deserve your attention:

1. Do all school personnel know what to do when an evacuation signal is given no matter where they are in the school building?
2. Do all school personnel know the evacuation signals? Exits? Returns?
3. Are you convinced that teachers have instructed students, at the beginning and middle of each school year, regarding procedures for evacuating the school building?
4. Do teachers and students know what to do while evacuating a room? (Example: Close all outside windows; close door after all have left the room; students line up in orderly manner; if exit is blocked, follow teacher; and routes to follow for each room).
5. Do the evacuation instructions emphasize orderliness, seriousness, and respect for potential danger?
6. Are copies of evacuation procedures given to each teacher and staff?
7. Are evacuation orders posted in each room?
8. Do you plan monthly evacuation drills at different times, under various circumstances, each month?

Figure 4–13
Inspection Blank for Schools

Prepared by
AMERICAN INSURANCE ASSOCIATION
Engineering and Safety Service
85 John Street, New York, N. Y. 10038

INSTRUCTIONS

Inspection to be made each month by the custodian and a member of the faculty at which inspection only Items 1 to 23 need be reported. At the quarterly inspection, a member of the fire department should accompany the above inspectors, and the complete blank should be filled out. The report of each inspection (monthly and quarterly) is to be filed with the Board of Education or School Commissioners.

Questions are so worded that a negative answer will indicate an unsatisfactory condition.

Date . . . .

Name of School . . . . Address . . . .

Class: Elementary . . . . Junior High . . . . Senior High . . . .

Capacity of School . . . . Number now enrolled . . . .

    1. Are all exterior exit doors equipped with approved panic hardware when serving 100 or more persons? . . . .
       Is the hardware tested each week? . . . . Is it readily operable? . . . .

    2. Are all outside fire escapes free from obstructions and in good working order? . . . . Are they used for fire drills?
. . . .

    3. Are all doors in smoke control partitions in operable condition? . . . . Free from obstruction? . . . .

    4. Is all heating equipment, including flues, pipes, ducts and steam lines:-
       (a) in good servicable condition and well maintained? . . . .
       (b) properly insulated and separated from all combustible material by a safe distance? . . . .

    5. Is the coal pile inspected periodically for evidence of heating? . . . .

    6. Are ashes placed in metal containers used for that purpose only? . . . .

    7 Is remote control provided whereby oil supply line may be shut off in emergency and is it readily accessible? . . . . . .

    8 Is an outside shut-off valve on the gas supply line provided? . . . . Is it readily accessible and marked? . . . .

    9 Has automatic heating and air-conditioning equipment been serviced by a qualified service man within the past year?
. . . .

  10. Are the following locations free of accumulations of waste paper, rubbish, old furniture, stage scenery, etc?
     attic? . . . . basement? . . . . furnace room? . . . . stage? . . . . dressing rooms in connection with
     stage? . . . . other locations? . . . . (explain "No" answers under Remarks.)

  11. Are spaces beneath stairs free from accumulation or storage of any materials? . . . .

  12. If hazardous material or preparation is used for cleaning or polishing floors: Is the quantity limited as much as practicable? . . . . Is it safely stored? . . . .

  13. Are approved metal cans, with self-closing covers or lids, used for the storage of all oily waste, polishing cloths, etc? . . . .

  14. Are approved safety cans with vapor-tight covers used for all kerosene, gasoline, etc., on the premises and are they stored away from sources of heat or ignition? . . . .
     Is it essential that such materials be kept on the premises? . . . .

  15. Are premises free from electrial wiring or equipment which is defective? . . . .
     (If answer is No, explain under Remarks.)

  16. Are only labeled extension or portable cords used? . . . .

  17. Is the correct size fuse being used in each electrical circuit? . . . .

(cont.)

Courtesy of the American Insurance Association.

18. Are electric pressing irons equipped with automatic heat control or signal and provided with metal stand? . . . .

19. Are sufficient proper type fire extinguishers provided on each floor so that not over 75 feet travel is required to reach the nearest unit? . . . .
In manual training shops and on stage. 30 feet or 50 feet depending on extinguisher rating? . . . .

20. Is date of inspection or recharge shown on tag attached to extinguisher? . . . .
Have fire extinguishers been inspected or recharged within a year? . . . .

21. Is the building equipped with standpipe and hose with nozzle attached? . . . .
Is the hose in good serviceable condition? . . . .

22. Where sprinklers are installed: Are all sprinklers clean and unobstructed? . . .
Are all sprinkler valves open? . . . . Has the system been thoroughly inspected within the past year? . . . .

23. Are large woolen blankets readily available in kitchens and science laboratories for use in case clothing is ignited?
. . . .

Remarks (Note any changes since last inspection)
The following items to be included in each quarterly inspection:-

24. Are there at least two means of egress from each story of the building? . . . .
Are these so located that the distance to any single exit measured along the line of travel, does not exceed:-
    From any point in any classroom, 150 feet? . . . .
    From any point in an auditorium. assembly hall or gymnasium, 150 feet? . . . .

25. Are all windows free from heavy screens or bars? . . . . , ...

26. Do all exit doors open in direction of exit travel? . . . .

27. Are all interior stairways enclosed? . . . .
Are doors to these enclosures of automatic or self-closing type? . . . . Are they unobstructed . . . . and in operable condition? . . . .
If automatic closing type. are they closed as routine part of fire exit drill? . . . .

28. Are windows within 10 feet above, 35' feet below and 15 feet horizontally of fire escapes glazed with wire glass?
. . . .

29. Are manual training, domestic science. other laboratories and the cafeteria so located that a fire in one will not make the means of agress from other nearby rooms or spaces unusable? . . . .

30. Are heating plant and fuel supply rooms separated from other parts of the building by fire-resistant walls or partitions, and fire doors? . . . .

31. Do all ventilating ducts terminate outside of the building? . . . .

32. State type of construction of any temporary buildings in the school yard . . . .
. . . .

33. Is nearest temporary building at least 50 feet from the main building? . . . .

34. State frequency of fire drills . . . . State average time of exit . . . .

35. Are provisions made for sounding alarm of fire from any floor of building? . . . .
Is sounding device accessible? . . . . Plainly marked? . . . .

36. Signs giving location of nearest city fire alarm box posted? . . . .
Give distance from the premises to box . . . .

      Inspector . . . . Title . . . .
      Inspector . . . . Title . . . .
      Fire Chief and/or Building Inspector . . . .

ATTACH COPY OF ANY "REMARKS" DEALING WITH INSPECTION FINDINGS

9. Do you keep a record of each evacuation drill? Does it include the date, time of day, evacuation time, and effectiveness?
10. Are all school exits clearly marked?
11. Is special attention given for the evacuation of special places like the school gym, auditorium, etc.?
12. Do you have special procedures for assisting handicapped students, teachers, or staff?
13. Do teachers and others know what to do if their specified exits are blocked when the order to evacuate is given?
14. Are procedures for returning to the school building provided to each teacher and staff member?

Accident Prevention

Part of the management responsibilities of a school principal is to assure the safety for school personnel. Accidents happen; some because of negligence, others because of happenstance. The best that a principal can do is try to instill in the faculty, staff, and students concepts of accident prevention. Be prepared! Be safety-minded! Don't be negligent! Think before you act! This is not an easy thing to do as you watch some students "burn rubber" getting out of the parking lots, or when you view children chasing each other around the playground swings as others are swinging. But try you must. Those in charge must be constantly on the check for conditions or activities that may contribute to accidents. Special attention should be given to areas such as showers, gyms, lavatories, halls, stairways, boiler room, swimming pool, parking lots, playground, and so on. Teachers of specific subjects such as industrial arts, physics, and chemistry should be aware of the dangers of power tools, chemical elements such as acids, electrical units, and the like.

A recommended form for securing data about student accidents appears in Figure 4-14. The information from forms such as this one can be used to plan safety and accident prevention programs.

HOW TO ORGANIZE AND MANAGE CUSTODIAL SERVICES

While the direct responsibility for the maintenance of plant and facilities belongs to the principal, it is carried out by the custodial staff. The importance of custodial personnel to the daily operation of the plant and to the educational program within the school cannot and should not be minimized. Therefore, both the principal and the custodial staff have specific responsibilities that are special to plant and facilities management.

Principal's Responsibilities

The principal's major responsibilities are threefold: to supervise, to administer, and to evaluate. As supervisor, the principal should define the custodian's job if the school district does not provide a job description.[6] A division of labor should also be developed if there is more than one custodian. And, most important, the principal should seek to have others respect and dignify the position of custodian. As the administrator of custodial services, the principal should comply with the following duties:

1. Cooperate with custodians; come to appreciate them for the services they provide.
2. Assist custodians by developing reasonable work schedules.[7]
3. Communicate with custodians by being open to their suggestions, listening to their problems and concerns, and sharing with them information about plant and facilities management.
4. Develop and demonstrate pride in the importance of each custodian's position and work efforts.
5. Mediate potential conflicts between custodians and teachers by using "work requests" and keeping teachers aware of each custodian's duties and problems.
6. Provide custodians with an office and workroom for maintaining records and reports and storing tools and equipment.

Figure 4–14
Student Accident Report Form

(check one)	RECOMMENDED	(check one)
☐ School Jurisdictional	**STANDARD STUDENT ACCIDENT REPORT**	Recordable ☐
☐ Non-School Jurisdictional		Reportable Only ☐

School District:
City, State:

General

1. Name			2. Address	
3. School	4. Sex Male ☐ Female ☐	5. Age	6. Grade/Special Program	
7. Time Accident Occurred Date:	Day of Week:		Exact Time:	AM ☐ PM ☐

Injury

8. Nature of Injury

9. Part of Body Injured

10. Degree of Injury (check one)
    Death ☐   Permanent ☐   Temporary (lost time) ☐   Non-Disabling (no lost time) ☐

11. Days Lost
    From School: From Activities Other Than School: Total:

12. Cause of Injury

Accident

13. Accident Jurisdiction (check one)
    School: Grounds ☐   Building ☐   To and From ☐   Other Activities Not on School Property ☐
    Non-School: Home ☐   Other ☐

14. Location of Accident (be specific)	15. Activity of Person (be specific)
16. Status of Activity	17. Supervision (if yes, give title & name of supervisor) Yes ☐ No ☐
18. Agency Involved	19. Unsafe Act
20. Unsafe Mechanical/Physical Condition	21. Unsafe Personal Factor

22. Corrective Action Taken or Recommended

23. Property Damage
    School $ Non-School $ Total $

24. Description (Give a word picture of the accident, explaining who, what, when, why and how)

Signature

25. Date of Report	26. Report Prepared by (signature & title)
27. Principal's Signature	

Student Accident Reporting Guidebook (Chicago: National Safety Council, 1966).

The principal's additional task is to evaluate the quality of work and the effectiveness of performance.

Custodians' Responsibilities

Like the principal, the custodians also have specific responsibilities.

1. They must work cooperatively with the principal, teachers, and school personnel.
2. They should demonstrate pride in their position and in their work.
3. They must show concern for the health and safety of all school personnel.
4. They must maintain high housekeeping standards.
5. They must be particularly helpful in times of emergencies, problems, and special school activities.
6. They must properly clean, repair, replace, and maintain the school plant and its facilities.
7. They must periodically inspect the building and equipment.
8. They must keep an up-to-date inventory of supplies and equipment.
9. They must anticipate and prevent many maintenance problems.
10. They should evaluate themselves and encourage others to evaluate their work.

Evaluating Principal-Custodial Relations

In order to help you and the custodians in your school determine the extent to which you cooperatively carry out some of the responsibilities previously identified, a rating scale has been constructed (Figure 4–15).

The purpose of such a scale is to help you and the custodian(s) evaluate some crucial factors important in a positive, pleasant working environment. It will also produce information that you and the custodian can discuss during follow-up conferences. For example, the scale may reveal that a cus-

todian feels that you don't keep the faculty informed about some "clean up" problems, but it doesn't reveal why the custodian feels this way; that is the purpose of the conference.

Evaluating Custodial Performance

Evaluating the performance of custodians, like that of other school personnel, must result from an accurate and comprehensive job description, continual and regular supervision, and the use of a written evaluation. Whether the evaluation is done by a principal or the head custodian, the evaluation instrument used should have resulted from input by the administration and the custodial staff.

Figure 4–16 shows a school district's evaluation scale that is based upon a comprehension job description. It should be noted that in this district's schools, where a head custodian does the evaluations, each custodian meets with the head custodian to discuss the evaluation—the quality of work performance and services. The intent is to show and help the custodians to find out how they are doing and what is expected of them. Hopefully, the result of the meetings is a cooperative approach toward obtaining higher quality performance which will lead to high quality school maintenance standards and services in each building. Each custodian, however, has the option to discuss any aspect of the job evaluation with the school principal. This procedure, which insures open communication and high morale, is worth your consideration.

Self-Evaluation/Teacher Evaluation

Self-evaluation is as valuable for a custodian as it is for the principal. Few administrators recommend self-evaluation procedures for classified personnel, yet the results can be informative and contribute to a more positive annual performance rating. The example shown in Figure 4–17 is easy to use and does not require a great deal of time to complete. The principal and custodian can add items to fit particular job requirements. The scale may be used

Figure 4–15
Principal-Custodian Rating Scale

Rate the extent to which you:	*Principal*		*Custodian*
1. Communicate	____	Great	____
	____	Some	____
	____	Little	____
	____	No	____
2. Establish maintenance plans	____	Great	____
	____	Some	____
	____	Little	____
	____	No	____
3. Schedule workload	____	Great	____
	____	Some	____
	____	Little	____
	____	No	____
4. Define job requirements and limitations	____	Great	____
	____	Some	____
	____	Little	____
	____	No	____
5. Work cooperatively to solve plant/facilities problems	____	Great	____
	____	Some	____
	____	Little	____
	____	No	____
6. Prepare budget for custodial needs	____	Great	____
	____	Some	____
	____	Little	____
	____	No	____
7. Prepare building and grounds repairs/replacements	____	Great	____
	____	Some	____
	____	Little	____
	____	No	____
8. Keep faculty/staff informed about custodial problems/duties/needs	____	Great	____
	____	Some	____
	____	Little	____
	____	No	____

Figure 4-16
Custodial Evaluation Form

ELMBROOK SCHOOLS

Merit evaluation of custodial/maintenance Personnel

MERIT RATING FORM

Name: _____ Work Location _____

Title _____ Period: From _____ to _____

Instructions: Read carefully the descriptive statements on the lower section of this page and on the other page. For each job element select and encircle the numerical value most nearly representing the degree of the employee's accomplishment. Do not rate the element "Supervisory Effectiveness" unless a significant portion of the employee's responsibility is in the supervision of other employees. After encircling the appropriate figure for each element, place corresponding figures in the right hand column and total.

	UNSATISFACTORY	AVERAGE		MAXIMUM	RATINGS
1. Technical Competence	1	2	3	4	5
2. Relationships	1	2	3	4	5
3. Reliability	1	2	3	4	5
4. Quantity	1	2	3	4	5
5. Work Interest	1	2	3	4	5
6. Supervisory Effectiveness	1	2	3	4	5

Total Rating _____

Signature: Rater _____ Reviewing Officer _____

To obtain rating, you are to divide the total rating by the number of classifications the employee was rated on. In most cases there will be five, but where the employee has supervisory responsibility, the employee will be rated for six classifications.

The following table is to be used in converting numerical ratings:

4.67-5.00	Excellent
4.00-4.66	Very Good
3.00-3.99	Good
2.00-2.99	Fair
0.00-1.99	Unsatisfactory

In appraising the several aspects of job performance, consider the following:

1. TECHNICAL COMPETENCE
(a) extent to which the employee possesses the knowledge and skills necessary to his position;
(b) his effectiveness in applying skills and acceptable techniques;
(c) comprehension of instructions and successful completion of assigned tasks;
(d) systematic approach to the duties of the position and thoroughness of accomplishment;
(e) recognition of problem situations and resourcefulness in developing ways and means of meeting them; and
(f) soundness of judgment.

2. RELATIONSHIPS
(a) employee's personal appearance and impression he generally makes on others;
(b) nature of response to guidance and extent to which he makes constructive use of criticism offered by superiors;
(c) the degree to which he cooperates and works with fellow employees;
(d) the tact and courtesy he exercises in dealing with the public;
(e) degree to which he understands his fellow workers and inspires their confidence and respect.

3. RELIABILITY
(a) degree of confidence and trust which may be placed in employees to carry out assignments without undue checking;
(b) sense of responsibility to the job and conscientiousness in performance;
(c) readiness to adjust to changing character of assignments and conditions of employment;
(d) temperament and emotional stability as they affect performance;
(e) regular attendance and punctuality; and
(f) loyalty to the standards and ideals of the School System.

4. QUANTITY OF WORK
(a) degree to which employee organizes his work effectively;
(b) accuracy of results with a minimum of waste, spoilage and loss of time;
(c) rate or production in relation to other employees in this category of position;
(d) ability to turn out a satisfactory amount of acceptable work under pressure; and
(e) degree to which he devotes himself steadily to the job.

5. WORK INTEREST
(a) his demonstration of originality in meeting new problems and developing ways to improve existing procedures;
(b) his recognition and utilization of opportunities to improve himself so as to perform his duties more efficiently;
(c) willingness to be personally inconvenienced when responsibilities of the job place unusual demands on his time or energy;
(d) his practice of keeping himself physically and mentally fit for the proper discharge of his duties;
(e) his readiness to accept special assignments beyond daily routine.

6. SUPERVISORY EFFECTIVENESS
(a) his effectiveness as a leader, manifested by his ability to inspire confidence, provide guidance, set appropriate standards and to follow through on performance.
(b) his interest and effectiveness in training subordinates for satisfactory quantitative and qualitative performance;
(c) adequacy of his over-all planning, his willingness to make appropriate delegation of responsibilities and to give the necessary authority for their proper discharge;
(d) soundness of judgment and validity of decisions;
(e) willingness to make decisions;
(f) extent to which his handling of subordinates develops and sustains a satisfactory level of employee morale.

Courtesy of the Elmbrook School District, Elmbrook, Wisconsin.

Figure 4–17
Custodian Self-Evaluation Scale

Directions: The purpose of this scale is to help you evaluate yourself in your day-to-day custodial duties in this school. Check the appropriate space following each item.

Items	Outstanding	Adequate	Needs Improving	Inadequate
1. Performance of duties	____	____	____	____
2. Speed of operation	____	____	____	____
3. Quality of work done	____	____	____	____
4. Ability to get along with others:				
a. Students	____	____	____	____
b. Teachers	____	____	____	____
c. Administrators	____	____	____	____
d. Other school personnel	____	____	____	____
5. Accept criticisms and suggestions	____	____	____	____
6. Physically healthy	____	____	____	____
7. Pride in your position	____	____	____	____
8. Positive attitude toward your work	____	____	____	____
9. Appearance	____	____	____	____
10. Attendance	____	____	____	____
11. List other items				

twice a year with a follow-up conference between the principal or head custodian and the custodian. The results may head off potential problems and will provide additional information that can be discussed during the conferences.

The self-evaluation process can take on added significance when the results are compared to an evaluation by those who are the recipients of custodial services and performance. To help you collect information from teachers and others about the custodial staff, a sample form appears in Figure 4–18.

In summary, a principal can bring three sets of data to the custodial evaluation conference: self-evaluation, teacher evaluation, and administrator evaluation. The information gleaned from these three sources should be extremely useful for obtaining or maintaining high quality performance and service.

A FINAL COMMENT

In the next decade, plant and facilities management will take on new dimensions. Principals will have to make better use of existing facilities. Decisions will have to be made about the closing of existing schools and what should be done with buildings no longer serving educational purposes. Plant and facilities management will require greater attention by you and your faculty for the creative use of existing facilities. The challenge will include the necessity for new and different ways to

Figure 4–18
Teachers/Others: Rating Scale of the Custodian

Performance Rating for:_____(Name and/or Position)

Directions: The rating sheet is designed to assist the principal in determining the efficiency and effectiveness of the custodian(s) in this school. Please indicate your rating by circling the appropriate number.

Items	Excellent	Good	Fair	Poor	Cannot Evaluate
1. Service to teachers	4	3	2	1	0
2. Understands duties	4	3	2	1	0
3. Carries out duties	4	3	2	1	0
4. Is efficient	4	3	2	1	0
5. Is cooperative	4	3	2	1	0
6. Is industrious	4	3	2	1	0
7. Is courteous	4	3	2	1	0
8. Contributes to school morale	4	3	2	1	0
9. Is punctual	4	3	2	1	0
10. Appearance	4	3	2	1	0
11. List other items					
_____	4	3	2	1	0
_____	4	3	2	1	0

Comments:

---

reduce vandalism of school property. The challenge will require greater attention to the personal safety and property of students and all other school personnel. The challenge will require principals to find ways to help a reduced custodial staff maintain quality service and high morale.

EVALUATION INSTRUMENTS

As a companion to the instruments described in this chapter, four useful evaluative resources are recommended as examples of the evaluative information you can find in the literature.

Rehabilitation of Existing School Buildings or Construction of New Buildings. E. B. Sessions (Chicago: Research Corporation of the Association of School Business Officials, 1964).

This bulletin contains criteria and questions relative to school building rehabilitation or new construction. School principals may use the questions listed for determining educational need (ten questions); examining changes in school population and location (thirty-two questions); examining school building rehabilitation (twenty-five questions); maintenance requirements (ten questions); and other information including a ceiling cost form for new construction.

"Staff Development and Performance Report." Irving Herrick, Director (Baltimore: Office of Developmental Projects, State Department of Education 21240).

The purpose of this evaluation instrument (also reported in *Nation's Schools Report,* 25 April 1977) is to assist each employee in improving job performance and to facilitate professional development. Using a question format, the form is designed to be used by both the employees (self-evaluation) and the supervisor. The form requires that the employee and supervisor meet to discuss the results. There is an overall performance rating scale and an employee reaction section.

The Administration of Non-Instructional Personnel in Public Schools. Louis Cohen (Chicago: Research Corporation of the Association of School Business Officials, 1964).

This booklet is a valuable resource on personnel management. It contains ten chapters ranging from selection to evaluation. The appendix provides school principals with examples of evaluation forms, including a Non-Instructional Occupation Characteristics Check List, a Job Satisfaction Form, a Personnel Application Blank, a Reference Check Form, a Medical Report Form, a Merit Rating Form, as well as several other forms relating to probation, personnel action, and evaluation.

"Checkpoints for Evaluating the School's Housekeeping Program." Charles E. Trotter, Jr. "Are You Touching All Housekeeping Bases?" *Nation's Schools* 92 (July 1973): 40–41.

The author provides a checklist in question form by which the school principal and custodian can rate administrative duties (nine questions); site and building exterior (nineteen questions); classroom cleaning (ten questions); special instructional areas (seven questions); administrative facilities (eight questions); cafeteria and kitchen (nine questions); corridor and stairs (eight questions); toilet and locker-room cleaning (ten questions); custodial service (nine questions); and fire safety (nine questions).

"Profile Rating Wheel: An Instrument to Evaluate School Facilities." Bureau of School Facilities Planning, California State Department of Education, Sacramento, California.

This instrument is designed to inform architects and school adminstrators of performance standards for new school construction.

"Laboratory Safety Checklist." Lab Safety Supply Co., Box 1363, Janesville, Wisconsin 53545.

Although this comprehensive checklist is designed for industry (based upon the Occupational Safety and Health Act-OSHA), it can be adopted for use in secondary school labs, workshops, and other laboratory and workshop facilities.

"Public School Energy Conservation Service (PSECS)." Educational Facilities Laboratories, Inc., 3000 Sand Hill Road, Menlo Park, California 94025.

PSECS provides a number of evaluation forms for assessing energy waste and/or conservation levels in a school. Self-help forms, energy use forms, and forms for assessing the efficiency of heating, water ventilation, lighting, and building structure are available.

ENDNOTES

1. See, for example, James Wolf, "Physical Facilities Guidelines for Handicapped Children," in *The Process of Special Education Administration,* ed. Charles H. Meisgeier and John D. King (Scranton, Penn.: International Textbook Co., 1970), pp. 488–505.

2. *NAEP Communicator* 2 (October 2, 1978), Washington, D.C.: National Association of Elementary School Principals.

3. *Energy Management: A Guide for School Districts* (Winneconne, Wisconsin: Wisconsin Association of School Boards, n.d.), introduction.

4. Ibid., p. 7.

5. William H. Roe and Thelbert L. Drake, *The Principalship* (New York: Macmillan Co., 1974), p. 223.

6. See, for example, Edward F. DeRoche and Jeffrey S. Kaiser, *Administering School Support Services*

(West Nyack, N.Y.: Parker Publishing Co., 1980), pp. 187–189.

7. Ibid., p. 195.

SELECTED REFERENCES

Abramson, Paul. "How Secure Are Your Schools?" *American School and University* 49 (June 1977): 29–33.

Baker, Joseph J., and Peters, Jon S. *School Maintenance and Operation.* Danville, Ill.: Interstate Printers and Publishers, 1963.

Davis, J. Clark. *The Principal's Guide to Educational Facilities Design, Utilization and Management.* Columbus, Ohio: Charles E. Merrill, 1973.

Disruptive Youth: Causes and Solutions. Reston, Va.: National Association of Secondary School Principals, 1978.

Energy Crisis. Chicago: Nation's Schools, 1975. (24 pp.)

Energy and Education Action Center. Washington, D.C.: U.S. Department of Health, Education, and Welfare. (The Center provides a variety of publications.)

Finchum, R. N. *Extended Use of School Facilities.* Washington, D.C.: U.S. Department of Health, Education, and Welfare, 1967.

Finchum, R. N. *School Plant Management.* Washington, D.C.: U.S. Department of Health, Education, and Welfare, 1960.

"How to Improve Your Custodial Program." *Nation's Schools* 93 (February 1974): 72–74.

Leggett, Stanton. "Sixteen Questions to Ask and Answer Before You Close a Small School." *American School Board Journal* 165 (April 1978): 38–39.

Leggett, Stanton: Brubaker, C. William; Cohodes, Aaron; and Shapiro, Arthur S. *Planning Flexible Learning Places.* New York: McGraw-Hill, 1977.

Lewis, James, Jr. *School Management by Objectives.* West Nyack, N.Y.: Parker Publishing, 1974.

Likert, Rensis. *New Patterns of Management.* New York: McGraw-Hill, 1961.

McGlade, Francis. *Adjustive Behavior and Safe Performance.* Springfield Ill.: Charles C. Thomas Publishers, 1970.

McPartland, James M., and McDill, Edward L. *Violence in Schools.* Lexington, Mass.: Lexington Books, 1978.

Neill, Shirley B. *School Energy Crisis: Problems and Solutions.* Arlington, Va.: American Association of School Administrators, 1978.

Pickhardt, Carl E. "Fear in the Schools: How Students Make Teachers Afraid." *Educational Leadership* 36 (November 1978): 107–112.

Stephan, Edward. "Energy Management." *American School and University* 47 (February 1975): 51–53.

Tonigan, Richard. "Do-It-Yourself Ideas for Principals Facing Plant Management Problems." *School Management* 16 (June 1972): 296–298.

Virkus, Robert N., ed. *Safety in the Secondary Science Classroom.* Washington, D.C.: National Science Teachers Association, 1978.

Walcott, Harry F. *The Man in the Principal's Office.* New York: Holt, Rinehart, and Winston, 1973.

5

EVALUATING AND IMPROVING INSTRUCTIONAL LEADERSHIP AND SUPERVISION

The genius of a good leader is to leave behind him a situation with which common sense, without the grace of genius, can deal successfully.

Walter Lippman

The major aim of instructional leadership and supervision is the improvement of instruction. The purpose of the content of this and the next chapter is to provide you with evaluative strategies to determine your and your teachers' effectiveness for improving instruction. To be the instructional leader /supervisor, you have to show evidence that you know what is going on in the classrooms in your school, that you can help teachers in the instructional process, and that you are a valuable resource to the teaching-learning process. It is not a question of teaching teachers how to teach. There are too many styles, too many personalities, and too many variations on the theme. The question is: What can you do to help teachers in your school do a better job of teaching?

This chapter does not pretend to be a definitive treatise on the supervision of instruction, but it will include a discussion of many of the major topics. It is assumed you will use the references at the end of this chapter.

THE CONFLICTING ROLE

Many writers have discussed what they feel to be a conflict between the administration role and the supervisory role of a school principal. The conflict is easily resolved by asking any school principal which of the two is he or she is able to give up. The answer, usually with an "are-you-kidding?" attitude, is neither. Like it or not, the principal is caught between the role of supervisor as a supportive, analytic, and nonevaluative endeavor to improve instruction and the evaluation of teacher effectiveness with the same aim. How does one resolve the conflict?

The general goal, whether it be evaluative or supportive, is the improvement of instruction. Therefore, there is supervision, in its broadest sense, designed to help teachers do a better job. It should be supportive, cooperative, humane, and helpful to teachers in improving the quality of instruction. Also, there is supervision that is evaluative. No matter what one may wish, the principal, like it or not, has to respond to administrative dictates—be they legal, professional, or social (public demand for accountability). And yet, evaluative supervision should also be supportive, cooperative, and humane.

The question is how to meld the two roles. The answer is with the teachers. Professional, knowledgeable teachers know that the principal must carry out both roles. Few teachers expect to go through a school year without being evaluated, whether it be formally or informally. The conflict arises, really, with teachers who are not performing up to standards (whoever sets the standards). Psychologically it is very difficult for a principal to help a teacher who has just been given a poor performance rating by that principal. If the teacher is new, without tenure, there is the opportunity to offer assistance with minimal dissonance between the two. The problem is more acute with the experienced, tenured teachers. Yet, based on the evaluative data, help has to be offered. It may be rejected. But the principal has a responsibility not only to the youngsters in class but to the teacher to respond to the information collected.

The conflict may be lessened if the principal meets the expectations of the teachers. Teachers expect to be consulted about supervision-evaluative programs. They expect to be consulted when an instrument is being selected, and they expect input and feedback. Teachers want as much objectivity in the process as is possible. They want to review the evaluation of their performance, and they expect the evaluator to meet and discuss results and circumstances that may have influenced the results.

Teachers also expect more than one evaluation by an evaluator. If these conditions are met by the principal, then the supervisory-evaluative program has a good chance for success.

WHAT IT TAKES TO BE AN INSTRUCTIONAL LEADER

In the minds of many, supervision and classroom visitation are synonymous. If there was ever a universal guilt feeling among principals, it certainly centers around classroom supervision. It is interesting to watch the reaction of principals as they bow their heads or lower their eyes when answering the question: How many times did you observe each teacher in your school this year?

The emerging role of instructional leadership and supervisor requires the accomplishment of many activities. If you are to engage in this role, you must perform the following:

1. Be resourceful to your faculty and staff; present to them new approaches, ideas, and materials for teaching and learning.
2. Be knowledgeable about research in learning and teaching and be able to "translate" it for your faculty.
3. Differentiate between the kinds of assistance provided new and experienced teachers.
4. Develop a supervisory program that develops and utilizes the talents of department heads or unit leaders, supervisors, and teachers.
5. Obtain and aid teachers in using effective instructional supplies and equipment.
6. Interpret the instructional program for parents and the community.
7. With a little help from your colleagues, identify instructional needs and objectives.
8. Encourage self-evaluation by serving as a model for teachers and students in promoting its value and use.
9. Evaluate the instructional program and the personnel in that program.

10. Encourage teachers to try new ideas, to experiment, to innovate, and to develop pilot programs.
11. Encourage and promote the professional development of your faculty through in-service programs, college courses, and other activities.

Make no mistake about it, instructional leadership requires a commitment on the part of the principal to improve instruction. It goes well beyond the lip-service most principals give to it. Implementation of these tasks will require time, energy, and planning. A principal who sets out to demonstrate to teachers and others that he or she wants to be viewed as the instructional leader of the school will be one who carries out these tasks:

- Helps people in the school and community define their instructional goals and objectives
- Facilitates the teaching-learning process
- Aims to develop effectiveness in teaching
- Builds a productive organizational unit
- Creates a climate for teacher growth and leadership
- Provides adequate resources for effective teaching.[1]

LEADERSHIP AND SPECIAL EDUCATION SERVICES

As most principals know, Public Law 94-142 is the primary law, supplemented by state laws, which secures educational services for exceptional learners. In essence, implementation of these laws has required new and different instructional leadership skills, administrative responsibilities, and a knowledge-base on the part of building principals.

These laws have insured free and appropriate public education for all handicapped people from ages three through twenty-one. They have given exceptional learners unprecedented new rights and responsibilities and have required that the schools and organizations within the community become integral parts of the state and local delivery systems.

In addition, these laws have brought about long-needed revisions in the education of the handicapped, requiring a restructuring of school programs and new rules for school personnel. For example, extensive teamwork is now required in all phases of educational planning and programming for handicapped students. The use of multidisciplinary teams consisting of administrators, psychologists, teachers, parents, nurses, social workers, and therapists is providing new challenges and additional demands on the supervisory and instructional leadership skills of building principals.[2] Thus, the specific responsibilities of building principals for educating "special" students is highlighted prior to an examination of ways and means for evaluating the principal's instructional leadership activities and supervisory programs. The tasks of instructional leadership are as applicable for programs and personnel in special education as they are to other school teachers and existing regular programs.

Principal's Responsibilities: A Checklist

The National Association of State Directors of Special Education published a manual that defines the primary roles of principals for the development and implementation of services for educating handicapped children.[3] These and other responsibilities have been rewritten into a checklist that you may use to determine the extent to which you are presently carrying out the listed tasks. After each item in the checklist you may use a scale ranging from "to a great extent," "to some extent," or "not at all." You may also wish to note your effectiveness in carrying out these responsibilities. For example, should you determine that "to a great extent" or "to some extent" you coordinate and administer special education services, you may wish, then, to judge the extent of your effectiveness: Are you very effective, somewhat effective, or not effective in carrying out this responsibility?

To what extent do you:

1. ____ coordinate and administer special education services in your school?
2. ____ require professional personnel to formulate special education program goals and objectives?
3. ____ recruit and select professional and paraprofessional personnel for the program?
4. ____ supervise personnel serving handicapped students in your school?
5. ____ know and disseminate state and school board policies, procedures, and guidelines for serving handicapped students?
6. ____ designate and implement educational programs and student activity programs for handicapped students in your school?
7. ____ engage in in-service training activities for yourself and other administrators?
8. ____ assist in the in-service training of professional and paraprofessional personnel?
9. ____ seek and receive referrals for students with suspected handicaps from teachers, parents, and others?
10. ____ serve as a member of screening and placement teams?
11. ____ institute appropriate screening and evaluation procedures for students who are referred?
12. ____ provide teachers with special assistance when requested?
13. ____ encourage home visitations by school personnel?
14. ____ attend to the management of student records and reports?
15. ____ implement due process procedures?
16. ____ assume final responsibility for the educational placement of handicapped students?
17. ____ help professional personnel provide handicapped students with educational and social activities with their nonhandicapped peers?
18. ____ make budget recommendations to the superintendent?
19. ____ serve as a liaison with community agencies and resources?
20. ____ participate in local agency plans for special educational services?
21. ____ inform the school's community of the needs and services for educating handicapped students?
22. ____ help teachers design individual educational plans for handicapped students?
23. ____ attend to the transportation needs of handicapped students in your school?
24. ____ plan and implement an evaluation of special education programs and services in your school?

Effective instructional leadership in carrying out these responsibilities requires that principals know and use the in-service opportunities available to them and their professional staff; that they know and use the numerous organizations and agencies concerned with educating and servicing handicapped people; and that they have knowledge of the terminology, concepts, principles, trends, and issues in this field.[5]

LEADERSHIP AND THE GIFTED/TALENTED

While programs and services for gifted and talented students have not, to date, received the legal, legislative, and financial support other special education programs have received, the principal's responsibilities are no less important. Many, if not all, the responsibilities listed in the previous section are applicable to the principal in organizing and administering programs and services for gifted and talented students.

It is not the intent to rewrite these responsibilities for your perusal. Substituting gifted/talented for handicapped student will enable you to use the preceding checklist. You should also consider using the self-assessment inventory suggested in the evaluation section of this chapter. The purpose here is to remind you of your responsibilities for those students in your school who are gifted and talented. In addition, you should be aware of current trends in your state and community as parents and others initiate legislative and judicial activities. Reynolds and Birch list eight such trends:

1. Special education is mandated (required by state law) for all school-aged gifted and talented children and youth.
2. It is the responsibility of each local school district, primarily, to see that the special education is forthcoming.
3. The state provides earmarked funds, over and above usual state educational support to local districts, to help pay for the required special education.
4. Teachers who have specialized in the education of gifted and talented pupils must be made available.
5. A professional certification is set forth for specialists in teaching the gifted and talented.
6. Special education for these pupils is to be conducted in the regular context, with regular and specialist teachers working as a team and offering consultation to each other.
7. Personalized education plans must be put in writing for each gifted and talented pupil and reviewed periodically.
8. Parents must be asked for permission to assess their children, must have access to all records about their children, and must be asked to consent to the inauguration of or change in any special education program for their children.[6]

With a perspective regarding the instructional responsibilities principals must assume for the programs and services for the handicapped, gifted, and talented students, it seems appropriate to discuss ideas for evaluating and improving a principal's instructional leadership and supervisory activities.

HOW TO EVALUATE YOUR INSTRUCTIONAL LEADERSHIP ACTIVITIES

The instructional leader attempts to improve the teaching-learning process by carrying out several specific activities related to it. For example, it is very important to seek agreement on both the purposes of instruction and the objectives of supervision. To do this requires the input and cooperation of teachers. You cannot be an instructional leader without the cooperation of the professional staff. Therefore, it is of value to assess yourself and to have the teachers assess your current attempts to improve instruction in order to improve the teaching and learning going on in your school. The rating scale in Figure 5–1 not only allows you to make such an assessment, but as you read it you will note excellent suggestions that should be part of your repertoire of activities toward the improvement of instruction.

The activities are not mere exercises. Consider whether or not you actually do anything to help teachers come together to share ideas about teaching and learning. There is evidence that they come together to decide where the bike racks will be placed or who will monitor study halls, but little evidence that teachers come together to discuss instruction. So, each activity in the list should be given serious consideration by you if you want to become the instructional leader in your school.

The Activities Rating Scale can be used as a pre- and post-assessment instrument with some conscious, directed activity in-between. For example, one principal used the scale to find out how his administrative team (himself, assistants, central office supervisor assigned to his school) rated on each item from their own and the teachers' point of view. They discovered that their perceptions and those of the teachers differed on several activities. For example, self-evaluation (item 4) was one activity where the ratings were different—a "B" grade was the average on the administrative scale, "D" was the average on the teachers' scale.

Figure 5–1
Instructional Leadership Activities Rating Scale

Principal:_____ Date:_____
School:_____

Directions for Self-Evaluation: Grade yourself on each activity using the scale below.

Directions for Teacher Evaluation: Grade your principal on each activity for improving the teaching-learning process using the scale below.

Scale: A—Excellent; B—Good; C—Fair; D—Poor; F—Does Nothing at All.

	Self-Grading	*Teacher-Grading*
1. Helps us identify the objectives/goals of instruction	A B C D F	A B C D F
2. Encourages us to share our ideas about curriculum and teaching	A B C D F	A B C D F
3. Keeps us aware of instructional materials and equipment	A B C D F	A B C D F
4. Promotes the use of self-evaluation techniques	A B C D F	A B C D F
5. Encourages us to try new methods of instruction	A B C D F	A B C D F
6. Helps us decide on the purposes of instructional supervision	A B C D F	A B C D F
7. Encourages and promotes the display of student work	A B C D F	A B C D F
8. Encourages teacher-student planning	A B C D F	A B C D F
9. Provides special funds for purchasing expendable supplies on short notice	A B C D F	A B C D F
10. Encourages us to use a variety of instructional media	A B C D F	A B C D F
11. Encourages us to use a variety of evaluative methods for assessing student learning and growth	A B C D F	A B C D F
12. Encourages us to attend workshops and visit other schools	A B C D F	A B C D F
13. Encourages our participation in in-service training programs	A B C D F	A B C D F
14. Promotes a school program that meets student needs and interests	A B C D F	A B C D F
15. Promotes our programs and progress throughout the community	A B C D F	A B C D F
16. Demonstrates and promotes the value of self-evaluation	A B C D F	A B C D F
17. Demonstrates and promotes community involvement in the school program	A B C D F	A B C D F
18. Provides instructional assistance (aides, tutors, etc.) for teachers	A B C D F	A B C D F

The principal summarized the data and provided each teacher and administrative team member with a written report of the summary with a request that all be prepared to discuss discrepancies and what they could do about it at the faculty meeting.

The approach, then, is to use the scale as a pre-test; discuss results with the faculty, implement some or all of their ideas and your ideas, and then retest—find out if there is improvement. Another suggestion is to focus in on one activity that may be rated poorly by teachers. Design ways to improve poorly rated items and then design an evaluation scale similar to those found in this book and find out if the teachers changed their minds. If not, then why? If they did, your strategies paid off.

HOW TO EVALUATE YOUR SUPERVISORY PROGRAM

It may be silly to ask and you may be offended, but before you can evaluate your supervisory program, you need to ask yourself if you have one. If you answer this question affirmatively, then consider these questions:

1. Is the program in writing?
2. Does it include specific objectives?
3. Does it include plans for observations, self-evaluation, and the like?
4. Does the program improve instruction?
5. How do teachers view the effectiveness of your supervisory program?

If you don't have a program of supervision, there are four critical questions that you must answer:

1. What are your reasons?
2. How do you improve instruction?
3. How do your teachers view you as an instructional leader/supervisor?
4. As the principal of the school, why do you neglect this important aspect of the job?

Two suggestions are discussed for principals who wish to evaluate existing supervision practices and its effectiveness.

Evaluating Instructional Leadership/Supervisory Practices

You and the faculty may wish to appraise the instructional leadership practices and the implications these have for the supervisory program in your school against a list of suggested criteria. Figure 5–2 can be used for this purpose.

Evaluating the Effectiveness of Your Supervision Program

If a supervisory program is effective, there should be certain objective evidence that can be used to support it. Some of the following conditions may be useful to you and imply further investigation. This can be done by you, a consultant, or a committee selected from your faculty and staff. There are many techniques that can be employed by you, the consultant, or the committee. Among them are checklists, rating scales, opinionnaires, surveys, logs, records, narratives, observations, polls, meetings, conferences, and interviews, all of which should seek evidence of an increase in:

- Student achievement
- Teacher morale
- Student-teacher relationships
- Student-teacher planning
- Student-teacher self-evaluation techniques
- Student performance—morale, grades
- The use of a variety of instructional materials
- The use of a variety of teaching-learning strategies
- The use of a variety of evaluation techniques
- Teacher knowledge of subject matter
- Teacher interest and reading of research
- The improvement of student behavior
- Interest in in-service programs
- Student attendance

Figure 5–2
Instructional Leadership Practices Scale

Name:_____ Date:_____
School:_____

Directions: Circle the number that represents your opinion concerning the extent to which each practice exists in the school.

In our school, the principal, faculty, and staff:	Definitely	Somewhat	Needs Improvement	No	Not Applicable
1. are actively involved in defining and clarifying educational goals and objectives.	1	2	3	4	5
2. insure that roles are clearly defined and understood.	1	2	3	4	5
3. define and understand working relationships.	1	2	3	4	5
4. have cooperatively defined and understand the role of specialized resource personnel.	1	2	3	4	5
5. understand clearly the authority-responsibility-power relationships.	1	2	3	4	5
6. share crucial rather than only routine decisions.	1	2	3	4	5
7. hold group discussions to clarify purposes and roles.	1	2	3	4	5
8. expect and encourage leadership to emerge from the group.	1	2	3	4	5
9. achieve status through group acceptance and competence.	1	2	3	4	5
10. view official leaders as being helpful.	1	2	3	4	5
11. expect leaders to help faculty/staff reassess their roles in terms of evidence from the sciences.	1	2	3	4	5
12. expect leaders to support school program and personnel as they work to improve both.	1	2	3	4	5
13. coordinate and support efforts for the improvement of instruction.	1	2	3	4	5
14. believe that the main function of the principal is to provide instructional leadership for her or his staff.	1	2	3	4	5
15. cooperatively develop rules of procedure.	1	2	3	4	5
16. cooperatively test these procedures to determine their effectiveness in achieving goals.	1	2	3	4	5

(cont.)

	Definitely	Somewhat	Needs Improvement	No	Not Applicable
17. modify the school structure when this is essential to facilitate the teaching-learning process.	1	2	3	4	5
18. cooperatively plan and decide program changes on the basis of objective data.	1	2	3	4	5
19. evidence high morale as we work together.	1	2	3	4	5
20. move toward mutually held goals.	1	2	3	4	5
21. utilize human relations skills.	1	2	3	4	5
22. who encounter teaching or other difficulties feel free to seek assistance.	1	2	3	4	5
23. encourage one another to attempt to achieve their potential.	1	2	3	4	5
24. establish a school climate conducive to creativeness, experimentation, and expression of individual skill and talent.	1	2	3	4	5
25. are eager to explore or experiment with suggestions made by the group.	1	2	3	4	5
26. use knowledge and data effectively in solving problems and resolving issues.	1	2	3	4	5
27. make provisions to help each member constantly acquire new skills, understanding, and attitudes.	1	2	3	4	5
28. have effectively established formal and informal channels of communication.	1	2	3	4	5
29. are informed of available resources and how to use them for improving instruction.	1	2	3	4	5
30. are encouraged to reach out beyond known resources for imaginative and creative solutions to problems.	1	2	3	4	5
31. effectively use resources from outside the group to help clarify goals, resolve issues, gain new insights, and develop new skills.	1	2	3	4	5
32. effectively use resources for improving instruction and contributing to faculty/staff growth inservice.	1	2	3	4	5
33. effectively use specialized resource persons (psychologists, guidance counselors, etc.) for assistance in improving instruction.	1	2	3	4	5

(cont.)

	Definitely	Somewhat	Needs Improvement	No	Not Applicable
34. effectively use available instructional materials and seek new resources.	1	2	3	4	5
35. have established procedures for evaluating the effectiveness of instructional leadership processes.*	1	2	3	4	5

*Adapted from a list of sixty-five criteria under eight categories from the Association for Supervision and Curriculum Development, *Leadership for Improving Instruction* (Washington, D.C.: National Education Association, 1960), pp. 164–168.

- Student interest and attitudes toward school and learning
- The sharing of ideas among teachers
- Discussion of teaching and learning
- The quality of questions asked by teachers and students
- Diagnostic and prescriptive teaching
- Student self-discipline and self-learning
- Classroom observations by principals, supervisors, and other teachers
- Supervisory conferences and meetings about teaching.

As principal, you should select appropriate instruments for evaluating each of these items. Following data collection, you must insure that a written report is prepared and disseminated to concerned parties. From this point on, it is important that the report be used and not filed away like many curriculum guides. The purpose of evaluation is to *do* something. The purpose of evaluating the supervisory program is to find out whether or not it is improving instruction (in the broadest sense) and to take action if it isn't or to maintain current activities if it is.

HOW TO DEVELOP AN EFFECTIVE SUPERVISORY PROGRAM

To help you supervise and actively participate in instructional improvement, it is recommended that you institute a plan called an *instructional improvement cycle* shown in Figure 5–3. This cycle contains three operational phases: a planning phase, an assessment phase, and an improvement phase.

The cycle is based upon communication and shared decision making by you and the faculty and by you and individual teachers. The essence of the cycle is feedback resulting from all or some methods such as self-evaluation, self-supervision, peer and student observation and evaluation, and principal/supervisor observation and evaluation.

Planning Phase

Developing plans for implementing a supervisory program in your school requires that you meet with the faculty and eventually individual teachers early in the school year. In fact, it may be best to hold a faculty meeting on the subject during orientation week. The faculty meeting should focus on the following topics:

- School district policies and procedures regarding teacher evaluation and supervision
- An explanation of this instructional improvement cycle should you decide to use it
- Discussion on district policies and the instructional improvement cycle.

Some of the points you should emphasize in the discussion include the following:

1. The focus will be on teacher performance, not personality.
2. Supervision of instruction will be a cooperative venture.

Figure 5-3
Instructional Improvement Cycle

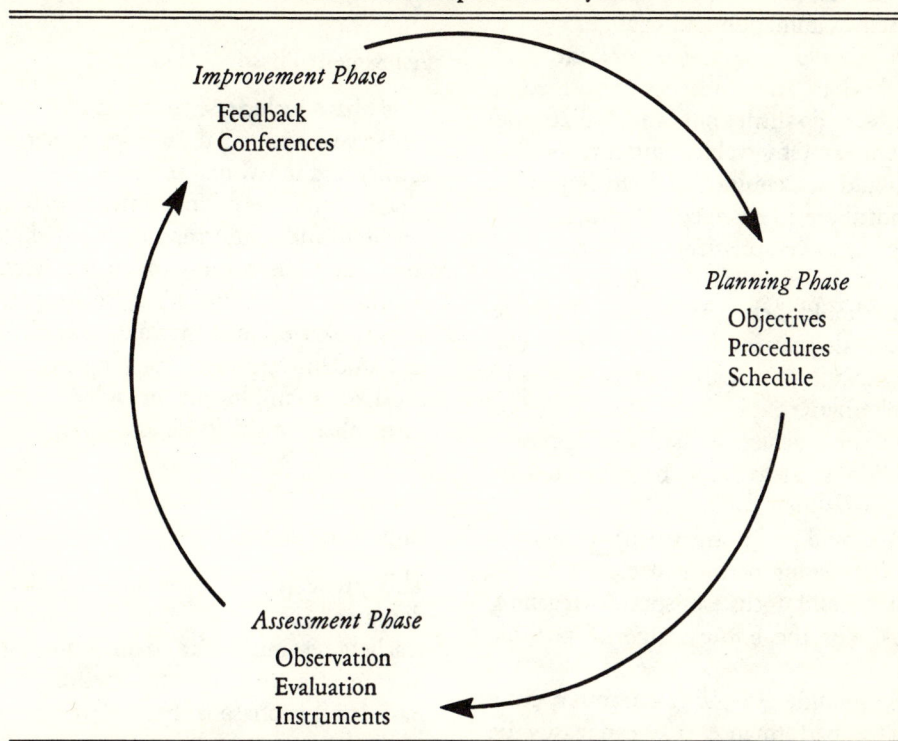

Improvement Phase
Feedback
Conferences

Planning Phase
Objectives
Procedures
Schedule

Assessment Phase
Observation
Evaluation
Instruments

3. The plan will vary according to the experience of the teacher; that is, new, inexperienced teachers will receive assistance that may be more comprehensive than experienced, tenured teachers.
4. The plan will emphasize feedback and two-way communication.
5. The plan will require that teachers decide which performance factor they wish to assess. For example, will teachers want to assess teacher performance in relation to pupil performance? Will student achievement, attitudes, and behaviors be factors to be assessed in relation to teacher performance? What factors will have to be assessed because of district policies?

The key to this instructional improvement cycle is feedback. The importance of feedback to

teachers as a group and individually should not be underestimated. Therefore, you should also include in your discussions with the faculty the value and importance of this concept. The following guidelines may be helpful to you for insuring an effective information exchange between you and the teachers:

1. Feedback should highlight the teacher's actual performance. Hearsay, assumptions, and other second-hand data should not be allowed and should be rejected by both you and the teacher.
2. Feedback should be as specific and as concrete as possible. The use of appropriate observational and self-evaluation techniques should help.
3. Feedback should not be judgmental. It does little good for a teacher to be told he or she is

not doing something well. It is better to describe the teacher's performance and encourage self-examination and change.

4. Feedback should emphasize present and future behaviors. How a teacher performed in the past will do little but antagonize and create excuses. Observable, current, performance should be examined with the hope that it will contribute to change in the future.

5. Feedback must emphasize the sharing of information, honestly and openly.

6. Feedback should help the teacher examine and create alternatives for instruction. The teacher, not the principal/supervisor, should suggest alternatives at least initially. It may be that after the teacher has had this opportunity, additional ideas could be presented by the principal/supervisor.

7. Feedback should permit the teacher to suggest changes in teaching performance.

8. Feedback should focus on specific teaching behaviors, not the entire range of possible behaviors.

9. Feedback should, first, focus upon specific behavior or performance that can easily be modified. In other words, help the teacher focus on teaching factors that can easily be changed. Successful experience in changing simple, specific factors will contribute to a feeling of success before the complex factors are considered.

10. Feedback requires summarization. Have the teacher prepare a written summary of the feedback sessions. From these, cooperatively prepare written objectives for use in the improvement phase of the cycle.[7]

In summary, the planning phase focuses upon a discussion with the faculty on the purpose of supervision and evaluation, the value of feedback, and the procedures that will best help each teacher improve performance. From this overview, you, your designee, or a supervisor meets with each teacher to determine those factors that should be observed and evaluated in relation to district requirements and the individual teacher's needs and suggestions.

Assessment Phase

This phase includes evaluation in terms of specific objectives; that is, those aspects agreed upon by faculty and individual teachers. The essence of this phase is the use of instruments that will provide teachers with information needed to improve instruction. A variety of instruments can and should be used, including self-supervision techniques, self-evaluation scales and checklists, peer and student ratings of teaching performance, and the like. Examples are provided in the improvement phase of this cycle and other chapters in this book.

Improvement Phase

This phase of the cycle requires that you, your designee, or your supervisor and individual teachers examine the data resulting from the instruments used in the assessment phase. The basis for this phase is the conference. One or more conferences with each teacher may be necessary.

The purpose of the conference(s) should be to review, analyze, and plan from the data collected during the assessment phase of this cycle. Since the conference is seen as central to this entire process, it is apparent that crucial to the conference and discussion held between a teacher and the principal/supervisor is the "chemistry" between both parties.[8] In other words, might previous interactions or current relationships have a bearing on the quality of the meetings to be held as a result of implementing this supervisory plan?

It is probably helpful to both you and each teacher to find out about this interaction. Figure 5–4 provides a scale to determine how each of you feels about the quality of interaction.

If, for example, you discover that a teacher expresses concern about your interaction with one another, it may be best to address this point directly, rather than proceeding with a discussion

Figure 5–4
Principal/Supervisor/Teacher Interaction Scale

How would you rate the way we presently interact with one another?

Principal/Supervisor to Teacher

	5	4	3	2	1	
Open						Close
Honest	5	4	3	2	1	Dishonest
Respectful	5	4	3	2	1	Disrespectful
Warm	5	4	3	2	1	Cool
Friendly	5	4	3	2	1	Unfriendly
Professional	5	4	3	2	1	Non-professional
Caring	5	4	3	2	1	Indifferent
Accepting	5	4	3	2	1	Rejecting
Democratic	5	4	3	2	1	Autocratic
Rational	5	4	3	2	1	Irrational
Sociable	5	4	3	2	1	Unsociable
Cooperative	5	4	3	2	1	Uncooperative

My principal/supervisor respects/honors/encourages my:	*Always*	*Often*	*Sometimes*	*Seldom/ Never*
Ideas	A	B	C	D
Accomplishments	A	B	C	D
Creativity	A	B	C	D
Professional talents	A	B	C	D
Self-direction	A	B	C	D
Initiative	A	B	C	D

of the plans for or results of the supervision/evaluation. A principal who is perceived to lack some of those qualities listed on the scale will have a very difficult time trying to establish relationships and strategies to help teachers change their behavior and improve instruction. It would be better for the principal to spend time and energy on methods to improve relationships with teachers.

Teacher Improvement Schedule

An example of a form that may be used to incorporate each of the three phases of the instructional improvement schedule is shown in Figure 5–5.

The Teacher Improvement Schedule can be used as part of the planning phase, and after a teacher proceeds through the cycle it is also useful in the improvement phase. The *objectives* are those performance items the teacher wishes to improve. They can be written as teacher objectives or in many cases as student learning objectives. In the *activities* column, the teacher describes what she or he will do to attain the objectives. The *assessment* column contains descriptions of or specific instruments to be used in evaluation of the objectives and activities. The *schedule* column will include appropriate days and dates for the use of assessment instruments, classroom visitations, videotaping of teaching, etc.; it provides a time schedule

for the assessment of each objective. The *constraints/circumstances* block is designed to allow the teacher and the principal/supervisor to identify or describe conditions that should be noted when they view the results. Some of these constraints/conditions might include such things as an unusually large class, many low achievers, lack of adequate instructional supplies, excessive student absences, classroom interruptions, and the like.

PLANNING PHASE FOR CLASSROOM OBSERVATION

"How often do you observe teachers in their classroom?" "Four times a year," responded most of the elementary principals in class. "Twice a year," responded secondary principals, "but once a year is not unusual."

Figure 5–5
Teacher Improvement Schedule

Objectives	Activities	Assessment	Schedule

Name:_____   Date:_____
School:_____   Evaluator:_____

Constraints/Circumstances

"How long are your observations?" The average visit lasted thirty minutes according to these principals.

"Why do you make classroom visits?" The true answer to the question, after we were able to sort through all the verbalization, was that the superintendent required it.

In a survey of high school principals, it was found that 38 percent of the sample observed several times a week, and 25 percent several times a year.[9] In any event your response to these three questions may reveal your attitudes and position about classroom observation. However, regardless of the variation in practice, classroom observation remains the heart of the supervisory process. Although there are varied ways to observe teacher performance, the physical presence of an observer remains the most popular method (audiotape and videotape are the other methods). Whether the observation is done by a principal to satisfy an administrative requirement and/or to actually try to improve instruction, some practical ideas may contribute to helping you improve your observation of teachers in their classrooms. (See, also, Jane Stallings' book described in the Evaluation Instruments section of this chapter.)

Purpose

The planning phase must include a pre-observation conference, the purpose of which is to:

- Establish a rapport with the teacher
- Find out about the teaching-learning situation
- Dispel fears
- Develop a helping relationship
- Establish the purposes of the observation
- Allow the teacher to identify the focus of the observations
- Possibly write a contract expressing the specifics of the visitation
- Agree on instruments that will be used during the observations (observation scale, audiotape, videotape)

- Agree on an observation schedule (include both scheduled and unscheduled visits)
- Agree on post-conference dates and times.

The Principal/Supervisor/Teacher Interaction Scale suggested in Figure 5–4 would be useful during pre-conference planning since it would help you determine the teacher's perceptions of the quality of your interactions with each other before specific planning questions are answered.

Questions to Answer

The pre-conference between you and the teacher might also include a discussion of the following questions if classroom observation is to be done by you and/or a supervisor:

1. What is the purpose of the visitation(s)?
2. What is your class like?
3. What lesson(s) will you be teaching?
4. What should I know about what preceded the lesson(s) you will be teaching?
5. What should I be looking for? What specific factors would you like me to observe?
6. What factors in your teaching do you feel should be improved?
7. How will we record the observation? What instruments should we use? Construct?
8. How long should I remain in your classroom during each visit?
9. How many visits should be scheduled? Unscheduled?

These and other questions should be discussed before the actual visitations. Whether a conference is necessary before each visitation should be a factor that you and each teacher decide. Since a post-conference is recommended following each visitation, it may not be necessary to hold pre-conferences before every scheduled or unscheduled visit.

One other factor may be important to clarify with the teacher before classroom observations take place. This is the question of whether or not notes should be taken by the observer during the observation. It may be a minor point but it is bothersome to an already nervous teacher.

There is a difference of opinion regarding note-taking during the visitation. Some authorities believe that notes should be recorded after, not during, the visit. I believe that notes should be taken during the visit because significant impressions, incidents, and situations may be lost if the principal waits until he or she leaves the classroom, hoping to get back to the office uninterrupted, to record such findings. The other obvious reason for note-taking is that the use of observation instruments or written descriptions of what is observed require immediate recording.

Clinical Supervision

One of the more effective methods of classroom observation is known as clinical supervision. Clinical supervision is designed to improve the teacher's performance in the classroom by focusing on actual classroom events, recording what actually happens rather than using a recording form developed prior to the observation. Clinical supervision recognizes the variety of teaching styles that you will encounter in your classroom observations. Clinical supervision places the teacher in the role of generator and interpreter of events; it recognizes the professional relationship and interactions between you and each teacher; and it requires the teacher to actively participate in her or his own professional improvement.

M. Cogan[10] specifies an eight-phase process for implementing clinical supervision strategies:

Phase 1. The teacher and supervisor (principal) establish a relationship, discuss clinical supervision as well as the role, purposes, and functions of the supervisor.

Phase 2. The supervisor plans a lesson(s) or unit with the teacher.

Phase 3. The teacher and supervisor plan strategies to be used during the observation of the teacher in the classroom.

Phase 4. The supervisor observes instruction or uses other techniques for recording classroom events (videotaping).

Phase 5. The teacher and supervisor analyze the recording of classroom events; separately at first and jointly later.

Phase 6. The conference is planned by the supervisor initially and later on, if feasible, joint planning may result.

Phase 7. The conference is held between supervisor and teacher.

Phase 8. During the conference, teacher and supervisor decide on the changes to be tried in the teacher's classroom performance or behavior and the cycle begins again.

The point here is to introduce you to this method of supervision. Obviously, it is expected that should you decide to implement clinical supervision ideas you will consult the appropriate resources.

ASSESSMENT PHASE FOR CLASSROOM OBSERVATION

By the time the assessment phase is implemented, you and each teacher will have decided which classroom observation method shall be used and which instruments will serve the purpose and the method. It should be noted that no one instrument alone would be used for an assessment of teacher effectiveness. Plans for using instruments that assess many facets of teaching and learning should be cooperatively developed. Three examples are described here.

Clinical Supervision

The advocates of clinical supervision suggest that the principal/supervisor describe in writing as many of the verbal exchanges that can possibly be recorded during the visit. These observation notes will become the basis for analysis and post-conference discussions. Eleven suggestions for the observation using clinical methods include:

1. Record what is said and done; record teacher-student talk verbatim.
2. Record your comments or questions on separate paper or in margins so that it is away from the raw data.
3. Record as objectively and as positively as you can nonverbal behavior.
4. Select a position in the classroom that gives you a good vantage point of the teacher but [one that] is not distracting to students.
5. Teachers should expect you to record (via note-taking) written data.
6. Do not intervene in the teaching in any manner.
7. Supplementally note the time in margins.
8. If most of the lesson is too quiet for verbatim recording, try to capture specific episodes.
9. Try a system that will allow you to identify specific students in your notes.
10. Stay for the entire lesson unless early departure has been arranged with the teacher.
11. Diagramming the teacher's and pupil's position in the classroom can be useful.[11]

Figure 5–6 is an example of an instrument that may be used for recording teacher-student behavior. You will have to duplicate several of these forms for one observation.

Figure 5–6
Sample Observation Form—Descriptive

Observer/Principal/Supervisor:_____

Class:_____ No. of Students:_____

Teacher:_____ Date:_____

Time of Observation: From:_____ To:_____

Objectives from pre-conference:

Subject of lesson:

Description of observation (include teacher behavior, student behavior, episodes, patterns):

Additional comments:

Concerns:

Questions:

Time:

Interaction Analysis

One of the more popular observation scales designed to record a teacher's verbal behavior is Flanders' Interaction Analysis.[12] This system of verbal analysis will help the observer help the teacher distinguish between direct and indirect verbal interaction occurring in the classroom. The instrument can be used with audiotape as well as with direct observation by a principal/supervisor.

The results, obtained by recording a number on the matrix every three seconds (twenty per minute), can be used by you and the teacher to examine specific classroom interaction factors posed in the following questions:

1. How much talking does the teacher do in the classroom?
2. Can the teacher be classified as direct or indirect in style?
3. How does the teacher react to student verbal behavior?
4. How much time does the teacher spend lecturing in class?
5. How much time does the teacher spend expanding on and using student ideas?
6. How do students react to the teacher's influence behavior?
7. Does the teacher accept, clarify, and use student emotion (ability to emphathize) in the interaction process?
8. How often and effective is the teacher's use of praise?
9. How often and effective is the teacher's use of criticism?
10. How effective is the teacher in communicating subject matter to students?
11. How effective is the teacher in soliciting student participation in class?[13]

Classroom Observation Record

In assessing teachers' classroom behaviors, Ryans developed the Classroom Observation Record which I have found to be easy to use and effective in discussing results with teachers (Figure 5–7).

The glossary describing each of the specific behaviors must be used with the scale.[14] The pupil behavior items may be useful to you for helping teachers observe and record pupil classroom behavior. The teacher behavior items have been used in a variety of ways to help teachers focus in on specific behaviors for self-analysis purposes. An example may be helpful. Teachers and principals who wish to explore in greater detail low or average ratings on any of the behaviors should use the items in the glossary, as suggested in Figure 5–8.

This instrument can be used to record by observation, videotape, and/or audiotape any one of the sixteen teaching behaviors. In the example, dull/stimulating behavior is shown. The purpose is to help the teacher gather additional evidence about the frequency of use of specific behaviors with examples of that behavior if it does occur. The Evidence/Episode/Example column enables the observer to describe what was observed. If videotape or audiotape is used for the analysis, the tape line (numbers) can be recorded in the column instead of a written description. In this way, the principal/supervisor and the teacher can go directly to that section of the tape that has recorded the specific behavior.

Question Approach

Several years ago, Briggs and Justman[15] suggested a procedure for observing classroom instruction that will be of value to the principal/supervisor as well as the teacher. The questions have been categorized to correspond to the sequence of teaching a lesson. It is suggested that the observer focus upon only a few of the questions during a visit to the teacher's classroom.

Purpose

1. What is the teacher's purpose? To what extent is it worthy? Definite? Specific with regard to this class? Attainable?
2. To what extent did the pupils share in proposing this purpose? To what extent do they com-

Figure 5-7
Classroom Observation Record

Teacher Characteristics Study

Teacher:_____ No.:____ Sex:_____

Class or Subject:_____ Date:____ City:_____

School:_____ Time:____ Observer:_____

Pupil Behavior   *Remarks:*

1. Apathetic	1 2 3 4 5 6 7 N	Alert
2. Obstructive	1 2 3 4 5 6 7 N	Responsible
3. Uncertain	1 2 3 4 5 6 7 N	Confident
4. Dependent	1 2 3 4 5 6 7 N	Initiating

Teacher Behavior

5. Partial	1 2 3 4 5 6 7 N	Fair
6. Autocratic	1 2 3 4 5 6 7 N	Democratic
7. Aloof	1 2 3 4 5 6 7 N	Responsive
8. Restricted	1 2 3 4 5 6 7 N	Understanding
9. Harsh	1 2 3 4 5 6 7 N	Kindly
10. Dull	1 2 3 4 5 6 7 N	Stimulating
11. Stereotyped	1 2 3 4 5 6 7 N	Original
12. Apathetic	1 2 3 4 5 6 7 N	Alert
13. Unimpressive	1 2 3 4 5 6 7 N	Attractive
14. Evading	1 2 3 4 5 6 7 N	Responsible
15. Erratic	1 2 3 4 5 6 7 N	Steady
16. Excitable	1 2 3 4 5 6 7 N	Poised
17. Uncertain	1 2 3 4 5 6 7 N	Confident
18. Disorganized	1 2 3 4 5 6 7 N	Systematic
19. Inflexible	1 2 3 4 5 6 7 N	Adaptable
20. Pessimistic	1 2 3 4 5 6 7 N	Optimistic
21. Immature	1 2 3 4 5 6 7 N	Integrated
22. Narrow	1 2 3 4 5 6 7 N	Broad

David G. Ryans, *Characteristics of Teachers* (Washington, D.C.: American Council on Education, 1960), p. 86.

prehend, approve, and adopt as their own the purpose proposed by the teacher?

3. How suitable for achieving the desired purposes is the plan of instruction which the teacher has prepared?

4. To what extent do the learning experiences proposed promise to help realize the desired purposes?

Preparation

5. Is the preparation by the teacher adequate?

6. To what extent have pupils been psychologically prepared, by assignment and otherwise, to participate in this learning experience?

7. What study was expected of the pupils? What direction was given to make it effective? What

Figure 5–8
Teacher Behavior Record

Teacher:_____ Observer:_____

Time of Observation: From:_____ To:_____ Day:_____

Subject of Lesson:_____ Class Size:_____

Teacher Behavior Observed: Dull/Stimulating*

Item	Regularly Repeated	Occasionally/ Partially	Seldom/ Never	Evidence/Episode/ Example
	Observed Teacher to Use This Behavior			
1. Uninteresting, monotonous explanations.	—	—	—	_____
2. Highly interesting presentation; got and held attention without being flashy.	—	—	—	_____
3. Assignments provided little or no motivation.	—	—	—	_____
4. Clever and witty, though not smart-alecky or wise-cracking.	—	—	—	_____
5. Failed to challenge.	—	—	—	_____
6. Enthusiastic; animated.	—	—	—	_____
7. Lacked animation.	—	—	—	_____
8. Assignments challenging.	—	—	—	_____
9. Failed to capitalize on pupil interests.	—	—	—	_____
10. Pedantic; boring.	—	—	—	_____
11. Took advantage of pupil interests.	—	—	—	_____

*David G. Ryans, *Characteristics of Teachers* (Washington, D.C.: American Council on Education, 1960), p. 89.

apparently did the pupils actually do in preparation for this lesson? What better could they have done?

Classroom Climate

8. What is the atmosphere of the classroom and what is the morale of the pupils as evidenced by their attitude toward each other, toward the teacher, and toward the work they are doing?

Organization and Development

9. Is the learning experience so organized as best to promote the purposes of instruction?
10. What concomitant learnings of wide educational importance does the teacher encourage and direct?
11. Are abundant and rich materials prepared by teacher or by pupils ready for use?
12. To what extent does the teacher, by recall of what has already been learned and by giving meaning to the new material by showing its relations to a large significant problem, create a readiness in the pupils?
13. Are the pupils obtaining adequate guidance from the teacher in directing their own learning? Does each pupil know what to do?
14. To what extent is the presentation of the new material adequate and clarified by explanation, by obvious order, by illustrations, by relation to the pupils' past experiences, and by application to pupils' needs, immediate or recognized as probable in the future?
15. What provisions are made for individual differences in interest, probable needs, special aptitudes, and ability? Does the teacher distribute efforts equitably among the pupils? Does he insure that every pupil is successful in something?
16. What is the amount and quality of participation by pupils? Do they demonstrate intelligent interest, the spirit of inquiry, open-mindedness, initiative, enthusiastic persistence, the ability to judge their own work, and satisfaction with nothing less than mastery in terms of the accepted purposes of the unit?

17. What are the teacher's responses to the proposals and activities of the pupils? Is he receptive, considerate, fair, tactful, and able to give them fruitful direction?
18. To what extent are pupils being trained to work both independently as individuals and cooperatively with others?
19. How ready is the teacher to modify his plan so as to seize opportunities as they appear and how resourceful is he to make the new plan effective?
20. What provisions are made to insure adequate understanding and retention of what is learned, in terms of individual needs?
21. What provisions are made to insure the ability to apply or use what is learned? To strengthen good habits of use in a new situation?
22. If tests are used, are they valid in terms of the purposes sought, significant to the pupils, and reliable in form? What is indicated for further teaching by the results?
23. What attempts are made to provide remedial instruction for those who need it?
24. What provision is made to incorporate the new learning into larger and more meaningful units?
25. To what extent is the teacher successful in revealing opportunities and direction for further growth on the part of pupils?

Results

26. Wherein are pupils better for the learning experience that they have just had?

The Teacher

27. What is outstanding in promise in the work of the teacher observed?
28. What immediate and what ultimate help does he need to strengthen his weaknesses so that his strengths may be increasingly effective?

Relation to the Unit and Other Goals

29. How is the unit of study contributory to the general purposes of education and to the special functions of the particular school?

The use of a question-type observation approach helps when the observer and the teacher discuss the subjective perceptions of the observer. For example, during a particular visit or two, the observer should have focused on two or more related questions (i.e., purpose of the lesson), then the discussion can be on what was observed via the written notations after each question, and from the teacher's point of view what was intended (if perceived differences exist). This question method, in addition to checklists, etc., should help the supervisor and the teacher appreciate teaching styles and the fact that there is no one best method of teaching.

IMPROVEMENT PHASE FOR CLASSROOM OBSERVATION

It is during this phase that data collected during the assessment phase are studied and analyzed in relation to the objectives established in the planning phase. The basis for the improvement phase is to provide feedback to each teacher resulting from the observations. The vehicle for doing this is the post-conference(s). How you conduct the conference is essential to its success. Like the pre-conference, it is important to establish rapport with the teacher, putting the teacher at ease and developing an atmosphere that demonstrates that you are genuinely interested in helping that teacher improve classroom instruction.

One caution should be mentioned. Although post-conference appears to be singular in effect, the fact is there may be more than one observation. It is easy to become trapped by what appears to be a rather mechanical procedure of a pre-conference, an observation, a post-conference—and presto! the teacher changes behavior. Change in teaching behavior takes time, effort, energy, and a feeling of a need to change. You may have to have several post-conferences with a teacher because change takes time. The teacher will need continuous feedback, additional observation, encouragement, and a commitment on your part to assist in the change.

Guidelines and Recommendations

The content and quality of the post-conference(s) is crucial to the supervisory and change process. To help you do a better job in post-conference sessions with teachers, the following questions are presented as guidelines:

1. How can you help the teacher analyze the data from the observation(s)?
2. How can you help the teacher use the data to identify strengths and weaknesses?
3. How can you help the teacher use the data to make a commitment to change?
4. How can you help the teacher create a willingness to try new ideas, whether they be from you, from the teacher, or from others?
5. How can you help the teacher feel confident and secure during the change process?
6. How can you help the teacher develop long- and short-term objectives for changing teaching behavior?
7. How can you help the teacher develop an evaluation plan that will assess the effects of the planned change?
8. How can you help the teacher want to self-supervise (videotape and audiotape) and self-evaluate teaching behavior?
9. How can you help the teacher evaluate your supervisory methods and procedures?
10. How can you help the teacher summarize the important factors resulting from the post-conference(s)?

These questions suggest several specific recommendations for the principal/supervisor:

1. The conference requires preparation. That is, both you and the teacher should have a clear idea of the purpose of the conference and the data to be discussed.
2. The conference setting should be pleasant, informal, and free from potential interruptions.
3. The conference should focus on the data at hand. Discussion should be purposeful, sincere, and honest.

4. The conference should focus on problem solving and feedback resulting from the analysis of the data.
5. The conference should emphasize interactions that require the active participation of the teacher. In other words, the teacher should not take a passive, listening role, but should, because of your methods, be actively engaged in the discussion.
6. The conference should include outcomes, recommendations, ideas, and future plans that are designed to help the teacher improve instruction.
7. The conference should include a written record of future actions, activities, and evaluation plans.
8. The conference should conclude on a positive, encouraging note.

These questions and recommendations should be carefully considered by every principal/supervisor. The importance of what you are doing is obvious. Here is your chance to help a teacher improve performance, the result of which should be a more positive learning situation for children and young people. A convenient report form incorporating these recommendations is shown in Figure 5–9.

Figure 5–9
Sample Post-Conference Report Form

Teacher:_____ Principal/Supervisor:_____
Date of Observation:_____ Date of Post-Conference:_____
Time of Observation:_____ Time of Conference:_____

Pre-Observation Conference Notes (see previous records):_____
Observation Conference Data (see records):_____

Instruments Used During Observation(s):

Data Discussed by Teacher and Principal/Supervisor:

Problems Identified:

Statement of Objectives:

Suggestions for Teacher Action

Methods of Evaluating Objectives/Actions

Schedule for Implementing Actions

_____   _____
    (Teacher's Signature)   (Principal's/Supervisor's Signature)

Post-Conference Evaluation

Every post-conference should be evaluated to insure that what was discussed, perceived, and written between the teacher and the principal/supervisor was agreeable to both parties. Figure 5–10 shows a post-conference evaluation form that may be used one or two days after the conference. This time span gives the teacher and the principal/supervisor time to think about what took place during the conference and what was recorded on the Post-Conference Report Form. It is also recom-

mended that both parties complete the form, share their ratings, informally discuss discrepancies, and file these reports for use in preparation for the next observation and post-conference.

SELF-SUPERVISION IDEAS

There are many ways for teachers to supervise and observe their own teaching behavior. Some require the assistance of an observer, others can be done by the teacher alone. Several examples will be de-

Figure 5–10
Post-Conference Evaluation Form

Directions: Please rate your feelings/values of the post-conference held between_____

_____ and _____on_____.
(principal/supervisor)   (date)

Circle the number that best represents your rating of the item: 1 represents a low rating; 10 a high rating.

How would you rate the_____of/during/from the conference?

1. Climate/atmosphere	1	2	3	4	5	6	7	8	9	10
2. Discussion/communication	1	2	3	4	5	6	7	8	9	10
3. Openness/honesty	1	2	3	4	5	6	7	8	9	10
4. Interaction/exchange	1	2	3	4	5	6	7	8	9	10
5. Analysis of data	1	2	3	4	5	6	7	8	9	10
6. Feedback you received	1	2	3	4	5	6	7	8	9	10
7. Contributions	1	2	3	4	5	6	7	8	9	10
8. Understanding/empathy	1	2	3	4	5	6	7	8	9	10
9. Recommendations	1	2	3	4	5	6	7	8	9	10
10. Suggestions	1	2	3	4	5	6	7	8	9	10
11. Plans/objectives	1	2	3	4	5	6	7	8	9	10
12. Plans/activities	1	2	3	4	5	6	7	8	9	10
13. Plans/evaluation	1	2	3	4	5	6	7	8	9	10
14. Results/outcomes	1	2	3	4	5	6	7	8	9	10
15. Degree of your satisfaction	1	2	3	4	5	6	7	8	9	10

_____   _____
(Teacher's Signature)   (Principal's/Supervisor's Signature)

scribed here with the hope that you will share this information with your teachers and adapt them to meet your needs and interests. In the first example, a selection from the literature is used to show how the Instructional Improvement Cycle can be easily implemented using many supervisory techniques.

Instructional Improvement Cycle: Teacher Feedback

You will recall the discussion of the ten guidelines for feedback earlier in this chapter. Using these guidelines, you might try B. Tuckman's idea, presented here in ten specific steps that you can follow within each phase of the Instructional Improvement Cycle.

Part of the basis for changing teachers, administrators, or anyone else is to create a dissonance between what a person would like to be and what that person actually is (in this case, between what an individual teacher is or would like to be and what that teacher is observed to be). The Tuckman Teacher Feedback Form (Figure 5–11) examines four factors: creativity, dynamism (dominance and energy), organized demeanor (quality organization), and warmth and acceptance. Notice how these factors relate and support those found in the studies reported in the next chapter on teacher evaluation.

Step 1. Meet with a group of teachers who are willing to share feedback about their teaching with others. Discuss the value of feedback and the purpose and use of TTFF. TTFF permits teachers to specify what they think makes a good teacher (their objectives) and then to obtain feedback on how they compare to the objectives, and finally, to consider ways to change.

Step 2. Have each teacher complete the TTFF describing the good/ideal teacher. Use the directions in Figure 5–12 and have each teacher compute scores for each of the four dimensions.

Step 3. Assessment Phase. Schedule teachers so that they are given the opportunity to observe one another via classroom visitation or videotape.

The teachers should decide when they are to be visited or when the tape should be made. The teachers decide whether or not they want more than one observation using the TTFF.

Step 4. If it is arranged so that a teacher is observed by more than one peer (and this is recommended), a summary of the ratings is given to the teacher.

Step 5. You, your designee, and the central office supervisor can also be included in the observation if the teachers agree.

Step 6. Improvement Phase. This phase requires that you arrange a meeting of the group, the purpose of which is to allow teachers to discuss the feedback—the dissonance between a teacher's TTFF rating and the group's TTFF rating of that teacher.

Step 7. The group of teachers should note the discrepancies and decide what each individual teacher can do in the classroom to overcome them.

Step 8. This "strength training" session will generate ideas and suggestions for individual teachers to consider so they can convert weaknesses to strengths.

Step 9. A teacher may take these suggestions and design specific objectives to correct the weakness (using the Teacher Improvement Schedule, Figure 5–5). At this stage the cycle begins again.

Step 10. Improvement can be ascertained by repeating the process when a teacher has tried out the ideas and asks for another peer review or a review by you and/or a supervisor.[16]

There are several variations you could implement using the TTFF. For example, for those teachers not wishing a peer review, you could go through the cycle by having the individual teacher complete the form; both of you review the information; then you and/or a supervisor use the form during actual classroom observation or in viewing a videotape of the teacher's performance. Following a summarizing of the data, a conference could be held in which you and the teacher review the information—the dissonance, if any—and then decide,

Figure 5-11
Tuckman Teacher Feedback Form (TTFF)

Teacher Observed:_____

Observer:_____ Date:_____

Directions: Place an X in that one space of the seven between each adjective pair that best indicates your perception of the teacher's behavior. The closer you place your X toward one adjective or the other, the better you think that adjective describes the teacher.

1. Original	___ ___ ___ ___ ___ ___ ___	Conventional
2. Patient	___ ___ ___ ___ ___ ___ ___	Impatient
3. Cold	___ ___ ___ ___ ___ ___ ___	Warm
4. Hostile	___ ___ ___ ___ ___ ___ ___	Amiable
5. Creative	___ ___ ___ ___ ___ ___ ___	Routinized
6. Inhibited	___ ___ ___ ___ ___ ___ ___	Uninhibited
7. Iconoclastic	___ ___ ___ ___ ___ ___ ___	Ritualistic
8. Gentle	___ ___ ___ ___ ___ ___ ___	Harsh
9. Unfair	___ ___ ___ ___ ___ ___ ___	Fair
10. Capricious	___ ___ ___ ___ ___ ___ ___	Purposeful
11. Cautious	___ ___ ___ ___ ___ ___ ___	Experimenting
12. Disorganized	___ ___ ___ ___ ___ ___ ___	Organized
13. Unfriendly	___ ___ ___ ___ ___ ___ ___	Sociable
14. Resourceful	___ ___ ___ ___ ___ ___ ___	Uncertain
15. Reserved	___ ___ ___ ___ ___ ___ ___	Outspoken
16. Imaginative	___ ___ ___ ___ ___ ___ ___	Exacting
17. Erratic	___ ___ ___ ___ ___ ___ ___	Systematic
18. Aggressive	___ ___ ___ ___ ___ ___ ___	Passive
19. Accepting (people)	___ ___ ___ ___ ___ ___ ___	Critical
20. Quiet	___ ___ ___ ___ ___ ___ ___	Bubbly
21. Outgoing	___ ___ ___ ___ ___ ___ ___	Withdrawn
22. In control	___ ___ ___ ___ ___ ___ ___	On the run
23. Flighty	___ ___ ___ ___ ___ ___ ___	Conscientious
24. Dominant	___ ___ ___ ___ ___ ___ ___	Submissive
25. Observant	___ ___ ___ ___ ___ ___ ___	Preoccupied
26. Introverted	___ ___ ___ ___ ___ ___ ___	Extroverted
27. Assertive	___ ___ ___ ___ ___ ___ ___	Soft-spoken
28. Timid	___ ___ ___ ___ ___ ___ ___	Adventurous

Bruce W. Tuckman, "Feedback and the Change Process," *Phi Delta Kappan* 57 (January 1976): 342. Copyright 1971, Bruce W. Tuckman.

together, ways the teacher can improve and how this attempt at improvement will be assessed.

The value of feedback has already been discussed. The value of this procedure for improving instruction is that the teacher:

- Sets or establishes personal objectives; identifies his or her own view of the ideal teacher
- Studies the results of the observation
- Uses this feedback to plan for change
- Tries to change.

Figure 5-12
Tuckman Teacher Feedback Form Summary Sheet

Teacher Observed:_____

Observer:_____ Date:_____

I. Item Scoring

   A. Under the last set of dashes on the sheet of twenty-eight items, write the numbers 7-6-5-4-3-2-1. This will give a number value to each of the seven spaces between the twenty-eight pairs of adjectives.
   B. Determine the number value for the first pair, Original—Conventional. Write it into the formula given below on the appropriate line under Item 1. For example, if you place an X on the first dash next to "Original" in Item 1, then write the number 7 on the dash under Item 1 in the summary formula below.
   C. Do the same for each of the twenty-eight items. Plug each value into the formula.
   D. Compute the score for each of the four dimensions in the summary formula.

II. Summary Formula and Score for the Four Dimensions

   A. Creativity

   $$\text{Item}(\ 1 + \ 5 + \ 7 + 16) - (\ 6 + 11 + 28) + 18$$
   $$(\_ + \_ + \_ + \_) - (\_ + \_ + \_) + 18 = _____$$

   B. Dynamism (dominance and energy)

   $$\text{Item}(18 + 21 + 24 + 27) - (15 + 20 + 26) + 18$$
   $$(\_ + \_ + \_ + \_) - (\_ + \_ + \_) + 18 = _____$$

   C. Organized Demeanor (organization and control)

   $$\text{Item}(14 + 22 + 25) - (10 + 12 + 17 + 23) + 26$$
   $$(\_ + \_ + \_) - (\_ + \_ + \_ + \_) + 26 = _____$$

   D. Warmth and Acceptance

   $$\text{Item}(\ 2 + \ 8 + 19) - (\ 3 + \ 4 + \ 9 + 13) + 26$$
   $$(\_ + \_ + \_) - (\_ + \_ + \_ + \_) + 26 = _____$$

Bruce W. Tuckman, "Feedback and the Change Process," *Phi Delta Kappan* 57 (January 1976): 343. Copyright 1971, Bruce W. Tuckman.

Some teachers will prefer the peer-group method, others will prefer another less publically-oriented method.

Audiotaping and Videotaping

Self-supervision through the use of audiotaping and videotaping procedures is a process whose time has come, but few have taken advantage of it. There is a much better chance for improving instruction when teachers are encouraged and trained to use self-supervision techniques.

Videotaping is an excellent and effective technique for observing classroom performance by teachers and students. It allows you and the teacher to observe the teaching together; discuss episodes taking place; evaluate teaching style; and assess teacher interactions with students, and student reaction to specific teaching behaviors. As pointed out by A. Simon,

The goals of video-tape self-appraisal and the clinical supervision scheme center around self-awareness and self-improvement and using videotape in the clinical supervisory situation provides the teacher and supervisor with immediate, accurate, concrete feedback.[17]

Audiotaping is also very effective and easier to manage than videotaping. Although not as dramatic as seeing oneself in action, audiotape is very effective for assessing teacher-student verbal interactions. Probably one of the best ways to convince you of the value of audiotaping and videotaping in the supervisory process is to share some examples with you. Both are effective methods for supervision and self-supervision. One of the advantages of these two mechanical devices is that their use strips the principal of an excuse that she or he is too busy to observe classroom instruction. Both devices provide a means for principals to "supervise" instruction at their convenience.

Audiotaping. The cassette tape recorder is as effective as any current supervisory method for recording the verbal behavior of teachers and students. Its major advantages are that it is inconspicuous in the classroom (compared to a visitor or videotape equipment); it can be operated with a minimum of teacher-student training and effort; it relieves the principal/supervisor from the chores of note-taking (or it is an excellent supplement to it); and it provides reliable feedback and instant replay of episodes needing study, classification, and analysis.

A suggested procedure for encouraging and implementing audiotaping of the verbal interaction taking place in the classrooms of your school follows:

1. Provide each teacher who wishes to try the idea with a tape recorder and one or more hour-long cassette tapes.

2. Have each volunteer teacher select a lesson of his or her choice for recording. Tape the lesson.

3. Provide each volunteer teacher with a copy of Flanders' Interaction Analysis (see previous reference) and train each individual how to use it.

4. Have each teacher play the tape and record the verbal interactions on the analysis chart. Have the teacher list conclusions, insights, and what was learned about personal verbal interactions and teaching.

5. If each volunteer teacher agrees, you or a supervisor should take his or her tapes and analyze each tape using the matrix as each teacher did.

6. Meet with each teacher to compare the data—the conclusions, insights, etc.

7. Where disagreement exists, replay parts of the tape, during a conference, so that both you and the teacher can analyze factors contributing to the discrepancies in the analysis.

One supervisor experimented with the tape recorder as a method of supervising teachers and concluded that combined with Flanders' Interaction Analysis, not only is it an excellent tool for collecting evidence of verbal interactions but it helps teachers develop self-knowledge about their teaching behavior and it detracts from teachers' arguments that the results and the observations were dependent upon the supervisor's own concept of teaching, subjective opinions, and/or whims.[18]

Videotaping. The use of videotaping for improving classroom instruction is finding its way into the research and into schools. In a study designed to assess the effects of feedback resulting from videotaping teachers' question-asking behaviors, teachers who used videotaping for self-analysis significantly decreased the percentage of rhetorical questions and increased the percentage of probing questions.[19]

The Video Inservice Program (VIP) is a Title III program designed to help teachers help themselves internalize change. The program is based upon the assumption that only the teacher can meaningfully change classroom behavior, and the results of the change will be improved learning by students.

The teacher self-appraisal technique of the Video Inservice Program is outlined in three levels:

Level 1

1. Introduce Planning
2. Introduce Taping
3. Introduce Self-Appraisal

Level 2

1. Teacher Selects Target Behavior—a new instructional behavior which is of interest to the teacher.
2. Modification of Plans and Training—a consultant helps the teacher in learning more about the selected instructional behavior.
3. Micro-Teach—the teacher may wish to "micro-teach" or practice the instructional behavior on a small group of students.
4. Self-Appraisal Plan—the teacher assesses ability to utilize the new behavior with his or her regular instructional class.

Level 3

1. Plan for Classroom Application
2. Classroom Teacher
3. Self-Appraisal (return to Level 2 for the selection of next target behavior).

The Teacher Self-Appraisal technique is but one aspect of the entire program which includes identifying and training personnel, setting goals, implementing strategies, evaluating progress, and personalizing learning. It is a good example of what the principal and teachers can do at the building level, with modifications, for using videotaping procedures for improving instruction.[20]

A FINAL COMMENT

Instructional change/improvement was the major focus of this chapter. It was suggested that change and improvement comes about when the principal takes an active role in designing, implementing, and evaluating instructional and supervisory activities and programs. The principal's responsibilities for special education programs and services was outlined; the intent being to demonstrate the unique and important role the principal has in instructional development and supervision in all phases of the teaching-learning process.

EVALUATION INSTRUMENTS

The instruments that follow can be used by principals and supervisors for observing teacher behavior in the classroom.

"Classroom Observation Schedule." Bureau of Educational Research, College of Education, University of Illinois, Urbana, Illinois 61801.

The Classroom Observation Record is a twenty-three-item instrument to be used by observers (principal/supervisors) for recording verbal behavior that has a simple cognitive focus. Observers will need practice using the instrument, probably by using it with audiotape recordings of lessons.

"The Teaching Evaluation Record." Educators Publishing Co., 97 Hodge Avenue, Buffalo, New York.

This instrument requires actual observation by administrator, supervisor, or other teachers. The thirty-two-item statements in the instrument are marked on a scale of 0–4. The recommended observation time is two full half-days early in the year and two full half-days during the spring of the year. The record can be used for diagnostic and rating purposes for all areas and grade levels of teaching.

"Flexible Use of Space Scale (FUSS)." R. T. Hyman, *School Administrator's Handbook of Teacher Supervision and Evaluation Methods* (Englewood Cliffs, N.J.: Prentice-Hall, Inc., 1975), pp. 101–104.

This scale enables an observer to rate on a three-point scale (limited, moderate, extensive) eight aspects of the classroom environment: diffusion of desks, use of floor for work area, decoration of walls and bulletin boards, decoration of ceilings, existence of display areas, partitions, and degree of student and teacher movement.

"Robeson Observation Code." Paul M. Allen et al., *Teacher Self-Appraisal: A Way of Looking Over Your Own Shoulder* (Worthington, Ohio: Charles A. Jones Publishing Co., 1970).

The Robeson Code enables a teacher to self-evaluate cognitive objectives (knowledge, comprehension, application, analysis, synthesis, evaluation); affective objectives (receive, respond, value); nonverbal expression (supportive, helping, receptive, routine, mattertive, unresponsive, disapproval); closed methods (information giving, mastery, problem solving, clarification); open methods (inquiry, dialogue); verbal expressions (supportive, helping, receptive, routine, inattentive, unresponsive, disapproval).

"Flanders' Interaction Analysis." Association for Productive Teaching, 1040 Plymouth Building, Minneapolis, Minnesota 55401.

This instrument enables the observer to classify and analyze the verbal communication in a classroom between teacher-class-student. Using a recording matrix, the observer notes teacher talk in two categories: response (accepts feelings, praises or encourages, accepts or uses ideas of pupils, asks questions, lecturing) and pupil talk in these same categories.

"Indicators of Quality." Institute of Administration Research, Teachers College, Columbia University, 525 West 120th St., New York 10027.

This instrument contains fifty-one polarized items used for measuring the quality of a classroom by an observer. The instrument is based on four characteristics judged to be basic to classroom quality: individualization, interpersonal regard, creativity, and group activity. The packet includes an orientation manual, instructions for observers, the instrument, score sheet, statistical data, interpretation guide, and a bibliography. It should be noted that this instrument is not recommended for teacher education. Rather, it can provide a school district score, against which an individual school's input may be correlated.

"A Self-Assessment Inventory for Guiding Education of the Gifted." Connie House, "Do you Need a Differentiated Program for Your Gifted Student? A Quiz." *Phi Delta Kappan* 61 (February 1980): 412–413.

This self-assessment is a twenty-five question checklist to help you find what kind, if any, program your school district offers gifted and talented students.

Jane A. Stallings, *Learning to Look: A Handbook on Classroom Observation and Teaching Models* (Belmont, Calif.: Wadsworth Publishing Co., 1977).

This valuable resource provides a variety of systematic observation instruments, scales, and checklists.

"Educational Leadership Appraisal." Educational Research Corporation, 85 Main St., Watertown, Mass. 02172.

This self-diagnostic instrument appraises one's leadership performance using twelve situational exercises. The leadership dimension includes management and organization, communication problem solving, task orientation, and interpersonal qualities.

"Georgia Principal Assessment System." Project R.O.M.E., University of Georgia.

This instrument is designed to assess performance of building principals. The Principal Performance Description Survey consists of four forms:

1. Principal's Form—assesses self-perceptions of how often and how well the principal performs one hundred tasks in five areas: curriculum and instruction, staff personnel, pupil personnel, fiscal management, and policies and procedures.
2. External Observer Form—a structured interview form designed to corroborate from observable evidence the principal's self-perceptions of performance.
3. Teacher Form—elicits teacher perceptions of principal's performance.
4. Superintendent Form—elicits superintendent's perceptions of principal's performance on forty-two behavior dimensions.

ENDNOTES

1. Association for Supervision and Curriculum Development, *Leadership for Improving Instruction* (Washington, D.C.: National Education Association, 1960), p. 29.

2. DeForest L. Strunk; Susan R. Winters; and Mary B. Blair, *Instructional Manual: Psychology of Exceptional Children Film Series* (San Diego: University of San Diego, 1980).

3. *Special Education Administrative Policies Manual* (Reston, Va.: The Council for Exceptional Children, 1977).

4. Edward F. DeRoche and Jeffrey S. Kaiser, *Administering School Support Services* (West Nyack, N.Y.: Parker Publishing Co., 1980), Chapter 5.

5. For an excellent resource, see Maynard C. Reynolds and Jack W. Birch, *Teaching Exceptional Children in All America's Schools* (Reston, Va.: The Council for Exceptional Children, 1979).

6. Ibid., pp. 235–236.

7. For other lists of characteristics/rules for feedback, see Ronald T. Hyman, *School Administrator's*

Handbook of Teacher Supervision and Evaluation Methods (Englewood Cliffs, N.J.: Prentice-Hall, Inc., 1975), Chapter 9; and Bruce W. Tuckman, "Feedback and the Change Process," *Phi Delta Kappan* 57 (January 1976): 341–342.

8. For conference behavior skills, see John R. Dettre, "Conference Behavior," *Bulletin of the National Association of Secondary School Principals* 58 (March 1974): 95–102.

9. Susan Abramowitz and Ellen Tenenbaum, *High School '77: A Survey of Public Secondary School Principals* (Washington, D.C.: National Institute of Education, 1978), p. 80.

10. Morris Cogan, *Clinical Supervision* (Boston: Houghton Mifflin Co., 1973), pp. 10–12.

11. Robert Goldhammer, *Clinical Supervision* (New York: Holt, Rinehart, and Winston, 1969), pp. 89–90.

12. Edmund J. Amidon and Ned A. Flanders, *The Role of the Teacher in the Classroom* (Minneapolis: Association for Productive Teaching, 1967); and Ned Flanders, "Intent, Action, Feedback: A Preparation for Teaching," *Journal of Teacher Education* 24 (September 1963).

13. Ibid., pp. 65–71.

14. David G. Ryans, *Characteristics of Teachers* (Washington, D.C.: American Council on Education, 1960), pp. 86–92.

15. Thomas H. Briggs and Joseph Justman, *Improving Instruction Through Supervision* (New York: Macmillan Co., 1952), pp. 339–341.

16. Bruce W. Tuckman, "Feedback and the Change Process," *Phi Delta Kappan* 57 (January 1976): 341–344.

17. Alan E. Simon, "Analyzing Educational Platforms: A Supervisory Strategy," *Educational Leadership* 34 (May 1977): 580–584.

18. Sr. M. Benita Dimas, *A Supervisor's Study of Classroom Instruction Through the Use of Audiotapes and the Flanders' System of Interaction Analysis.* Master's essay, Marquette University, 1969.

19. Charles H. Adair and Allan R. Kyle, *Effects of Feedback on Teacher Behavior* (Atlanta, Georgia: Southeastern Educational Laboratory, 1969).

20. *Video Inservice Program* (Milford, Nebraska: Educational Service Unit No. 6) pamphlet, n.d.

SELECTED REFERENCES

Alfonso, Robert J.; Firth, Gerald R.; and Neville, Richard F. *Instructional Supervision: A Behavior System.* Boston: Allyn and Bacon, 1975.

Beegle, Charles W., and Brandt, Richard M., eds. *Observational Methods in the Classroom.* Washington, D.C.: Association for Supervision and Curriculum Development, 1973.

Bishop, Lesless J. *Staff Development and Instructional Improvement.* Boston: Allyn and Bacon, 1976.

Black, James M. *The Basics of Supervisory Management, Mastering the Art of Effective Supervision.* New York: McGraw-Hill, 1975.

Blumbers, Arthur. *Supervisors and Teachers: A Private Cold War.* Berkeley, Calif.: McCutchan Publishing, 1974.

Bradford, Eugene J.; Doremus, Albert F.; and Kreismer, Clifford F. *Elementary School Evaluation: Administrator's Guide to Accountability.* West Nyack, N.Y.: Parker Publishing, 1972.

Crosby, Muriel. *Supervision as Co-operative Action.* New York: Appleton-Century-Crofts, 1957.

Educational Leadership 34 (May 1977). (The theme of this issue is Instructional Supervision.)

Erger, Donald V., and Israel, Benjamin. *New Directions in Educational Leadership.* Farmingdale, N.Y.: Carley Press, 1975.

Feyereisen, Kathryn V.; Fiorino, A. John; and Nowak, Arlene T. *Supervision and Curriculum Renewal: A Systems Approach.* New York: Appleton-Century-Crofts, 1970.

Harris, Ben M. *Supervisory Behavior in Education.* Englewood Cliffs, N.J.: Prentice-Hall, 1975.

Harris, Ben M., and Valverde, Leonard A. "Supervisors and Educational Change." *Theory Into Practice* 15 (October 1976): 267–273.

How to Evaluate Administrative and Supervisory Personnel. Arlington, Va.: American Association of School Administrators, 1977.

Hymans, Ronald. *School Administrator's Handbook of Teacher Supervision and Evaluation Methods.* New York: Prentice-Hall, 1975.

Lucio, William H., and McNeil, J. D. *Supervision: A Synthesis of Thought and Action.* New York: McGraw-Hill, 1969.

Niedermeyer, Fred C. "The Testing of a Prototype System for Outcome-Based Instructional Supervision." *Educational Administration Quarterly* 13 (Spring 1977): 34–50.

Olds, Robert. *Self-Evaluation for Teachers and Administrators.* Westerville, Ohio: School Management Institute, 1973.

Oliva, Peter F. *Supervision for Today's Schools.* New York: Thomas Y. Crowell Company, 1976.

Raubinger, Frederick M.; Sumption, Merle R.; and Kamm, Richard M. *Leadership in the Secondary School.* Columbus, Ohio: Charles E. Merrill, 1974.

Sergiovanni, Thomas J., ed. *Professional Supervision for Professional Teachers.* Washington, D.C.: Association for Supervision and Curriculum Development, 1975.

6

EVALUATING TEACHERS AND TEACHING

The best way to improve instruction is to improve teaching, and the only way to improve teaching is to change teacher behavior.

Donald M. Medley

The effective school principal continually works at lessening the gap between what is and what ought to be. In the previous chapter, ideas for evaluating and improving the supervisory program were presented. This chapter focuses attention on teacher evaluation.

GUIDELINES FOR EVALUATING TEACHERS

A recent task-force study recommended several guidelines that principals should follow in evaluating the performance of teachers. These guidelines were developed with one state's laws in mind, but they probably have applicability to other states as well. Not only do the guidelines have legal implications, they suggest a common sense approach to teacher evaluation. The guidelines fall into two categories: procedural considerations and the contents of the evaluation form.

Procedural Considerations

The teacher performance evaluation process must:

- Involve the superintendent, principals, and teachers
- Identify the number (of teacher evaluations per year) and area of emphasis (personal characteristics, instructional role, etc.)
- Clearly state the purposes for the evaluation
- Include pre- and post-conference regarding the evaluation
- Fully inform teachers about the scope of the evaluation process; i.e., classroom observation, conferences, other documentation to be gathered by the principal (daily journals, memorandums, etc.)

- Spell out causes for termination of a teacher contract following state law and local collective bargaining agreements
- Be based on factual descriptions, not interpretations or conclusions; that is, the use of evaluative information other than the performance evaluation, or (principal's daily journal, etc.) must be complete, objective, and defensible
- Be open to teacher review
- Represent a fair sampling of the teacher's performance; i.e., show a pattern of performance over a period of time
- Inform the teacher, as early as possible, about any deficiencies in performance
- Provide the teacher with opportunities to correct deficiencies
- Guarantee equal treatment regardless of personal status, race, sex, and age.

Evaluation Form

Several suggestions were outlined regarding the evaluation form itself. In summary, the evaluation form must:

- Define incompetency; causes for which a teacher contract can be terminated
- Define the values on the scale used; i.e., which end is high or low on a 1 to 5 scale
- Rate single characteristics only; don't combine two terms in a single statement
- Include a written glossary defining the characteristics, attitudes, and behaviors to be evaluated
- Be cautious about cumulative numerical ratings; that is, assigning equal weight to all evaluative items
- Not be based solely on open-ended statements
- Include a comment section where the principal's comments reflect the strengths and shortcomings already listed on the rating scale
- Provide explicit instructions on how the form is to be used
- Have a clear statement of the purpose of the evaluation

- Include space for a teacher review statement and teacher signature.[1]

Using these guidelines as the basis for evaluating teacher performance, a three-phase evaluation plan will be outlined.

PLANNING PHASE FOR TEACHER EVALUATION

The previous chapter outlined an instructional improvement cycle for use in the supervision of instruction. This cycle is also applicable to the evaluation of teachers since both the supervision and evaluation of instruction go hand in hand.

You will recall that the instructional improvement cycle had three phases: a planning phase, an assessment phase, and an improvement phase. Teacher evaluation plans will be discussed for each of these phases. In an earlier chapter, it was suggested that the principal use a committee pattern for assessing the many aspects of schooling. An evaluation committee was suggested with various subcommittees; i.e., subcommittee on teacher evaluation. Whether you use a subcommittee format or involve all teachers in the planning phases, it is important that some mechanisms be established to enable all teachers to study and discuss the purposes of teacher evaluation.

The following guidelines are worthy of consideration as you, the subcommittee, and/or faculty plan the teacher evaluation program.

1. The first step in designing your teacher evaluation program is to insure that the faculty understands the two purposes for evaluating teacher performance from the principal's point of view:
   a. Instructional improvement is dependent upon the willingness of teachers to improve their teaching, which essentially means helping them change their behaviors.
   b. Teachers must be evaluated for administrative purposes.

2. The plan is based upon democratic processes:
   a. A sharing of ideas and problems
   b. Open communication
   c. Fairness and justice
   d. Desire for objectivity.
3. The plan requires the principal and teachers to identify performance standards and/or objectives.
4. The plan is shared with the community and is subject to review, at any time, by principals and teachers.
5. The evaluation plan is designed to help teachers improve professionally and enhance the quality of instruction.
6. The evaluation plan is a continuous process.
7. The plan is shared and discussed with new teachers and published in the teachers' handbook.
8. The plan is based upon self-appraisal techniques as well as appraisal by others (principal, supervisor, students, peers).
9. The plan focuses upon the quality of human relations—understanding, concern, care, self-respect, and the like.
10. The evaluation plan provides information about the faculty as a whole and individual teachers specifically; information on the individual teachers is confidential.
11. The evaluation plan does not permit comparison of one teacher with another.
12. The evaluation plan uses multiple evaluations, several kinds of instruments, and includes a variety of supervisory techniques (direct observation, audiotape, videotape).
13. Conferences follow most, if not all, the evaluation strategies.

These guidelines can be helpful to you and the faculty when initiating a teacher evaluation program.

Characteristics of Successful Programs

Those who have a teacher evaluation program may wish to consider A. Brighton's suggestion that there are certain characteristics present in successful teacher evaluation programs, and the absence of one or more of the characteristics greatly diminishes the chance of success. The following checklist is designed to help you determine which characteristics are present in your current teacher evaluation program. Place a checkmark before one of the two statements for each item that best describes your teacher evaluation program.

1. ____ (A) Teachers, principals, and supervisors are actively involved in planning and reviewing our program.
   ____ (B) Administrators institute the program with little or no participation by teachers.
2. ____ (A) There is little or no preparation by faculty and administrators before implementing our teacher evaluation program.
   ____ (B) We plan, study, and prepare professional personnel before instituting our teacher evaluation program.
3. ____ (A) This school's education goals and objectives have been established and generally accepted.
   ____ (B) Educational goals and objectives are unpublished, generally unknown, and not clear.
4. ____ (A) Teaching has been defined and job descriptions developed.
   ____ (B) Teachers are not clear or at least vaguely aware of their responsibilities.
5. ____ (A) We rate teachers primarily for administrative purposes.
   ____ (B) We rate teachers primarily to improve instruction and help teachers succeed.
6. ____ (A) It is clear to all personnel who will make the evaluations.
   ____ (B) Personnel are generally not clear on who has the responsibility for evaluation.

7. ____ (A) Teacher evaluation is based on non-classroom activities, teacher traits, hearsay, or conformity to raters' values.

____ (B) Teacher evaluation is based on observation of teachers' classroom performance.

8. ____ (A) Teacher evaluation is recorded on a cooperatively developed or selected instrument.

____ (B) Teacher evaluation is recorded on an instrument selected by the administration.

9. ____ (A) Teacher evaluation records are not readily available to teachers.

____ (B) Teacher evaluation records are available to teachers.

10. ____ (A) The teacher evaluation program includes informal conferences between the evaluator and teacher.

____ (B) The teacher evaluation program includes no conferences, or, if there is one, it is a formal, administrator-controlled one.

11. ____ (A) Administrator's rating is final with no provision for reviewing ratings of observations.

____ (B) Disagreement on any item provides for conferences, reviews, and provision for other observers or evaluators.

12. ____ (A) Provisions are made for developing supervisors'/principals' skills and competencies in teacher evaluation.

____ (B) Teacher evaluation is conceived as an addition to the principals' task without concern for qualifications or work load.

13. ____ (A) No provisions are made for assessing the effectiveness of principals/supervisors in the teacher evaluation program.

14. ____ (A) The teacher evaluation program itself is evaluated periodically.

____ (B) The teacher evaluation program is seldom evaluated.

15. ____ (A) The teacher evaluation program is changed whenever the evaluation suggests it should be changed.

____ (B) The teacher evaluation program as implemented continues unchanged or with minor administrative changes from year to year.[2]

There are seven basic questions that usually arise in discussions with principals and teachers that are worth considering:

1. Why should we evaluate teachers in this school?
2. What should be evaluated?
3. How will the evaluation be done?
4. Who should do the evaluating?
5. When and where will the evaluation take place?
6. What will be done with the results of the evaluation?
7. What will be our plans and procedures following the evaluation of teachers in this school?

These questions provide an overview of teacher evaluation and are noteworthy for discussion and planning. Answers to each of these questions will be found in the instructional improvement cycle discussed in this chapter. The importance of involving teachers in any evaluation-accountability plans cannot be overstated.

It is unreasonable, undemocratic, and increasingly unworkable to give teachers no control over setting the standards for which they should be held accountable. It would be equally unrealistic to give them sole control. The pressure is on teachers as well as administrators and board members to consider seriously ways of satisfying the public's legitimate demand for some system of accountability that will improve teaching performance where it needs to be improved.[3]

This improvement will result from strong, positive leadership from the person in the front office.

The next two components of the planning phase for teacher evaluation that deserves your attention are what is to be evaluated and by whom.

Deciding What to Evaluate

To be straightforward about it, you and your teachers can evaluate many aspects of teaching and instruction. Here are some factors that can be evaluated:

- Teacher's characteristics
- Teaching techniques and methods
- Teacher's performance
- Teacher's relationships with students
- Teacher's use of instructional media
- Teacher's instructional methods, i.e., grouping, teacher-centered, student-centered, individualizing
- Teacher talk, verbal interactions
- Teacher's questions—kind, quality
- Teacher's knowledge of learning principles
- Teacher's knowledge of child and adolescent growth and development
- Teacher's ability to write instructional objectives
- Teacher's evaluation procedures—testing, grading
- Teacher's classroom climate
- Teacher's classroom management skills
- Teacher's ability to handle discipline problems
- Teacher's ability to teach concepts of the subject.

The question before you and your teachers is what should be evaluated. Part of the answer to this question will depend upon your district's policies and union negotiation regarding teacher evaluation. The teacher performance evaluation instrument will contain items that teachers and administrators feel are important to the instructional

process. This means that you and the faculty must decide together what factors, performance objectives, and characteristics are worthy of evaluation with the intent that the effort will contribute to the improvement of instruction. Several examples will be provided in the next section of this chapter (assessment phase). The discussion that follows will be limited to three interesting factors related to teaching and to evaluation: teacher characteristics, teacher competencies, and teacher evaluation in relation to student achievement. Why? Most inquiries I receive about the topic of teacher evaluation, be they from teachers, administrators, or parents, can be summarized in three questions:

1. What are the characteristics of good, effective teachers?
2. What competencies and skills do effective teachers demonstrate?
3. What effect do teachers have on student achievements?

Answer to these three questions may be helpful to you and your faculty as you proceed in the planning phase to decide what to evaluate.

Teacher Evaluation and Student Achievement

One of the most intriguing questions and perhaps one that most administrators and teachers ask is: What effect do teachers have on student achievement? For whatever reason, principals and others would like a definite answer to the question—teachers either do or do not affect student achievement.

Common sense and some research suggest that teachers do make a difference and that certain teacher variables seem to relate to student achievement. To suggest otherwise is to ignore observational evidence, testimony, and logic. The problem is one of trying to relate teacher performance and student learning to evaluation and accountability. There are too many variables on both sides that prevent accurate, significant teacher evaluation when student achievement is the major objective.

A review of teacher effectiveness studies on student learning summarized by Dunkin and Biddle[4] and Rosenshine and Furst[5] show a lack of definitive results that could be used by principals or anyone else for teacher evaluation purposes.

However, there are some teacher variables worth considering that seem to relate to student learning. They are presented here to help you and your faculty in planning for the evaluation of teaching performance and the improvement of instruction.

Effective teachers (who have some influence on student achievement) are those who demonstrate the following qualities:

1. They are clear in their presentations of the concepts of the subject matter.
2. They use a variety of approaches in techniques and materials during instruction.
3. They teach their lessons with enthusiasm.
4. They are task-oriented and businesslike.
5. They give students opportunities to learn the material being taught.
6. They use student ideas and provide a supportive emotional climate.
7. Their use of criticism is limited and not over-used.
8. They provide students with an overview of the lesson or unit; that is, they use structuring statements that tell the students what has happened and what is to happen during the lesson or unit.
9. They use a variety of questions that encourage both the lower and higher cognitive levels with emphasis on "high-level" questions.
10. They "probe" students, through questioning and other methods, to elaborate on their answers to questions, problems, and issues.
11. They help students with their perception of the level of difficulty of the instruction.[6]

These criteria are worthy of note when evaluating teachers, but they should be treated with caution should you attempt to relate them directly to student achievement or use them for administrative purposes (i.e., evaluating probationary teachers, retention, etc.).

Few principals would assess teacher performance solely on the basis of student achievement. Yet, it is possible to include student achievement, as measured by standardized achievement tests and/or criterion-referenced tests, as part of a teacher's performance rating. In fact, some school districts are beginning to use this information not only in the teacher evaluation program, but also as a part of the evaluation profile of individual school principals. (Recall the discussion of principal behavior and teacher-student productivity.) A school district's plan for evaluating teachers which includes the use of student achievement test data is described in the improvement phase section of this chapter. It is probably inevitable that the accountability movement will include a greater interest in matching student achievement with teaching performance. This demand will have to be challenged by school principals if student achievement begins to become the major criterion for determining the effectiveness of a teacher's performance.

Deciding Who Should Evaluate

There are six potential evaluators that you and your faculty should consider:

- The principal
- The teacher
- The students
- The teacher's peers
- The school district's supervisor and/or coordinator
- The department chairperson, unit leader, master teacher.

Your evaluation plan should include a description of the role of all six of these potential evaluators. The case has been made for the role of the principal as an evaluator of teacher effectiveness. While the supervisor (central office) can be of assistance in the evaluation of teachers and teaching, many prefer that the role be one outside of evaluation; namely, a consultant role, helping teachers with methods, procedures, and materials of instruction, serving as a master teacher by demonstrating methods and techniques that may be of value to a teacher or group of teachers. Supervisors should help both principals and teachers by engaging in the evaluation process as an important third party who serves as a consultant to both the teacher(s) and the principal. A similar role can be assumed by department chairpersons, unit leaders, and/or master teachers. In other words, if the situation allows it, three parties are engaged in the evaluation process: principal, supervisor, and department-unit leaders.

Your evaluation plan may include three additional sources for teacher evaluation: peers, students, and the teacher.

Peer Evaluation

Realistically, peer evaluation, regardless of its merits, will probably be the one component to be questioned by the faculty. Although peer evaluation can be of great value for instructional improvement,[7] the concerns, cautions, and fears it may generate among your faculty may not be worth the effort. Therefore, for experienced-tenured teachers, the opportunity for peer evaluation should be encouraged but left on a volunteer basis. If one teacher wants colleagues to observe the way she or he uses the discussion method, then you should do what needs to be done to enable that teacher to provide assistance, ideas, and suggestions. However, peer evaluation should, in my opinion, be a requirement for all new teachers during their first two years of teaching. Here are some suggestions:

1. All new teachers should be told about peer evaluation before they are employed.
2. Experienced teachers on your faculty should be selected by you from a list of recommended teachers that is submitted by the faculty.

3. You and the selected teachers (two or three depending on the size of the school) should meet and plan the evaluation process—the what, when, where, and how.
4. Peer evaluators should be given time to do the job; therefore, substitute teachers or teacher aides should be utilized to relieve class assignments at the appropriate time.
5. Peer evaluation should take place once a month for two years between October and May.
6. Classroom observations should be scheduled for at least one-half hour.
7. Conferences should be held before and after the peer evaluator observes the new teacher.
8. Conferences between the principal and peer evaluator should be held regularly to compare data, schedule meetings with the new teacher, and make recommendations.

Student Evaluation

A poll by the National Education Association showed that 50 percent of the elementary and secondary teachers surveyed favored formal student evaluation of teachers, while the remaining 50 percent were opposed. Students can and should evaluate their teachers for the following reasons:

1. Students are the continual recipients of what the teacher does.
2. Students are exposed to methods, styles, and procedures that they can react to, and, within limits, they can provide valuable feedback to the teacher.
3. Teachers are in the learning business, and it makes sense to find out from learners how well this business is being transacted.
4. Student evaluation of teachers will demonstrate to students the value of feedback, and of knowing strengths and weaknesses.
5. Feedback from student evaluations will provide additional data to the teacher that may help improve teacher instruction and performance.

There are several guidelines that should be followed when and if you and your teachers decide to have students evaluate instruction:

1. Student evaluation of teachers should be on a volunteer basis only.
2. Student evaluation of teachers should be anonymous.
3. Student evaluation of teachers should be on a continuous-periodic basis throughout the school year.
4. Student evaluation of teachers should be promoted as a sense of self-improvement.
5. Student evaluation of teachers should not be used for administrative decisions about the teacher.
6. Data collected from student evaluation remain with the teacher.
7. The teacher decides whether to share the results with you during conferences.
8. Teachers should be given opportunities to share their experiences using student evaluation with the faculty should they desire to do so.
9. Teachers should be encouraged to use a variety of instruments, at different times throughout the year, to obtain student reaction to their methods, assignments, and the like.
10. Teachers should try to identify specific aspects of their performance for student evaluation. For example, a procedure for student evaluation of a teacher's skill in asking questions (memory, convergent, divergent, evaluative) has been suggested, as well as a procedure for student evaluation of teacher directiveness.[8] A variety of instruments are presented in the section under the assessment phase of the instructional improvement cycle as examples of student evaluation of teachers and teaching.

Self-Evaluation

Like self-supervision, self-evaluation can be a powerful method for changing behavior and improving instruction. "Do as I do, not as I say."

Therein lies the strategy for implementing teacher self-evaluation methods. You, as principal of the school, must demonstrate the value you place on self-evaluation. Several administrator self-evaluation methods have been described in previous chapters. It would be foolhardy to promote self-evaluation methods among your teachers without using self-evaluation as part of your plan for evaluating how you administer the school.

Purposes of self-evaluation. The purposes of teacher self-evaluation are:

- To change teacher behavior
- To improve instruction
- To improve specific aspects of a teacher's performance
- To initiate experimentation; to get teachers to try new things, new ideas
- To promote an attitude that "we can do it better."

Self-evaluation, although effective for new and inexperienced teachers, may be the most significant part of a teacher evaluation plan for experienced, tenured teachers.

There is a multitude of behaviors, performances, and activities that can be evaluated through self-evaluation methods. For example, some teachers use self-evaluation methods to determine

- Student achievement
- Student attitudes, interests, self-concepts, etc.
- Instructional methods
- Value, purpose, importance of student assignments
- Testing procedures
- Student knowledge of instructional goals and objectives
- Classroom climate
- Independent learning activities (learning centers, etc.)
- Student reaction to texts and other materials

- Time spent with individual students, groups, whole class
- Teacher-pupil relationships
- Teacher behavior as perceived by students
- Parent attitudes about the teacher
- Relationship with the administration
- Relationship with teachers in the building.

Self-evaluation techniques have also been used to assess out-of-class activities and professional activities such as:

- College courses
- Independent readings, professional readings
- In-service programs, workshops attended
- Trips of an educational nature
- Extra-school activities (chaperone, class-supervisor, etc.).

A procedure for self-evaluation. The principal and faculty should give some attention to the procedures used for implementing self-evaluation plans. For example, it would be helpful to have teachers:

- Read about self-evaluation procedures (see references)
- Learn to write objectives as specifically as possible
- Examine existing self-evaluation instruments
- Learn to construct their own self-evaluation instruments
- Learn to use observational techniques (see self-supervision in previous chapter)
- Plan self-evaluation methods for the entire faculty, groups within the faculty, as well as individual teachers.

A suggested procedure for implementing self-evaluation plans, whether for groups or individuals, follows.

1. Self-Evaluation Objective:
   a. I (We) would like to self-evaluate . . .
   b. Therefore, my (our) objective(s) is (are) . . .

2. Self-Evaluation Methods:
   a. To self-evalute this objective(s), I (we) will . . .
3. Self-Evaluation Instrument(s):
   a. To self-evaluate this objective(s), I (we) will use the following instrument(s) . . .
4. Self-Evaluation Schedule:
   a. To self-evaluate using this instrument(s), I (we) will utilize the following schedule . .
5. Self-Evaluation Results:
   a. The results of this self-evaluation are summarized as follows:
6. Change:
   a. Based upon the results, I (we) plan to take the following action(s) . . .
   b. Therefore, my (our) new objective(s) for self-evaluation is (are) . . .

ASSESSMENT PHASE FOR TEACHER EVALUATION

Once you and your faculty have implemented the suggestions in the planning phase for teacher evaluation, you should have settled on the why, what, who, and when aspects of the plan. The recurring issue is how to evaluate teachers.

The following instruments serve as illustrations of teacher-administrator prepared materials for evaluating teachers and/or aspects of teaching. They can be used for external or self-evaluation purposes. They can be adapted to suit your particular needs. Commercially-prepared instruments are available, and a summary of some of these is provided.

Teacher Evaluation Profile

The evaluation profile in Figure 6–1 uses factors found in the research regarding successful, effective teaching and basic principles of learning. This profile is to be completed by the principal/supervisor. Directions would require the evaluator to shade in the bar graph under each personal characteristic and to place a check along the line for each item under Methods, Learning Environment, and Learning Processes. The checks can then be connected with a line that will provide a "picture" profile of the teacher. The profile is designed to be used by the principal but, with some adaptation, it can serve as a self-evaluation and/or student evaluation instrument. If this is done, the bar graphs can be shaded in with colored pencils to reflect the ratings of the teacher, the principal/supervisor, and the students. Lines of different colors could be used on the other items of the profile.

It should be noted that other items may be added to the profile. For example, methods of instruction could be detailed. Items from the chapter on classroom climate might be added to the section on learning environment.

Figure 6–1
Teacher Evaluation Profile

Personal Characteristics

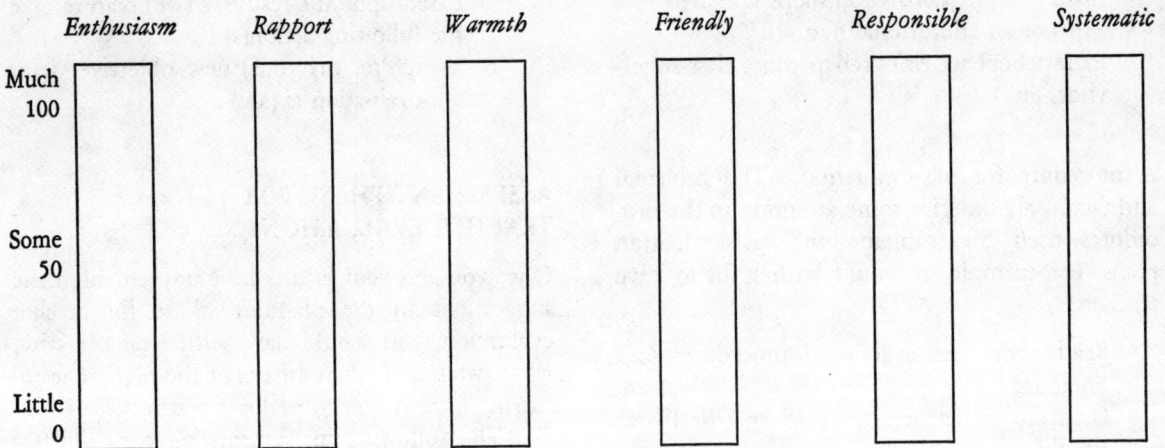

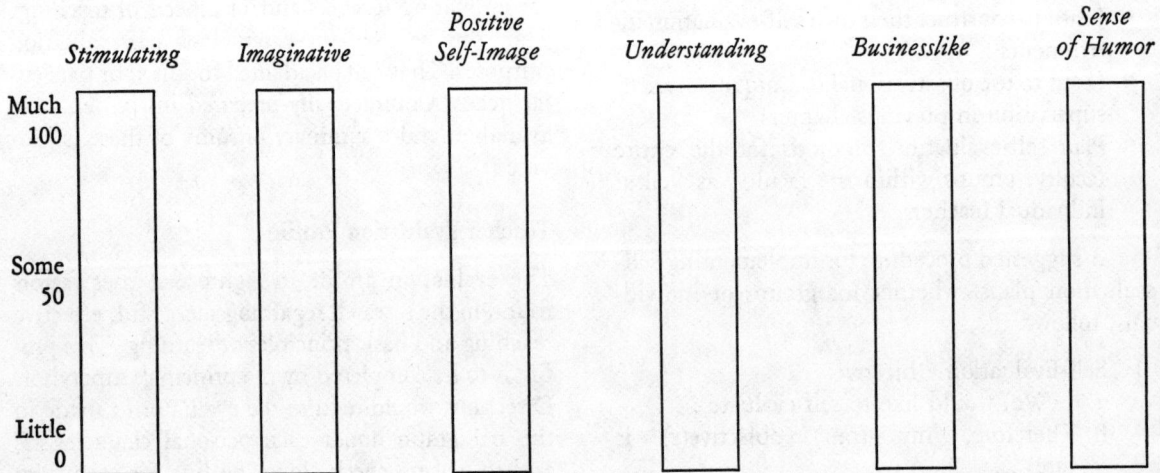

	Enthusiasm	Rapport	Warmth	Friendly	Responsible	Systematic
Much 100						
Some 50						
Little 0						

	Stimulating	Imaginative	Positive Self-Image	Understanding	Businesslike	Sense of Humor
Much 100						
Some 50						
Little 0						

(cont.)

Teaching Performance: Methods

	Never/ Limited		Sometimes/ Moderate		Always/ Extensive

1. Objectives of each lesson are clear.

0	25	50	75	100

2. Uses multiple texts.

0	25	50	75	100

3. Uses a variety of instructional methods.

0	25	50	75	100

4. Assesses student progress frequently.

0	25	50	75	100

5. Uses diagnostic evaluative methods.

0	25	50	75	100

6. Uses a variety of instructional resources.

0	25	50	75	100

7. Assignments are interesting.

0	25	50	75	100

8. Presents subject matter interestingly.

0	25	50	75	100

9. Lessons are presented clearly.

0	25	50	75	100

10. Methods include a review of what is to be taught and learned.

0	25	50	75	100

11. Questions asked of students are more than memory/recall.

0	25	50	75	100

12. Focuses instruction on student learning.

0	25	50	75	100

13. Asks student opinion on difficulty of lesson.

0	25	50	75	100

14. Methods require students to think about their ideas, opinions, and answers.

0	25	50	75	100

15. Methods require students to try to attain teacher-student objectives.

0	25	50	75	100

16. Methods are task-oriented and well-planned.

0	25	50	75	100

17. Methods encourage student discussion and debate.

0	25	50	75	100

18. Demonstrates flexibility in teaching.

0	25	50	75	100

(cont.)

Teaching Performance: Methods

	Never/ Limited		Sometimes/ Moderate		Always/ Extensive

19. Methods reflect that teacher sees things from student point of view.

0	25	50	75	100

20. Utilizes an informal, easy teaching style.

0	25	50	75	100

21. Methods reflect a sound knowledge of subject matter.

0	25	50	75	100

22. Personalizes teaching.

0	25	50	75	100

23. Is willing to experiment; to try new things.

0	25	50	75	100

24. Methods are democratically oriented.

0	25	50	75	100

25. Methods emphasize productive learning.

0	25	50	75	100

Teaching Performance: Learning Environment

	Never/ Limited		Sometimes/ Moderate		Always/ Extensive

1. Maintains an aesthetically pleasant classroom.

0	25	50	75	100

2. Involves students in helping with classroom decor.

0	25	50	75	100

3. Involves students in classroom cleanliness.

0	25	50	75	100

4. Involves students in creating a positive learning environment.

0	25	50	75	100

5. Provides areas for quiet study; independent work.

0	25	50	75	100

6. Provides areas for small group discussions and work.

0	25	50	75	100

7. Uses classroom space and equipment effectively.

0	25	50	75	100

8. Involves students in classroom managerial tasks.

0	25	50	75	100

9. Involves students in daily clerical tasks.

0	25	50	75	100

10. Demonstrates concern for safety and security of students and materials.

0	25	50	75	100

(cont.)

Teaching Performance: Learning Processes

	Never/ Limited		Sometimes/ Moderate		Always/ Extensive

1. Encourages creative, imaginative work from students.

0	25	50	75	100

2. Encourages independence in student learning.

0	25	50	75	100

3. Provides opportunities for students to learn the material.

0	25	50	75	100

4. Encourages and uses students' ideas and suggestions.

0	25	50	75	100

5. Encourages and uses students' questions.

0	25	50	75	100

6. Promotes and uses students' curiosity.

0	25	50	75	100

7. Capitalizes on students' interests.

0	25	50	75	100

8. Plans motivational activities for students.

0	25	50	75	100

9. Uses problem-solving techniques.

0	25	50	75	100

10. Involves students in unit and lesson planning.

0	25	50	75	100

11. Promotes cooperation in group learning.

0	25	50	75	100

12. Works with students in developing long- and short-term objectives.

0	25	50	75	100

13. Involves students in arranging groups.

0	25	50	75	100

14. Promotes cooperation and responsibility in group work.

0	25	50	75	100

15. Encourages students to respect each others talents, abilities, interests, and needs.

0	25	50	75	100

16. Involves students in the evaluation of their work.

0	25	50	75	100

17. Promotes self-evaluation methods.

0	25	50	75	100

18. Helps students assess progress toward specified objectives.

0	25	50	75	100

(cont.)

Teaching Performance: Learning Processes

	Never/ Limited		Sometimes/ Moderate		Always/ Extensive
19. Helps students identify barriers to achieving objectives.					
	0	25	50	75	100
20. Helps students identify barriers to learning subject matter content.					
	0	25	50	75	100
21. Helps students develop effective study skills and habits.					
	0	25	50	75	100
22. Praises more than criticizes students.					
	0	25	50	75	100

Student Evaluation of Teachers

Many of the instruments already suggested in this and other chapters can easily be adapted and used as student evaluation instruments, at least for students who can read. Since reading ability in the primary grades limits the use of instruments previously described, some alternate examples may be helpful.

Teacher evaluation—Primary grades. Can students in the primary grades evaluate teachers? Listen to children as they leave school each day, or on the last day of school you can hear them shouting to one another, "Who did you get?" In some cases, you can hear a teacher's name mentioned—groans! Another teacher is named—cheers! Yes, primary grade children (and their parents, for that matter) can evaluate (some authorities prefer the word *rate*) teachers, however informally and impressionistically.

To formalize the process somewhat, one instrument is presented as an illustration of what might be used by primary grade teachers. Obviously, the results are to be treated cautiously. Nevertheless, they can reveal information that will be useful to primary grade teachers.

Figure 6–2 shows a form that has been used successfully with primary grade students. The teacher can read the directions and items to the children. Students place an X on the face that best describes how they feel.

Figure 6–2
Primary Grade Student Evaluation of Teacher/Class

How do you feel about:

1. your teacher?

2. helping your teacher?

(cont.)

3. your classmates?

4. your work in class?

5. the work I give you?

6. the way I teach you?

7. the things we do in class?

8. our working together?

9. the way I teach you to read?

10. the way I teach you mathematics or numbers?

11. the worksheets we use?

12. the workbooks we use?

(cont.)

13. answering in class?

14. your reading group?

15. how I like you?

16. the time I give you to do things?

17. the way I discipline you or your friends?

18. the way I talk to the class?

19. the way I look?

20. the way I test what you have learned?

Teacher evaluation—Upper grades. Students in the upper grades (four through twelve) can and should be given opportunities to evaluate their teachers. To initiate such a program would require teacher volunteers. Properly promoted, with volunteer teachers sharing the benefits they derive from student evaluation, many skeptical teachers may be willing to give it a try. Students are very perceptive and thus can rate many aspects of the teaching-learning process. Students can be effective evaluators of the total teacher performance or of specific aspects of teaching such as methods, assignments, effectiveness of learning results, teacher-made tests, and the like. Student evaluation of teachers

Figure 6-3
Upper Grade Student Evaluation of Teacher/Class

	Yes	No	Sometimes
1. Do you always know what I want to do?	——	——	——
2. Is reading easy for you?	——	——	——
3. Do you have many different things to do?	——	——	——
4. Do I like you?	——	——	——
5. Do you like me?	——	——	——
6. Do your classmates like you?	——	——	——
7. Do you like your classmates?	——	——	——
8. Do you like the way I teach reading?	——	——	——
9. Do you like the way I teach math or numbers?	——	——	——
10. Do you like the way I teach you other subjects?	——	——	——
11. Do you like the way I discipline your classmates?	——	——	——
12. Do you like the tests I give you?	——	——	——
13. Do you always know what I want you to do?	——	——	——
14. Do you like the assignments I give you?	——	——	——
15. Do you like my voice?	——	——	——
16. Do I make school work interesting for you?	——	——	——
17. Do I help you when you need it?	——	——	——
18. Do I give you enough of my time?	——	——	——
19. Do you like to help me?	——	——	——
20. Do you like to help your classmates?	——	——	——
21. Do you like to share your ideas?	——	——	——
22. Do you understand my directions?	——	——	——
23. Do you feel good about being in this class?	——	——	——

should be done anonymously. Figure 6–3 is an example of a student form for evaluating the teacher and the class.

Evaluating Specific Aspects of Teaching

Not all evaluating instruments have to assess the broad range of teacher-teaching behaviors. Instruments can be designed to evaluate specific aspects of teaching. In fact, it may be more helpful to teachers to focus in on certain aspects of teaching and instruction so that planning for change can be more specific and concrete. For these reasons, two examples follow. I have used several of the instruments with principals and teachers as they work toward the goal of improving instruction. The first

example is designed to help teachers evaluate instructional methods, the second helps them examine processes they use in their teaching. These examples are presented here to help your teachers evaluate themselves on the many factors that influence teaching and instruction.

Instructional methods. In this example, a competency statement will be the focus of the evaluation. The competency is stated as follows: A competent teacher uses a variety of instructional methods. An instrument was designed to help teachers determine the extent to which various instructional methods are used (Figure 6–4).

The instrument serves as a self-evaluation tool initially. Some teachers have used the instrument

Figure 6–4
Instructional Methods Questionnaire

Teacher's Name:_____

Grade Level or
Subject Taught:_____

Competency: Effective teachers use a variety of instructional methods. Therefore, a competent teacher will plan and use a variety of instructional methods.

Question: How often do you use each of the following in your classes?

Methods	Very Often	Often	Some-times	Seldom	Never	Example of How and When It Was Used
1. Cassette tapes	___	___	___	___	___	
2. Demonstration by teacher	___	___	___	___	___	
3. Differentiated assignments	___	___	___	___	___	
4. Discussion	___	___	___	___	___	
5. Display of student work	___	___	___	___	___	
6. Flexible grouping	___	___	___	___	___	
7. Field trips	___	___	___	___	___	
8. Films	___	___	___	___	___	
9. Filmstrips	___	___	___	___	___	
10. Game-type activities	___	___	___	___	___	
11. Peer teaching	___	___	___	___	___	
12. Independent study	___	___	___	___	___	
13. Inquiry techniques	___	___	___	___	___	
14. Learning centers/stations	___	___	___	___	___	
15. Learning packets	___	___	___	___	___	
16. Lecture	___	___	___	___	___	
17. Multilevel materials	___	___	___	___	___	
18. Newspapers, magazines, etc.	___	___	___	___	___	
19. Outside speakers	___	___	___	___	___	
20. Group projects	___	___	___	___	___	
21. Individual projects	___	___	___	___	___	
22. Role playing	___	___	___	___	___	
23. Small group instruction	___	___	___	___	___	
24. Student aides (tutorial)	___	___	___	___	___	
25. Student demonstrations	___	___	___	___	___	
26. Videotapes	___	___	___	___	___	
27. Debate	___	___	___	___	___	
28. Student self-evaluation	___	___	___	___	___	
29. Student-teacher planning	___	___	___	___	___	
30. Other	___	___	___	___	___	

as a student evaluation tool as well. In this case, the question on the form can be changed to: "How often does your teacher use the following methods in class?" If the form is to be used by a principal/supervisor, the question may read: "How often have you observed each of these methods being used by the teacher?"

Using this instrument, the teacher can analyze the data and then write an objective (e.g., I will attempt to use more group-type activities during the next term). The teacher designs procedures for implementing this objective and may have to develop a new instrument to determine whether or not he or she attained the objective. A similar procedure can be used by teachers to evaluate the processes of teaching and learning.

Teaching processes. Teachers have voiced concern and confusion about teaching processes as they relate to the teaching of content. As a means of self-evaluation and a procedure to generate discussion at faculty and in-service meetings, the Teacher's Process Scale was used (Figure 6–5). The purpose of the scale is to help teachers identify teaching processes and then to determine the extent to which they use the process in their teaching (directly or indirectly). One of the interesting findings, for example, and one that creates a dilemma for teachers, is the fact that many will say they use a particular process (i.e., questioning, listening, etc.), but they seldom teach it directly; that is, they do not have lessons on helping students learn to question, to listen, to clarify data, to make generalizations, and so on. Asked if they expect youngsters to learn these processes indirectly usually brings a resounding "no." Asked why they don't teach most of the processes directly usually leads to interesting discussions, rationales, and eventually a request to be helped to do it.

An Example of Teacher Self-Evaluation

One principal and his faculty designed a self-evaluation instrument to help identify their strengths and weaknesses. First, the teachers identified characteristics that they believed described the talented teacher. The following thirteen characteristics were identified:

1. A person who has confidence, radiates it, and fosters confidence in others.
2. A person who enjoys other people as well as life itself.
3. A person who can effectively communicate with other people.
4. A person who treats students as he would like to be treated.
5. A person who is flexible.
6. A person who recognizes students as individuals and utilizes their talents to form a cohesive group.
7. A person who is open-minded and willing to change.
8. A person who does not over-react to minor problems.
9. A person who develops within the students a feeling of accomplishment.
10. A person who encourages and directs creativity in the students.
11. A person who is knowledgeable about new methods of education and ready to try them.
12. A person who encourages the learner to approach learning with an open mind.
13. A person who has well-defined purposes of education.[9]

The teachers and principal designed a self-evaluation instrument called "My Thoughts." For each of the thirteen characteristics, five statements were developed. Each statement was designed so that a talented teacher would tend to disagree with the statement. The self-evaluation instrument and scoring procedure are shown in Figure 6–6.

The principal reported that his staff completed the instrument with an understanding that he would not see any individual's results or score. Faculty, he discovered, discussed results among themselves and about 20 percent of the teachers

Figure 6-5
Teacher's Process Scale

School: _____   Subject(s) and Grade: _____

As a teacher, how often do you use and teach each of the following processes in your class(es)?

Process	Very Often	Often	Sometimes	Seldom	Never	Process Taught: Specifically	Indirectly	Not at All
1. Questioning								
2. Reading								
3. Discussing								
4. Observing								
5. Collecting Data								
6. Identifying Variables in the Data								
7. Listening								
8. Confering, Reporting, Interviewing								
9. Classifying Data								
10. Discovering Principles								
11. Making Hypotheses								
12. Drawing, Photography, Lettering, etc.								
13. Analyzing the Material								
14. Displaying, Exhibiting, Graphing, Mapping								
15. Generalizing from Data								
16. Recognizing the Material								
17. Making Relationships								
18. Testing Data for Social and Personal Use								
19. Creating and Imagining								
20. Other								

Figure 6-6
Self-Evaluation Instrument

As you perceive your role as a teacher you have some rather definite thoughts about yourself, your job, and your students. The statements below are similar thoughts that teachers might have. Place a checkmark on the line after each statement to indicate how you feel.

	Strongly Approve	Approve	Disapprove	Strongly Disapprove
1. A teacher should often change his purposes and goals of education to meet the daily demands of the classroom.	——	——	——	——
2. The idea of questioning everything is ridiculous. Tested knowledge, proven solutions, and the experience of the teacher should be the core of learning.	——	——	——	——
3. Is my job one of keeping kids happy or educating them? Sure, I know many of the new methods, but most are not worth using if a good solid education is to be achieved.	——	——	——	——
4. Today's students have very little imagination and seem to be interested in very little.	——	——	——	——
5. A pat on the back may be a good idea now and then but it borders on dishonesty to compliment a student for poor or messy work even if some progress is evident.	——	——	——	——
6. This is a job of emotions. If a minor emotional upset occurs immediately before school, I tend to have a difficult day with my job and with the students.	——	——	——	——
7. When my friends talk about their jobs, I just listen. Who would be interested in hearing about my being a teacher?	——	——	——	——
8. I think that sports, music, and other activities should be considered secondary to academic matters in the school curriculum.	——	——	——	——
9. Students enjoy hearing of the interests and accomplishments of teachers. Some of my most interesting lessons develop when I weave my own experiences into the discussion.	——	——	——	——
10. There is a place where my responsibility ends. I give my classes outlined notes. These are gone over in class with the homework and from this point it is the student's responsibility to get the correct information.	——	——	——	——
11. Students realize that I, the teacher, deserve a special right to do as I wish in my classroom.	——	——	——	——
12. I insist that all students in the class conform to the same or nearly the same standards. Everyone is equal.	——	——	——	——

(cont.)

	Strongly Approve	Approve	Disapprove	Strongly Disapprove
13. Although I believe in student participation, my more experienced views must be projected most of the time.	—	—	—	—
14. Lesson plans are too restricting. Often my best classes have no structure and are open discussions on un-related topics.	—	—	—	—
15. I encourage my students to have opinions, support them and stand by them. This develops a firm char-acter and not the wishy-washy attitude one sees in the world today.	—	—	—	—
16. What my students need is more self-discipline and a greater sense of responsibility, not new, "innovative" programs.	—	—	—	—
17. Creativity cannot be taught or developed. I believe it is one of those talents that some people have and some do not (like the ability to sing, for example). So—some teachers readily produce creative lessons while others must be satisfied with grinding out edu-cation.	—	—	—	—
18. Achievement in learning is its own reward. Achieve-ment should not be unduly rewarded and never rewarded in a material way.	—	—	—	—
19. I find the only way to handle today's youth is to act quickly and decisively at all times no matter what situation arises.	—	—	—	—
20. I think most teachers should seem somewhat unsure of themselves so they do not appear too authoritarian.	—	—	—	—
21. I believe that a teacher should have a strict code which he lives by and from which he rarely deviates.	—	—	—	—
22. Like most teachers, I am a loner. After spending the day with kids and lunch with teachers, I need to be alone most nights and week-ends.	—	—	—	—
23. Reading is the only true road to acquiring an educa-tion. I cannot and should not be expected to teach students with less than grade-level reading ability.	—	—	—	—
24. I can apply the Golden Rule to a few students, but the minute I treat others as equals they will walk all over me.	—	—	—	—
25. It is not fair to the students in my classes who want to learn to keep the two or three students in each class who do nothing but disrupt the class.	—	—	—	—
26. The attitudes of kids and parents are changing so much that each year I find my job more difficult.	—	—	—	—

(cont.)

	Strongly Approve	Approve	Disapprove	Strongly Disapprove
27. A good teacher need not worry about goals in education as long as he develops a good rapport with the students.	___	___	___	___
28. Teachers must above all train the students to respond to just a few certain keys of learning and from these all others will come.	___	___	___	___
29. The old, tried and true methods of teaching are the best for me and the students because they are what has been successful. The real question is, why fool around with success?	___	___	___	___
30. Deviation from accepted classroom methods indicates to me that the student is not listening or following directions.	___	___	___	___
31. My tests are planned to be difficult and several always fail. Students must be constantly challenged to do better.	___	___	___	___
32. I will not tolerate any kind of foolishness in my classes. If one begins talking out of turn, it is just a beginning for all of them.	___	___	___	___
33. I feel uncomfortable with some classes. It's not just a few students, but most in the class are not pleasant to work with.	___	___	___	___
34. I find the best setting for learning is an orderly, quiet classroom.	___	___	___	___
35. Some days I question my choice of a profession while other days I question whether or not teaching is a profession.	___	___	___	___
36. If students would pay attention and think with me, they would have no trouble learning.	___	___	___	___
37. I teach five (5) straight classes and would enjoy a cup of coffee about 11 o'clock. To say that it is unfair for me to drink coffee in class when the students do not have a like privilege is not treating me as a professional adult.	___	___	___	___
38. With classes so large I am forced to teach to the average ability of the class, knowing this is the best way to reach most of the students.	___	___	___	___
39. Little of value develops from parent-teacher committees since most parents do not understand the process or goals of education.	___	___	___	___
40. Teachers are expected to teach so many things nowadays—citizenship, creativity, human worth, etc.—that I don't know what is truly important myself.	___	___	___	___

(cont.)

	Strongly Approve	Approve	Disapprove	Strongly Disapprove
41. Students seem to think on a superficial level, thereby making open discussion an impossible situation.	___	___	___	___
42. Teaching often becomes a drag. Some days I feel like a tape recorder and each year is becoming a rerun.	___	___	___	___
43. Projects, unusual types of book reports, creative writing, and the like tend to make education play instead of the hard work that is necessary to learn.	___	___	___	___
44. The quality of a paper is important. If it is messy work, I refuse to accept the paper no matter what preparation the student did. Neatness is also important.	___	___	___	___
45. Sending students to the office is a safety value for me. When I become irritated, it is the best solution for both the students and me.	___	___	___	___
46. I wouldn't try student-teacher planning with Junior High students as they are too young to help decide things.	___	___	___	___
47. There is no reason for a student to do poorly in my tests if they have properly studied for them.	___	___	___	___
48. There are certain types of children who clash inevitably with my personality. I can do nothing about this.	___	___	___	___
49. The students may not understand every word I use; however, denying my vocabulary makes a farce of my education.	___	___	___	___
50. I will demand to be respected by the students no matter what. When they are adults, they will demand the same.	___	___	___	___
51. I do not give extra help to students who do not work hard or who cause problems in my class. The students must earn the extra time I give to them.	___	___	___	___
52. Because of the many changes that are taking place in education, I find my job becoming less rewarding.	___	___	___	___
53. At times I am most confused when I try to relate what I do in the class to the major goals of education.	___	___	___	___
54. Real knowledge doesn't change. Theories may prove to be wrong, but real knowledge does not change. And, it is this real knowledge that is the basis of my course.	___	___	___	___
55. Professional magazines always propose ideal methods which I don't have the time or facilities to prepare.	___	___	___	___
56. A social studies project, just like everything a student does in art class, is naturally creative.	___	___	___	___

(cont.)

	Strongly Approve	Approve	Disapprove	Strongly Disapprove
57. I would like to give no grade lower than a "C" but standards are important and, when a student fails, he simply fails.	——	——	——	——
58. I should not overlook little things students do is wrong. They do these things to show their disrespect for the teacher.	——	——	——	——
59. When things don't work out well, it bothers me that the students sense the lack of confidence which I feel.	——	——	——	——
60. I could readily individualize instruction if we had strict homogeneous grouping. The plans and methods would then be geared to the various ability levels. It would be heavenly.	——	——	——	——
61. Teaching junior high kids is okay, but their immaturity makes discussion of a serious topic difficult.	——	——	——	——
62. There are times when the students and I are not on the same wave length. The generation gap is essentially a language barrier.	——	——	——	——
63. When a student acts like a dope, I see nothing wrong in calling him a knucklehead.	——	——	——	——
64. My goal is to best serve the welfare of the overall student group and its goals supersede that of the individual.	——	——	——	——
65. The suggestion of students evaluating the teacher or the curriculum makes my blood boil.	——	——	——	——

Score Sheet*

A. Count the number of checkmarks under the *Strongly Disapprove* column, and multiply by 2. A_____
B. Count the number of checkmarks under the *Disapprove* column. B_____
C. Add A and B. C_____
D. Count the number of checkmarks under the *Strongly Approve* column, and multiply by 2. D_____
E. Count the number of checkmarks under the *Approve* column. E_____
F. Add D and E. F_____
G. Score—Subtract F from C. =====

Suggested Evaluation of Score:

110 +	You are too good to be true!
90–109	You are most talented.
80–89	You are talented.
70–79	You are average.
60–69	Improvement in several areas is needed.
Below 60	You are in trouble.
Negative Score	Seek other employment for your mental health.

*Edward T. Richardson, "My Thoughts: A Self-Evaluation Instrument," *Bulletin of the National Association of Secondary School Principals* 59 (December 1975): 10–16.

shared their scores and item analysis with him. Teachers were interested and willing to talk about results, and it appeared that the results were more accurate than either the principal or teachers thought they would be. As a follow-up to teacher self-ratings on each item, the faculty used the form shown in Figure 6–7, the contents of which was included in principal-teacher conferences early in the school year.

IMPROVEMENT PHASE
FOR TEACHER EVALUATION

The major purpose of the planning and assessing phase of this teacher evaluation plan is to obtain information that can be utilized in the improvement phase where plans are established to improve teaching and learning. Post-conferences are as important in the teacher evaluation phase as they are in the observation phase described in the previous chapter. In the previous chapter, guidelines for conferences between the principal and teacher were

identified. These guidelines are applicable to post-conference plans in the teacher evaluation phase as well. A few additional suggestions may be helpful:

1. You and each teacher should agree, within the parameters of union/association rules and school board policies, on what evaluative data are to be retained in the teacher's file, both at school and at the central office.
2. Post-conferences, like those recommended in the previous chapter, should focus on the results of the data collected and what the data reveal about teacher behavior and performance.
3. Teacher evaluation data usually have an administrative purpose as well as an instructional purpose, and this should be reemphasized during the post-conference. In other words, teachers should know how the evaluation data will be used by the principal.
4. All instruments as well as records of post-conference results should be cosigned by both the teacher and you.

Figure 6–7
A Teacher's Objective*

The talent I desire to improve is

The following materials or activities have helped me to improve this talent:

As I look back through the year, I feel my improvement in this talent has been:

Signed _____

*Edward T. Richardson, "My Thoughts: A Self-Evaluation Instrument," *Bulletin of the National Association of Secondary School Principals* 59 (December 1975): 16–17.

5. Teacher evaluation should result in the improvement or maintenance of instruction. To accomplish this, it is recommended that a plan of action be implemented that would include the following procedures:

   a. Objectives—Based upon the evaluative data, the principal helps the teacher write some specific objectives for improving concepts of the teacher performance.

   b. Methods—The principal helps the teacher decide what methods might best lead to the accomplishment of objectives.

   c. Instruments—The principal helps the teacher select or construct evaluation instruments that will help assess progress in attaining the objective.

   d. Schedule—The principal helps the teacher develop a schedule for trying out the methods, evaluating progress, and recording and reporting results.

   e. Results—The principal helps the teacher analyze and interpret the results of the evaluation and other aspects of the situation that the teacher brings to the conference in relation to the objectives.

   f. Change—Based upon an interpretation of the results, the teacher and principal make judgments about the teacher's performance relative to the objectives and decide whether new objectives should be identified or existing objectives should be retained for further pursuit.

These suggestions for improvement focus on individual teachers. It is also possible to plan, evaluate, and improve instruction on a faculty-wide basis. An example will illustrate the point. Teachers in a particular high school, in the middle of the year, decided with the principal's help and suggestions to evaluate student perceptions of teaching methods and assignments. Two instruments were selected; one instrument was actually designed by a group of teachers. The two instruments were administered to all students and codi-fied in such a way that results could be analyzed for each teacher and for the faculty as a group. The results were given to the principal, who, with the help of a central office supervisor, developed a profile for the staff and for each teacher. The profile was discussed at one faculty meeting. Each teacher's profile was discussed with that teacher only if she or he wished to to do so. Teachers with low ratings were offered specific assistance. At two faculty meetings, the principal and supervisor led the teachers in discussing the faculty profile and ways to improve areas of weakness. It was easy for the principal and supervisor to give examples of areas of low ratings (based on actual individual teacher performance without identifying the teacher). They asked the faculty to "brainstorm" ways to improve in a particular area. The teachers' list of ideas was recorded, typed, and distributed to each teacher. The supervisor and teachers with low ratings selected items that might be tried in the classroom. One point of this improvement idea is that not only did the teachers with low ratings get individual help from the principal and the supervisor, but they, like their colleagues, also benefited from the collective ideas of the faculty.

Evaluating the Evaluation Plan

Obviously, there is no one best teacher evaluation plan. There are limitations because of time, personnel, and the instruments used. A school's teacher evaluation plan should be evaluated periodically. One way to accomplish this task is to use an incomplete sentence format. The following incomplete sentences are designed for teachers. The results should be given to the principal, summarized by him or her, distributed to the teachers, and discusssed at faculty or inservice meetings:

1. Teacher evaluation . . .
2. Because of the teacher evaluation plan, morale at this school is . . .
3. The principal's part in teacher evaluation. . . .
4. The instrument we use . . .

5. Our teacher evaluation procedures . . .
6. Evaluation of my teaching . . .
7. One major problem with our teacher evaluation program . . .
8. Our school's teacher evaluation program needs . . .
9. One major strength of our teacher evaluation program . . .
10. Experienced teachers feel that the teacher evaluation program . . .

Teacher Evaluation and Improvement: A Summary and Example

The instructional improvement cycle for both the supervision and evaluation of instruction has, as its goal, the improvement of teaching and learning. As suggested earlier, the planning phase should include time for both you and your faculty to come together to discuss:

- Guidelines for successful teacher evaluation programs
- The characteristics of successful teacher evaluation programs
- The characteristics of good, effective teachers
- Who should evaluate teachers in your school.

The need to engage in discussions on these very important topics cannot be underscored enough. When you, supervisors, teachers, and others appreciate the value of diagnosing teacher strengths and weaknesses, only then can each take steps towards the improvement of instruction.

The assessment phase will flow naturally from discussions held during the planning phase. In the assessment phase, you and your teachers can cooperatively plan who will evaluate teaching; how will it be done; when will it be scheduled; what kind of evaluation instrument will be used; what factors, characteristics, methods will be evaluated; and what will be done with the results of the assessment.

The improvement phase will serve administrative purposes and performance improvement purposes. No doubt you are in a school district that requires evaluation of teachers for purposes of retention, reassignment, and other decisions including performance improvement. It is during this phase that the data obtained during the assessment phase are used in individual conferences and general faculty meetings to write individual and group objectives to correct weaknesses and capitalize on strengths.

The Kalamazoo (Michigan) Public Schools uses a multicomponent approach to teacher evaluation and improvement that has applicability to individual schools. It highlights some of the major points discussed in the instructional improvement cycle of this and the previous chapter.

This district developed a Teacher Performance Profile (TPP) consisting of six components: student ratings; principal evaluation; peer ratings; parent ratings (elementary level only); self ratings by principals, students, and peers; and student achievement data. The purpose of TPP is to provide each teacher relevant feedback about his or her performance which will contribute to professional growth and serve as the formal evaluation of teachers by their principals.

Some of the specifics of the Teacher Performance Profile may be instructive:

1. Students in grades 2 through 12 rate their teachers using the *Teacher Image Questionnaire;* ratings of kindergarten and first-grade teachers are optional.
2. Probationary teachers are evaluated twice each year by the school principal using the *Teacher Evaluation Form;* tenured teachers are evaluated using the form once each year.
3. Peer ratings are optional. Those teachers who wish peer ratings submit a list of at least five peers who are knowledgeable of the teacher's performance. At least five but no more than fifteen teachers compare the peer rating group, and this group must be approved by

the principal. The *Peer Image Questionnaire* is used for peer ratings.

4. Each spring, parents rate their child's teacher as part of a parent-teacher conference on a scale from poor to excellent.

5. Each teacher rates herself or himself using the *Teacher Image Questionnaire,* the *Teacher Evaluation Form,* and the *Peer Image Questionnaire* (if applicable).

6. With regard to student achievement data, the procedure includes:

   a. Administration of an achievement test in September (pre-test) and May (post-test) for grades 1 through 6

   b. Administration of an achievement test each May for junior high school students

   c. The use of teacher-made objective-referenced tests and the administration of an achievement test at the beginning of each year is part of the plan at the secondary level.

All of these factors go into the teacher profile. The data are used by the principals and teachers in conferences held at the beginning and end of each year with the aim of helping teachers grow professionally.[10]

A FINAL COMMENT

Most school districts have a method of teacher evaluation that is a result of negotiations between the teachers' union and the board of education. In most cases, the plan includes an agreement on the assessment form to be used, the number of scheduled and unscheduled classroom visitations, the use of the results, procedures for appeal of a decision, and the like. One administrator summarized the usual procedure, saying, "I can't get anything done this week. It's my week for teacher evaluation." This means, one supposes, that he visits all classrooms, meets with each teacher, files his report, and breathes a sigh of relief.

This may be overstating the case, but the point is that system-wide evaluation of teachers is only effective if something is done at the building level.

> Systemwide evaluation should be focused on school-by-school achievement (a kind of annual building accreditation), and the evaluation of individual certificated teachers should be done only by colleagues in the building—with records kept only in the building. Schools differ so much from place to place, and local working conditions are so important to professional activities, that it makes sense to place trust in the teachers in the building and their principal, to let them work with their clients (parents and students) in developing appropriate goals for their school, and to infer the appropriate professional performance attendant on these goals.[11]

EVALUATION INSTRUMENTS

Here is a review of several teacher evaluation instruments that you and your faculty may wish to examine.

> "Teacher Image Questionnaire." Educator Feedback Center, Western Michigan University, Kalamazoo, Michigan 49001.

This eighteen-item questionnaire assesses student perceptions and is recommended for Grades 7–12. It takes about fifteen minutes for students to complete, and it measures reactions varying from poor to excellent in such categories as fairness, control, attitudes towards students, anxiety, sense of humor, etc. The Center provides an analysis of the responses and develops an image profile for each teacher.

> Croft Educational Series. 100 Garfield Avenue, New London, Connecticut.

In its Action Folio No. 5, "Evaluating Your Teacher," this service provides several scales that are useful. There is a five-item questionnaire that a teacher could use daily to obtain feedback about the class/lesson entitled, "Daily Student Reaction Form." There are examples of teacher evaluation scales, checklists, rating reports, and self-rating forms.

"Teacher Classroom Climate Questionnaire." Judith A. Agard et al., ATS Associates, Inc., 1521 New Hampshire Avenue, N.W., Washington, D.C. 20036.

This instrument is a sixty-seven-item teacher report inventory of selected aspects of the socio-emotional climate and instructional conditions in a teacher's classroom. There are six scales: cooperation/diversification, friction, rigidity/control, individualization, difficulty, and cooperation. Teachers should take about fifteen to twenty minutes to complete the scale by circling a five-point response scale.

"Classroom Activities Questionnaire, 1969." Joe M. Steele, University of Illinois—Urbana, Curriculum Laboratory, 1201 West Springfield Avenue, Urbana, Illinois 61801.

This thirty-item Likert-type questionnaire assesses student perception of activities in their classroom. There are twenty-five questions on which students react ranging from strongly agree to strongly disagree. Two questions examine student preparation for the class and the amount of teacher-talk. The final three questions ask students to comment about the class, listing three things they like best about the class and three things they would like to change.

"Self-Evaluation Checklist for Teachers in Secondary Education." Sterling G. Callahan, Chicago: Scott, Foresman and Co., n.d.

This four-page booklet is a self-evaluation instrument by which secondary teachers can evaluate themselves with respect to five major categories: the teacher as a person, professional and academic preparation, professional attitudes, relationship to the community, and attitudes toward self-improvement. A scale from A to E is used to rate each item under each category.

"The Purdue Teacher Opinionnaire." H. H. Remmers and G. N. Wright, Purdue University, University Book Store, 360 State Street, West Lafayette, Indiana 47906.

This instrument is designed to measure teacher morale regarding ten factors: teacher rapport with the principal, satisfaction with teaching, rapport among teachers, teacher salary, teacher load, curriculum issues, teacher status, community support of education, school facilities and services, and community pressure. Teachers can complete the instrument in twenty to thirty minutes.

"*The Teaching Evaluation Record.* Educators Publishing Company, 97 Hodge Avenue, Buffalo, New York.

The *Teaching Evaluation Record* is a thirty-two-item rating scale designed to determine teacher effectiveness through observation. Each item is rated on a scale from 0–4 with a description of the evidences the observer should look for before scoring the item. It is recommended the scale be used for diagnostic and evaluative purposes with two full half-days early in the school year and two full half-days in the spring as the amount of observation time.

ENDNOTES

1. "15 Things to Remember Evaluating Teachers." *The Executive Educator* 2 (January 1980): 18–19.

2. Staynor Brighton, *Increasing Your Accuracy in Teacher Evaluation* (Englewood Cliffs, N.J.: Prentice-Hall, 1965), pp. 36–37.

3. Donald W. Robinson, "Editorial," *Phi Delta Kappan* 53 (November 1972): 193.

4. Michael J. Dunkin and Bruce J. Biddle, *The Study of Teaching* (New York: Holt, Rinehart and Winston, 1974).

5. Barak Rosenshine and Norma Furst, "Research on Teacher Performance Criteria," in *Research in Teacher Education: A Symposium,* ed. B. Othanel Smith (Englewood Cliffs, N.J.: Prentice-Hall, 1971), Chapter 3.

6. Ibid., pp. 44–54.

7. "Should Pupils Evaluate Teachers? Teacher Opinion Poll," *Today's Education* 61 (April 1972): 16.

8. See James H. Hogg and William W. Wilen, "Evaluating Teachers' Questions: A New Dimension in Students' Assessment of Instruction," *Phi Delta Kappan* 57 (November 1976): 281–282; and Bruce W. Tuckman, "A Technique for the Assessment of Teacher Directiveness," *Journal of Educational Research* 63 (May-June 1970): 395–400.

9. Edward T. Richardson, "My Thoughts: A Self-Evaluation Instrument," *Bulletin of the National Association of Secondary School Principals* 59 (December 1975): 9.

10. David E. Bartz, *A Multi-Component Approach to Evaluation for Teacher Improvement* (Kalamazoo, Mich.: Kalamazoo Public Schools, 1978). This booklet describes the entire plan and includes copies of instruments used in teacher evaluation.

11. William H. Drummond, "Involving the Teachers in Evaluation," *National Elementary Principal* 52 (February 1973): 32.

SELECTED REFERENCES

Bolton, Dale L. *Selection and Evaluation of Teachers.* Berkeley, Calif.: McCutchan Publishing Corp., 1973.

Bryant, Gerald, and Haack, Frank. "Appraisal: Peer-Centered and Administrator-Centered." *Educational Leadership* 34 (May 1977): 608–612.

Duke, Daniel L. "What Can Students Tell Educators about Classroom Dynamics?" *Theory into Practice* 16 (June 1977): 262–269.

Eckard, Pamela J., and McElhinney, James H. "Teacher Evaluation and Educational Accountability." *Educational Leadership* 34 (May 1977): 613–618.

Edwards, Clifford H.; Getz, Howard G.; Lewis, Franklin G.; Lorber, Michael A.; and Pierce, Walter D. *Planning, Teaching, and Evaluating: A Competency Approach.* Chicago: Nelson-Hall, 1977.

Evaluating Teacher Performance. ERS Circular No. 2. Washington, D.C.: National Education Association, 1972.

The Evaluation of Teachers. Washington, D.C.: Pi Lambda Theta, 1967.

Gage, N. L. *The Scientific Basis of the Art of Teaching.* New York: Teachers College Press, 1978.

Gage, N. L. "The Yield of Research on Teaching." *Phi Delta Kappan* 60 (November 1978): 229–235.

Herman, Jerry J. *Developing an Effective School Staff Evaluation Program.* West Nyack, N.Y.: Parker Publishing Co., 1973.

Maier, Norman R. F. *The Appraisal Interview; Three Basic Approaches.* La Jolla, Calif.: University Associates, 1976.

McNeil, John C., and Popham, W. James. "The Assessment of Teacher Competence." In *Second Handbook of Research on Teaching,* ed. Robert W. Travers. Chicago: Rand McNally and Co., 1973.

McNeil, John D. *Toward Accountable Teachers.* New York: Holt, Rinehart and Winston, 1971.

National Elementary Principal 52 (February 1973). (The theme of this issue is evaluating school personnel.)

Pine, Gerald J., and Boy, Angelo V. "Necessary Conditions for Evaluating Teachers." *Bulletin of the National Association of Secondary School Principals* 59 (December 1975): 18–23.

Popham, W. James. "Pitfalls and Pratfalls of Teacher Evaluation." *Educational Leadership* 31 (November 1974): 141–146.

Redfern, George B. *How to Evaluate Teaching.* Worthington, Ohio: School Management Institute, 1972.

Rogers, Carl. "Questions I Would Ask Myself If I Were a Teacher." *Education* 95 (Winter 1974): 138–139.

Sergiovanni, Thomas J. "Reforming Teacher Evaluation: Naturalistic Alternatives." *Educational Leadership* 34 (May 1977): 602–607.

7

EVALUATING CURRICULUM: PROGRAMS AND MATERIALS

When God made Heaven and God made Earth,
He formed the seas and gave Man birth.
His heart was full of jubilation:
But he made one error—no Evaluation!
Oh, He said, "That's Good!" and He meant
it, too.
But now we know that that won't do.
Even something that we know is best,
We've got to prove by a pre-post test.

Newsletter, NASA

Curriculum evaluation and improvement is a district-wide function involving teachers, administrators, and others from each of the schools within the district. The district-wide approach to curriculum improvement and evaluation must be maintained because of the advantages provided individual schools in relation to such factors as resources, articulation, scope and sequence, objectives, coordination, and so on. District-wide curriculum evaluation and improvement is usually accomplished by subcommittees (i.e., mathematics program committee, social studies committee, etc.) who report to a steering committee who publish a plethora of guides, manual, bulletins, and handbooks.

But no matter what happens at the district level, the individual teacher, with curriculum guide in hand or in the bottom drawer of the file cabinet, implements that program as soon as the door to the classroom is closed and teaching begins. It is the task of the individual school principal and teachers to insure that the district's curriculum be interpreted and implemented in their classrooms. Although the individual school is not autonomous, it should be recognized that curriculum changes will best result when individual building principals and teachers are involved in evaluation, decision-making, and implementation processes.

CURRICULUM EVALUATION AND IMPROVEMENT CYCLE

You work in a school and district that is already operating with some kind of a curriculum. Whether or not it is doing the job (whatever that means), and whether or not you and others are satisfied with the curriculum you have, is the major point of this cycle. So we begin the quest for curriculum improvement through the process of evaluation.

Step 1: Acknowledge the Presence of a Curriculum

This means that you and your faculty have a statement of the district's goals and objectives; that you have tried and are trying to implement these through the curricular and cocurricular programs; that these have been translated into specific objectives relating to student behaviors; that these objectives, competencies, and performance standards are implemented by the teachers in your school; that the resources are available to teachers to implement the curriculum; and that you and your teachers, either formally or informally, continually evaluate the curriculum.

Some questions you and your faculty may want to ask and answer about the objectives of your current curriculum include the following:

1. Are the objectives of the curriculum based upon district goals and objectives?
2. Are the objectives stated in such a way that we can determine achievement?
3. Are the objectives really attainable?
4. Do we know why we want to achieve these objectives?
5. Are there additional objectives that this curriculum might be accomplishing?
6. Do the objectives reflect the program we have?
7. Are the objectives the focus of the program or is the focus centered around curriculum material (i.e., textbooks)?

Step 2: Survey of Curriculum Practices

To determine whether or not the school's existing curriculum stands up to a test of some of the basic principles of curriculum improvement, you and your teachers should complete the scale shown in Figure 7–1.

Figure 7–1
Survey of Curriculum Practices

School:_____

Subject or Grade:_____

Position:_____

Directions: Please give us your opinion of each of the statements below. Circle the number that indicates your general reaction and use the comment space for specific opinions. Thank you for your time and cooperation. Your name is not necessary.

Item	Not Applicable	No Opinion	Definitely	Sometimes	Not at All
1. There is a rationale for our present curriculum. Reason/Comment:	0	1	2	3	4
2. Our curriculum is evaluated regularly. Reason/Comment:	0	1	2	3	4

(cont.)

Item	Not Applicable	No Opinion	Definitely	Sometimes	Not at All
3. There is evidence of curriculum innovation and change in our school. Reason/Comment:	0	1	2	3	4
4. Our curriculum is designed to promote an interest in learning. Reason/Comment:	0	1	2	3	4
5. In general, the curriculum is based upon the content of the textbooks we use. Reason/Comment:	0	1	2	3	4
6. Administrators encourage teacher innovation and experimentation. Reason/Comment:	0	1	2	3	4
7. In our school, most teachers feel they have to cover the material by the end of the year/semester. Reason/Comment:	0	1	2	3	4
8. Meetings to discuss the educational program are held regularly. Reason/Comment:	0	1	2	3	4
9. In most cases, teachers are encouraged to cooperatively plan for instruction. Reason/Comment:	0	1	2	3	4
10. In general, the curriculum is planned partly on the needs and interests of the students. Reason/Comment:	0	1	2	3	4

(cont.)

Item	Not Applicable	No Opinion	Definitely	Sometimes	Not at All
11. There is a flexible time schedule for the educational program. Reason/Comment:	0	1	2	3	4
12. Our educational program is based upon written instructional objectives. Reason/Comment:	0	1	2	3	4
13. There is evidence of teacher-pupil planning. Reason/Comment:	0	1	2	3	4
14. There is evidence that a variety of teaching methods are being used. Reason/Comment:	0	1	2	3	4
15. In general, our educational program promotes special talents of students. Reason/Comment:	0	1	2	3	4
16. In general, our educational program meets the individual needs of the students. Reason/Comment:	0	1	2	3	4
17. Our grouping procedures are based upon a sound educational rationale. Reason/Comment:	0	1	2	3	4
18. In most cases, instructional materials are selected according to the purposes of the program. Reason/Comment:	0	1	2	3	4

(cont.)

Item	Not Applicable	No Opinion	Definitely	Sometimes	Not at All
19. There is evidence that the curriculum is designed to promote the intellectual and social needs of students. Reason/Comment:	0	1	2	3	4
20. There is evidence that the curriculum is designed to promote physical and aesthetic needs of students. Reason/Comment:	0	1	2	3	4
21. The scope and sequence of the curriculum is a result of careful study. Reason/Comment:	0	1	2	3	4
22. There is evidence of curriculum articulation from kindergarten through grade twelve. Reason/Comment:	0	1	2	3	4
23. Teachers representing various levels meet regularly to discuss curriculum practices. Reason/Comment:	0	1	2	3	4
24. In our instructional program, most subjects are taught in isolation; that is, there is little effort to develop interrelationships. Reason/Comment:	0	1	2	3	4
25. Most teachers know what study habits and attitudes should result because of the educational program. Reason/Comment:	0	1	2	3	4

(cont.)

Item	Not Applicable	No Opinion	Definitely	Sometimes	Not at All
26. Most supporting services (library, guidance, remedial, etc.) help teachers and learners to achieve the objectives of the educational program. Reason/Comment:	0	1	2	3	4
27. Others (specific): Reason/Comment:	0	1	2	3	4

The purpose of the survey is to generate analysis and discussion about its results. For example, in using the scale with a school's faculty, one would ask for evidence regarding a rational for the existing curriculum, innovation, and articulation (continuity for learning experiences from one grade to another). In another example, teachers usually have great difficulty specifying the needs and interests of students. In several cases, additional meetings and some in-service opportunities have been provided to meet this and another need, namely, examination of curriculum trends and innovations.

Some additional questions include:

1. Does the curriculum appear likely to contribute to the achievement of the objectives?
2. Is the curriculum (process and content) well-planned, with concern for articulation, scope and sequence, etc.?
3. Is the curriculum clear and understandable to those responsible for its implementation?

Step 3: Survey of Student Needs

As a result of an examination of existing curriculum and the practices used to implement these programs, several needs may be identified. Through the scale or questions, teachers may express needs to develop skills in writing objectives, further study the needs of students, work on the problems of articulation, examine grouping practices, and re-examine instructional objectives. Let's examine student needs as an example. Teachers may wish to examine students' needs in relation to the existing curriculum.

The scale shown on Figure 7–2 may be helpful. The scale requires teachers to judge the extent to which the current program meets the needs listed.

The result of steps one, two, and three is to help teachers identify areas of dissatisfaction, concern, and need for change in the existing curriculum. Some questions in this regard would be:

1. Have you and your teachers identified real problems or are they pseudo-problems?
2. Are the areas of concern or dissatisfaction worthy of further study?
3. Do these areas of concern need further clarification?
4. Have you and the faculty defined the problems in writing for all to react to?
5. Is the dissatisfaction a concern of most of the faculty or a small part thereof?

Figure 7–2
Scale for Evaluating the Curriculum: Student Needs

School:_____ Grade or Subject:_____ Position:_____

Directions: Using the scale below, rate how you feel the educational program is meeting the needs of students. Thank you for your time and cooperation.

0—Does not apply

1—Cannot judge; no opinion

2—Program *definitely* meets this need

3—Program *sometimes* meets this need

4—Program *seldom* meets this need

5—Program *never* meets this need

		0	1	2	3	4	5
1.	Need for proficiency in basic skills	0	1	2	3	4	5
2.	Need to recognize and appreciate people of all races, nationalities, and creeds	0	1	2	3	4	5
3.	Need to be concerned about the welfare of others	0	1	2	3	4	5
4.	Need to live and work cooperatively with others	0	1	2	3	4	5
5.	Need to develop one's creative and critical thinking habits	0	1	2	3	4	5
6.	Need to learn about one's environment	0	1	2	3	4	5
7.	Need to learn about the interrelationship which exists in the environment	0	1	2	3	4	5
8.	Need to use leisure time effectively	0	1	2	3	4	5
9.	Need to find satisfaction and success in learning	0	1	2	3	4	5
10.	Need for physical and mental health	0	1	2	3	4	5
11.	Need to find affection and approval from adults and peers	0	1	2	3	4	5
12.	Need to assume individual responsibility for behavior	0	1	2	3	4	5
13.	Need to be independent	0	1	2	3	4	5
14.	Need for a positive self-concept	0	1	2	3	4	5
15.	Need to promote activities and/or musical talents	0	1	2	3	4	5
16.	Need to learn at his or her own rate	0	1	2	3	4	5
17.	Need to develop special interests and abilities	0	1	2	3	4	5
18.	Need to understand and appreciate living in a democracy	0	1	2	3	4	5
19.	Need to learn about various occupations	0	1	2	3	4	5
20.	Need to learn about marriage and family life	0	1	2	3	4	5

Comments or reasons may be noted on the back of this sheet.

Step 4: Objectives and Content Defined

As a result of dissatisfaction with all or part of the curriculum, this step requires that you and the teachers do one or all of the following:

- Write new objectives for a specific (new/old) program
- Write additional objectives for a specific program
- Modify existing objectives
- Identify the content of the program.

Whether the objectives call for a modification, addition, or a completely new program, they should be defined to meet the guidelines implied in the following questions:

1. Are the objectives written in behavioral, operational, or other specific terms?
2. Do the objectives state the evidence that will be accepted to determine achievement?
3. Do the objectives include an acceptable minimal level of performance/achievement?

4. Do the objectives suggest methods of evaluation?
5. What content is necessary for the implementation of these objectives?

One of the major problems a principal or committee may encounter in this area is that the objectives do not exist, or, if they do, they are stated in terms that defy evaluation. Teachers are not skilled in writing clearly defined objectives. One effective way to encourage teachers to write clearly defined, operational objectives is to have them examine their course-instructional objectives. One example that has proven to be of some value is shown in Figure 7–3. Using this instrument, you, your department chairperson, or a committee would assume responsibility for collecting course objectives from each teacher.

All questionnaires would be returned to the appropriate party, who would assume responsibility for analyzing and collating the objectives as follows:

1. The objectives should be analyzed to determine whether the objectives are well written.
   a. Does each objective tell about what the learner will be doing?
   b. Does the objective indicate the kind of performance expected of the learner?
   c. Does the objective tell how the learner wil be evaluated?
2. The analysis should also show whether the objectives for one subject taught by several teachers, at the same grade level, are similar, or do teachers have different objectives? To find this out, a committee or the teachers

Figure 7–3
Survey of Instructional Objectives

Directions: This survey is designed to determine the objectives for each subject matter area taught in this school. Please answer each question carefully. The information you provide will be of great value to the Subcommittee on Curriculum Evaluation.

1. School:_____ Grade(s):_____
2. Subject(s) that you currently teach:_____
3. Write the *major objectives* for each subject you teach.

   Subject/Course   *Objectives*

A. _____   _____
                  _____
                  _____
                  _____

B. _____   _____
                  _____
                  _____

C. _____   _____
                  _____
                  _____

D. _____   _____
                  _____
                  _____

themselves can collate the objectives for each subject by listing all of the objectives that are common to most teachers in one column; and, in a second column, list the objectives that were not commonly stated by most teachers. In this way, teachers can note and maybe establish some priority objectives for the subject(s) they teach.

Step 5: Program Design

As a result of the statement of objectives, a program should be created. You and the teachers must decide whether the program will be a new one and/or an addition or modification to the existing program. Answers to the following questions should serve as the foundation for each program:

1. Is the program based upon the objectives stated?
2. What learning experiences will best achieve these objectives?
3. Is the program developed in enough detail to insure that it will be implemented, if approved?
4. Does the program include learning experiences, activities, and opportunities that may make a difference?
5. Does the program identify needed financial and personnel resources?
6. Does the program include a list or description of alternatives?
7. Does the program include methods and procedures for ongoing evaluation?
8. Does the program include the knowledges, skills, and attitudes students will be learning?
9. Does the program consider problems of articulation, scope and sequence, and organizing experiences for teaching and learning?

Step 6: Controls and Constraints

You are well aware of "the best laid plans of mice and men." The realities of a situation are not something principals and teachers can ignore. Curriculum evaluation and improvement in individual schools and school districts require a realistic look at possible controls and constraints. It would be best for you and your teachers to examine the program with regard to the following possible control or constraint factors:

- Instructional time and scheduling
- Finances
- Facilities
- Administrative or board of education
- Political
- Parental
- Professional (Do the teachers have the expertise, training, skills to carry out the program?)
- Special interest groups
- Resources and personnel
- Other

Step 7: Alternatives—Projects

This step requires that you and the faculty identify and select possible alternatives. These alternatives should be ready when and if one or more of the constraints prohibits implementation of the entire program. It may also be helpful to have the alternatives accurately described so that one or more may be selected for a trial implementation. For example, rather than implement a school-based career education program, you and the faculty may wish to "test" components of the program in the different grades or subject matter areas for a period of time with appropriate evaluation strategies. Should the entire program be approved, then you can proceed to the next step of this cycle regarding program evaluation.

The alternatives selected are tried and tested by creating projects and pilot programs. The projects must be based on one or more objectives of the entire program. In other words, the projects are an attempt to arrive at promising solutions to curriculum improvement. The projects are selected as a result of the constraints placed upon the possibility of implementing the entire program.

Step 8: Project Evaluation

In essence, you want to find out to what extent the pilot program or your total program:

- Meets its objectives
- Is worthy of implementation
- Was evaluated objectively and selectively
- Should be modified.

The questions to be asked in this step of the cycle have been suggested as follows:

1. Do the results of the new program warrant incorporation into the existing program?
2. Are the results such that another test-run with some modification is warranted?
3. Are the results so bad that the program or goal ought to be dropped?[1]

Step 9: Implementation

After all of the questions have been answered in the first eight steps, program implementation requires:

- The encouragement, enthusiasm, and participation of all teachers in the new program
- The need for adequate inservice training programs
- An adequate financial commitment for materials, supplies, consultants, etc.
- Continued support and commitment by school administrators.

Some questions to guide you at this stage include:

1. Have you provided teachers with appropriate orientation and in-service opportunities for implementing the curriculum plan?
2. Is the budget for the curriculum plan sufficient for implementing the plan without "cutting corners"?
3. Have opportunities been provided teachers to practice using materials and techniques of the plan?

4. Are in-service sessions planned throughout the first year of the plan for evaluating and identifying problems, strengths, and weaknesses?

Step 10: Continuous Assessment

The instructional program implemented as a result of the evaluation and pilot program and projects needs ongoing evaluation. Thus, you and the faculty should be continually using the following questions as criteria for assessing each program offered in your school.

Criterion 1: Are the program objectives of your school based upon the district's goals and objectives?

Criterion 2: Are the program objectives written in clearly defined, operational terms?

Criterion 3: Are the courses in the program contributing to the achievement of school objectives?

Criterion 4: Are the personal and social needs, interests, talents, skills, and problems of all students being met by the curriculum?

Criterion 5: Does the curriculum reflect the needs of the local community and society at large?

Criterion 6: Does the curriculum provide for the development of student attitudes, values, skills, knowledge, and understanding?

Criterion 7: Are the curriculum materials and resources sufficient to meet teacher and student needs and interests?

Criterion 8: Are the curriculum materials appropriate for the programs offered and the objectives identified?

Criterion 9: Is there articulation of the subject matter and the objectives among grade levels (i.e., K–12 curriculum)?

Criterion 10: Is there an attempt to correlate/integrate skills, objectives, and content among the subjects (i.e., use of content in one subject to reinforce content in another subject; prevention of fragmentation; etc.) in the curriculum?

HOW TO EVALUATE AN EXISTING PROGRAM OR A NEW PROGRAM

Most of the principals and teachers I have worked with in curriculum matters seemed to be faced with two tasks: one is the task of evaluating and improving an existing program, the other is the task of creating new programs. For example, the school board in one district has asked the superintendent to have the principal and teachers in a particular school evaluate its reading program. The reason for this was a direct result of a report in the local newspaper about reading achievement test scores in all schools. This particular school recorded the lowest group mean scores when compared to the other schools in the district. Another school district is considering the implementation of a drug education program and has asked one of its schools to develop and try out a program for possible implementation in all of the schools.

These two conditions, evaluating and changing existing programs and/or creating totally new programs, suggest that some pattern may be useful to teachers and principals.

The procedure that follows differs somewhat from the curriculum evaluation and improvement cycle discussed earlier because in this case the focus is on a program within the curriculum or a program that has not been incorporated into the total school curriculum as yet. The following overlay will guide you and the faculty toward program evaluation and improvement:

Step 1: Assess the Present Situation

Existing Program

1. What factors require that you and your teachers examine this program?
2. In general, do you and your teachers feel there is a need for changing or revising this program?
3. What evidence is there that this program needs examination?

New Program

1. What factors are influencing the creation of the program?
2. Do you and your faculty feel there is a need for this program?

3. What evidence is available to support the creation of this program?

Assessment

Existing Program

_____

_____

4. Who will do the evaluation?
5. How will you organize the faculty for implementing this evaluation phase?

New Program

_____

_____

Existing Program		*New Program*
	6. When will the evalua-tion begin? End?	
_____		_____
	7. What factors will you and the faculty want to assess?	
_____		_____
__knowledge __skills __other (specify:____)	a. cognitive factors	__knowledge __skills __other (specify:____)
__attitudes __opinions __interests __needs __self-concept __self-esteem __values __other	b. affective factors	__attitudes __opinions __interests __needs __self-concept __self-esteem __values __other
__decision making __communication __organization __morale __policies and procedures __leadership __teacher effectiveness __quality of services provided teachers and learners __class size __attendance __other (specify:____)	c. administrative factors	__decision making __communication __organization __morale __policies and procedures __leadership __teacher effectiveness __quality of services provided teachers and learners __class size __attendance __other (specify:____)
__school climate __classroom climate __quality of teacher-student relationships __socioeconomic level of students' families __occupation of parents __kind and quality of neighborhood __violence __vandalism __other (specify:____)	d. environmental	__school climate __classroom climate __quality of teacher-student relationships __socioeconomic level of students' families __occupation of parents __kind and quality of neighborhood __violence __vandalism __other (specify:____)

Existing Program   *New Program*

                          8. On the basis of the fac-
_____

8. On the basis of the factors you and your faculty checked, who will be evaluated? Will you use sampling techniques? How will you determine your sample?

9. On the basis of the factors you and your faculty selected and the sample identified, how will you assess the sample?
   surveys, polls
   questionnaires
   ability tests
   standardized achievement tests
   criterion-referenced tests
   anecdotal records
   observation of student in and out of class
   attendance, truancy, drop-out records
   vandalism records
   records of violence in school and community
   self-evaluation instruments
   self-concept instruments
   school climate scales
   leadership behavior scales
   case histories
   rating scales
   checklists
   records of student awards and performances

Existing Program		*New Program*
	records of student participation in school and community programs and activities	
_____	motivation assessment instruments[2]	_____
_____		_____
_____	10. On the basis of the evidence (data) you and your faculty have collected, what judgments can you make regarding the program?	_____
_____	11. What conclusion can you and your faculty draw from the evidence and judgments?	_____

Step 2: Decide on Objectives

Existing Program

1. Using the results from Step 1, what revisions or modifications are recommended?
2. Have you and your teachers specified objectives based on the answer to the above question?
3. Are the objectives stated in operational, performance terms?
4. Are the objectives stated in a way that will help you when you have to evaluate the extent to which they have been achieved?

New Program

1. Using the results from Step 1, what is recommended?
2. Have you and your teachers specified objectives based on what was recommended above?
3. Are the objectives stated in operational, performance terms?
4. Are the objectives stated in a way that will help you when you have to evaluate the extent to which they have been achieved?

Step 3: Decide on Learning Experiences

Existing Program

1. What learning experiences in the existing program can be retained because they will contribute toward the achievement of the objectives?

New Program

1. What learning experiences will teachers have to develop that will contribute toward the achievement of the objectives?

Existing Program

2. What learning experiences would teachers have to revise? Delete? Add?

3. What subject matter content has to be revised, modified, dropped, added?

4. What classroom situations will give students the chance to express the behaviors implied in the objectives?

5. What classroom situations will give students the chance to express the behaviors implied in the objectives?

6. What out-of-school situations will give students the chance to express the behaviors implied in the objectives?

7. What situations, experiences, and activities will give students the opportunity to use and apply their knowledge, skills, and learnings?

New Program

2. What subject matter content will teachers have to develop that will contribute to the learning experiences of the students?

3. What skills will teachers have to identify that will contribute to the learning experiences of the students?

4. What classroom experiences will teachers create and implement that will help students express behaviors implied in the objectives?

5. What classroom experiences will teachers create and implement that will help students express behaviors implied in the objectives?

6. What other school experiences will teachers create and implement to give students a chance to express behaviors implied in the objectives?

7. What activities, experiences, and situations will give students the opportunity to use and apply their knowledge, skills, and learnings?

Step 4: Organize Experiences for Teaching and Learning

Although the ideal would be to organize the learning experiences in such a way that they contribute maximally to teaching, learning, and attaining the objectives, there are realities that cannot be ignored. For example, your school operates in an existing organizational plan imposed by the school system itself. The organizational pattern within your school may influence the way teachers have to organize learning experiences for students. A high school may operate on a departmentalized plan with traditional or modular scheduling patterns. Elementary and middle-junior high schools may be organized in a variety of ways: the traditional self-contained classroom, a departmentalized structure,

a block-schedule plan, nongraded and/or continuous progress patterns, and open-classroom approaches with a traditional or nontraditional organization scheme.

Therefore, five central questions will help you and your teachers focus on ways to organize the learning experiences in your school.

1. What is the best way to organize the learning experiences?

2. What changes in our existing organization may be required?

3. Are these changes easily implemented? Realistic? Practical?

4. What can be accomplished within each department, each level (primary, etc.), each grade to organize learning experiences in such

a way that we account for concerns about scope, sequence, repetition, reinforcement, articulation, etc.?

5. How will organizational changes affect teaching loads, class sizes, and materials and resources?

PROGRAM EVALUATION PROFILE

Many principals have expressed concern about newspaper reporting of achievement tests scores, particularly in reading and mathematics. The current emphasis on achievement, literacy tests, minimal competency tests, and competency-based education programs may be contributing to a curriculum that emphasizes cognitive-achievement factors rather than maintaining a balance between these factors and affective-aesthetic factors. School principals should continually provide their own reports to the public, one that shows the importance and value of all programs in the school curriculum.

School principals have asked for a plan, an "overlay" scheme, a procedure that they can share with their teachers that is applicable to all programs yet enables them to evaluate specific programs.

Two previous examples serve this purpose, but an additional example with emphasis on the content for a public report may be helpful. A profile for evaluating a specific program such as social studies, art, music, reading, career education is outlined below.

Program Description

The content for this section of the profile includes a description of the school, its students, the community the school serves, the income range and occupations of parents, and other variables or descriptions that you feel would be valuable for readers to know as they read the profile report.

This section would also include the program to be evaluated or already evaluated and the grades in which the evaluation took place (i.e., seventh- and

eighth-grade art program, or primary-grade reading programs, or social studies program for high school freshmen).

Program Objectives

The content of this section of the profile would include objectives for knowledge, skills, attitudes, understandings, and appreciations. It would be best that these objectives be stated in operational, student performance terms.

You and your faculty should establish the conditions of attaining the standards established for this program. In other words, attention should be given to the criteria against which the results from program evaluation will be compared. Thus, the faculty would consider the program as meeting the list of objectives if a certain percentage of students reach a certain level of performance or effectively demonstrate a particular skill. For example, a performance statement or standard might be: Seventy percent of the students in American History will have demonstrated some out-of-school political or community service activity. Or: Eighty percent of the students in the seventh- and eighth-grade mathematics programs will have scored above the national norms on achievement tests in both computation and reasoning.

Program Content

This section of the profile would include the content of the subject matter—the concepts, knowledge, etc., that students are to learn or should have learned. For many programs, this will be the table of contents of the texts used; for others, it will be the content described in the curriculum guide. The content to be included would be limited to the specific program and to objectives of the program.

Program Processes

This section would include the processes students learn—the attitudes, interests, skills. Some of the specific processes would include listening, note-taking, questioning, verifying, classifying, summarizing, deciding, solving, constructing, creating, performing, etc. Attitudes might include such factors as tolerance, respect, sensitivity to others, fairness, equality, sense of humor, and so on. The processes to be evaluated would be limited to the objectives of the program.

Program Evaluation

This section of the profile would include only those factors which you and your teachers want to evaluate. You may for one reason or another decide not to evaluate every objective of the program. But once you decide on what objectives will be evaluated, you should decide on how you are going to evaluate these and when the evaluation will take place. There are several evaluation designs you may consider. For example, you may plan an ongoing evaluation: that is, certain factors will be evaluated throughout the implementation of the program and the results will be "tested" against the objectives and appropriate changes made. Or, you may wish to create a pre-post test situation (with or without control groups) whereby comparisons will be made (gain-score analysis) between pre-test results and post-test results. Or, you may decide to evaluate at the end of each school year (or every two years) and compare the results to the criteria or standards of performance selected by the faculty.[3]

You and your teachers must then attend to the factors to be evaluated—the "what" of evaluation. Following a decision on what is to be evaluated, consideration must be given to who is to be evaluated. In the examples here, we are talking about student evaluation, but your objectives may call for parent evaluation, teacher evaluation, etc.

Evaluation Package

This section of the profile would include instruments needed to assess those factors that have to be evaluated in order to determine the extent to which the objectives have been accomplished. Included in the package would be a variety of instruments such

as standardized achievement tests, objectives-referenced tests, criterion-referenced tests, observation scales, checklists, etc. The outline for this section would include each objective, factors to be evaluated for each objective, and the instruments needed or used for evaluating the factors for each objective.

Data Analysis

This section of the profile reports the data in summary form. But well before this section of the report is prepared, you and your faculty should have examined the data, decided how best to summarize them, and, most important, what it means in terms of student-teacher performance, program emphasis, alternatives, and changes. You and the faculty should discuss such questions as: What did we find? What do the data show us? What does it mean? What conclusions can we draw from the data? What recommendations appear likely? What alternatives should be considered? What additional questions should be asked? What factors should be discussed?

Program Report

This section of the profile deals with the public report. It will include program description, objectives, evaluation, and results. Who will prepare the report, how it will be prepared, and what will be reported are decisions to be made by you and your faculty. Besides a brief description, a statement of objectives, and evaluation procedures, the program report should include a summary of the results and what they mean. Also reported should be constraints and cautions when interpreting the data, and limitations of the evaluation. Included should be concerns of the faculty, future plans, role of parents and community, and alternative programs or changes being considered by you and the faculty.

The report should not be lengthy, and wherever possible data should be presented graphically. However, before the written report is distributed widely throughout the community or in cooperation with the publication of the report, meetings should be arranged with parent-teacher groups, groups of parents (PTA, etc.), and community groups. Discussions of the report and of the alternatives and their impact on personnel, finances, and resources would serve as the agenda for the meetings.

EVALUATING AVAILABILITY AND CONDITION OF INSTRUCTIONAL MATERIALS

Building principals must insure that teachers have appropriate materials for teaching and learning. The use of an annual checklist regarding the condition of existing supplies and equipment and the availability of these to teachers may be worthy of examination. To help you complete this task, two examples are provided. Figure 7–4 is a checklist to be used for assessing the condition of equipment and supplies. Figure 7–5 shows a sample form that may be used to find out whether teachers feel that the materials they have are adequate or not.

CLASSROOM USE AND VALUE OF INSTRUCTIONAL MATERIALS

Students learn from instructional materials just as they learn from teachers. A good book is still one of the most rewarding learning experiences. An effec-

Figure 7–4
Audio-Visual Equipment and Supplies: Condition Form

Directions to Teachers: Please evaluate the audio-visual equipment and supplies in the school by placing the appropriate number after the item and checking whether the item should be replaced or repaired. 1—excellent condition; 2—good condition; 3—poor condition; 4—do not have.

Item		Replace	Repair	Comments
1. Overhead projectors				
2. Filmstrip projectors				
3. 16 mm projectors				
4. Masterfax copier				
5. Mimeograph				
6. Tape recorders				
7. Phonographs				
8. Film screens				
9. Television sets				
10. Music equipment				
11. Maps				
12. Charts				
13. Other_____(Specify)				

14. Is there sufficient audio-visual materials in this school?
    Yes__ No__ If no, please explain:

15. In what ways could audio-visual materials and equipment be more useful to you?

Figure 7–5
Teacher Evaluation Form—Instructional Materials

Directions: Please rate the instructional materials available to you and your students using the following scale: 1—adequate; 2—needs improving; 3—not adequate; 4—does not apply.

Comments

1. Library resources
2. Reference books (encyclopedias, etc.)
3. Textbooks in science
4. Textbooks in arithmetic
5. Textbooks in reading
6. Textbooks in social studies
7. Textbooks in_____(Specify)
8. Tradebooks
9. Paperbacks
10. Supplementary material (newspapers, magazines, etc.)
11. Programmed learning material
12. Science equipment and/or kits
13. Classroom supplies
14. Professional literature
15. Films
16. Filmstrips
17. Overhead transparencies
18. Records
19. Slides
20. Tape recordings
21. Pictures
22. Maps, charts
23. Dioramas, models, etc.
24. Other (Specify:_____)

tive film can be instructive as well as emotive. A good filmstrip can reinforce new ideas or concepts, or it can be used to introduce students to new learnings. A recording can effectively bring the sounds and voices of people from the past into the classroom. The point is that each classroom should be rich with materials for teaching and learning.

One of the tasks of principals, especially those faced with budgeting restrictions, is to periodically survey the faculty regarding the use and value of the instructional materials in their classrooms. Figure 7–6 shows a survey form that may be useful for this purpose.

After each teacher in your school completes the survey form, a discussion of the results is recommended. Many times, one discovers from the results of the survey that a sharing of materials prevents duplication and creates opportunities for purchasing needed or additional supplies and equipment. This procedure helps you practice the principle that those who use the material should have a voice in the selection of the materials.

Figure 7-6
Survey of Use and Value of Instructional Materials

School:_____ Grade or subject:_____

Date:_____

Directions: We would like your opinion of the use and value of instructional materials provided by this school for this year only. Please check the appropriate space after careful thought.

Material	Frequency of Use					Value		
	Often	Very Often	Some-times	Seldom	Never	Absolutely Necessary	Useful, Not Necessary	Could Do Without It
1. Textbooks	___	___	___	___	___	___	___	___
2. Workbooks	___	___	___	___	___	___	___	___
3. Supplementary books	___	___	___	___	___	___	___	___
4. Reference books, encyclopedias	___	___	___	___	___	___	___	___
5. Duplicated materials	___	___	___	___	___	___	___	___
6. Newspapers and magazines	___	___	___	___	___	___	___	___
7. Models and mockups	___	___	___	___	___	___	___	___
8. Chalkboard materials	___	___	___	___	___	___	___	___
9. Drawing and construction materials	___	___	___	___	___	___	___	___
10. Television programs	___	___	___	___	___	___	___	___
11. Radio programs	___	___	___	___	___	___	___	___
12. Motion picture films (16mm)	___	___	___	___	___	___	___	___
13. 8mm film loops (single concept)	___	___	___	___	___	___	___	___
14. Overhead transparencies	___	___	___	___	___	___	___	___
15. Videotapes	___	___	___	___	___	___	___	___
16. Recordings	___	___	___	___	___	___	___	___
17. Programmed materials (self-instruction)	___	___	___	___	___	___	___	___
18. Picture, drawings, and paintings	___	___	___	___	___	___	___	___
19. Slides	___	___	___	___	___	___	___	___
20. Filmstrips	___	___	___	___	___	___	___	___
21. Maps, charts, graphs	___	___	___	___	___	___	___	___
22. Posters, cartoons	___	___	___	___	___	___	___	___
23. Others (Specify)	___	___	___	___	___	___	___	___

EVALUATING TEXTBOOKS

Textbooks continue to be the basic, most used resource in the curriculum. There are times throughout the life of a textbook (usually three to five years) that evaluation of its effectiveness would be worth the time and effort. Although many of the questions in Figure 7–7 are applicable to use when selecting a textbook, they are presented here as an example of an instrument that you and your teachers may use for evaluating the texts currently in use.

In addition to the textbooks, teachers should also evaluate the teacher's edition to each textbook series to determine how it helps in their teaching. Some questions worth answering with the teacher's edition in hand are:

1. Does it contain a reprint of the pages of the student's text?

Figure 7–7
Teacher Survey of Textbooks

Directions: Place a checkmark on the appropriate line. Please feel free to add any other comments on the bottom of this form.

	Yes	No	Not Applicable
1. Has the text contributed to helping you and the students attain the course objectives?	—	—	—
2. Does the content of the text cover all or most of the content of your course?	—	—	—
3. Does the text do the job you expected when you selected it?	—	—	—
4. Is the text a recent (within five years) copyright?	—	—	—
5. Is the text content up-to-date?	—	—	—
6. Does the content accurately portray minority groups?	—	—	—
7. Does the content accurately reflect ethnic cultures and life styles?	—	—	—
8. Is the content free of racist materials and connotations?	—	—	—
9. Is the content free of sexist materials and connotations?	—	—	—
10. Is there satisfactory development of concepts, generalizations, and relationships?	—	—	—
11. Are the concepts, generalizations, and relationships clearly and accurately presented?	—	—	—
12. Are the concepts, generalizations, and relationships developed from the concrete to the abstract when and where appropriate?	—	—	—
13. Do students find the text interesting to read?	—	—	—
14. Do most students find the text easy to read?	—	—	—
15. Does the text highlight new and difficult words in some way?	—	—	—
16. Are graphs and tables clearly illustrated and easy to read?	—	—	—

(cont.)

	Yes	No	Not Applicable
17. Are diagrams and scale drawings clearly illustrated and easy to read?	—	—	—
18. Does the text have a table of contents?	—	—	—
19. Does the text have an index?	—	—	—
20. Does each main idea begin each chapter or sub-section?	—	—	—
21. Are there chapter summaries?	—	—	—
22. Are summaries appropriately placed throughout the chapter?	—	—	—
23. Is each chapter summarized?	—	—	—
24. Does each chapter contain a review of the concepts, generalizations, and relationships?	—	—	—
25. Are motivating social or personal situations or issues used to introduce new ideas?	—	—	—
26. Are quotations or other authoritative sources used to highlight the concepts or content?	—	—	—
27. Does the text contain recommended readings for students?	—	—	—
28. Are end-of-the-chapter activities interesting and stimulating?	—	—	—
29. Do end-of-the-chapter activities require students to apply the concepts or content to other situations?	—	—	—
30. Do end-of-the-chapter activities emphasize creative problem solving?	—	—	—
31. Do end-of-the-chapter activities provide for the immediate practice of a skill?	—	—	—
32. Do end-of-the-chapter questions include several forms such as true-false, multiple choice, and essay?	—	—	—
33. Is the text attractive, colorful, and well-designed?	—	—	—
34. Is the type-size easy for students to read?	—	—	—
35. Does the text make use of center heads, side heads, and/or italics to help students in their reading?	—	—	—
36. Is the text binding strong enough to withstand student use over a number of years?	—	—	—
37. If a text contains controversial issues, are these presented objectively and accurately reflecting representative points of view?	—	—	—
38. Does the text provide material or examples of how the concepts or content is correlated with other subjects?	—	—	—
39. Are the directions in the text clear and complete?	—	—	—
40. Is the page-paper of the text of such quality that it will stand up to student use over a number of years?	—	—	—

2. Does it provide answers to all questions and problems?
3. Does it provide a bibliography?
4. Does it provide useful reading references for each chapter?
5. Does it include a list of films, filmstrips, tapes, recordings, and games?
6. Does it provide teaching ideas?
7. Does it provide lesson plan outlines and samples?
8. Does it provide an overview of the semester's or year's work?
9. Does it provide discussion questions?
10. Does it provide examples of overhead transparencies that can be made or purchased?
11. Does it provide actual or sample tests?
12. Are suggestions for student activities and projects provided for each chapter?

These kinds of questions help teachers pay greater attention to instruction—its objectives, content, material, and evaluation.

EVALUATING SEX STEREOTYPING OF MATERIALS

The Committee on Sexism and Reading of the International Reading Association has developed a checklist (Figure 7–8) to assist teachers in analyzing educational materials for sex stereotypes and related language usage.[4] Teachers or groups evaluating materials for sex stereotyping should take a particular item (textbook, workbook, tradebook, etc.) and use the questions shown in Figure 7–8.

STUDENT EVALUATION OF INSTRUCTIONAL MATERIALS

Are textbooks, workbooks, films, and the like used, selected, and purchased for the benefit of the teacher or the learner? In other words, are the textbooks that your teachers select purchased for them to teach from, or are they selected and purchased as a learner resource? You may say that a textbook ser-ies in your school is purchased for the benefit of both the teacher and learner. Then answer this question: Do students in your school or district serve on selection committees, or, at the very least, have the opportunity to evaluate the instructional material they use? The point is that students' perceptions of the value or lack thereof of the materials used in class are worthy of examination regardless of what salespeople say about their product.

A teacher may find a textbook, film, or record to be very interesting and challenging from the teacher-training point of view, but if students in the class do not share this perception, then one could easily question the value of the instructional resource to the learner. There may be few opportunities to find this out beforehand. So, if it seems appropriate for students to be involved in the selection process, then their judgments of the material used in class should be sought. There are several reasons for both approaches. First, learners need to develop skills in discerning what kinds of resources will help solve specific kinds of problems. Second, practice in evaluating instructional materials will help students develop critical reading, viewing, and listening skills. Third, when learners have an opportunity to select and evaluate learning resources, they may take seriously the value of using instructional materials for independent learning of knowledge and skills. Fourth, the involvement of students in selecting and evaluating instructional materials may help teachers help students to read and study more effectively.

What instruments would help you and your teachers involve students in the evaluation of instructional materials? The first example is a checklist that teachers may use for student evaluation of a film, filmstrip, recording, or a television or radio program. The teacher would suggest that students write in the instructional resource being evaluated on the line above the list of questions and that each question should be answered with a "yes" or "no." The teacher should also recommend that students add any qualifying comments they wish after each question.

Figure 7–8
Analysis of Sex Stereotypes in Educational Materials

	Almost Always	Occasionally	Rarely
1. Are girls and boys, men and women, consistently represented in equal balance?	___	___	___
2. Do boys and girls participate equally in both physical and intellectual activities?	___	___	___
3. Do girls and boys each receive positive recognition for their endeavors? Females	___	___	___
Males	___	___	___
4. Do boys and girls, fathers and mothers, participate in a wide variety of domestic chores, not only the ones traditional for their sex? Females	___	___	___
Males	___	___	___
5. Do both girls and boys have a variety of choices and are they encouraged to aspire to various goals, including nontraditional ones if they show such inclination? Females	___	___	___
Males	___	___	___
6. Are both boys and girls shown developing independent lives, independently meeting challenges and finding their own solutions? Females	___	___	___
Males	___	___	___
7. Are women and men shown in a variety of occupations, including nontraditional ones? When women are portrayed as full-time homemakers, are they depicted as competent and decisive? Females	___	___	___
Males	___	___	___
8. Do characters deprecate themselves because of their sex? (Example: "I'm only a girl.") Do others use denigrating language in this regard? (Example: "That's just like a woman.") Females	___	___	___
Males	___	___	___
9. Do the illustrations stereotype the characters, either in accordance to the dictates of the text or in contradiction to it? Females	___	___	___
Males	___	___	___
10. Is inclusionary language used? (For example, "police officer" instead of "policeman," "staffed by" instead of "manned by," "all students will submit the assignment" instead of "each student will submit his assignment," and so on.)	___	___	___

From Committee on Sexism and Reading, "Guide for Evaluating Sex Stereotyping in Reading Materials," *The Reading Teacher* 31 (December 1977): 288.

*(Item)*_____

1. Did the ____ contribute to the objectives of the lesson or unit?
2. Did the ____ interest you in the content of the lesson?
3. Is the ____ worth repeating?
4. Did the ____ reinforce the content you have been learning?
5. Did the ____ expand on, add to, the content you have been learning?
6. Did the ____ relate to content you have been studying?
7. Did the ____ help you better understand the content of the lesson or unit?
8. Did the ____ give you some new ideas?
9. Did the ____ hold your interest and attention?
10. Did the ____ seem boring and useless?
11. Did the ____ make you want to read additional materials to find out more about the subject?
12. Did the ____ help you raise questions that you would like answered?
13. Did the ____ answer some of the questions you had before seeing/listening to it?
14. Did the ____ help you develop problem-solving, reading, and/or study skills?
15. Did the ____ give you some ideas of projects you would like to work on?

A second example suggests two ways teachers can obtain students' perceptions of textbooks, workbooks, study sheets, and the like. Some questions teachers might ask:

1. What do you like about this textbook?
2. What do you dislike about this textbook?
3. What changes would you like made in this textbook?
4. Is this textbook too easy or too difficult for you to read?
5. Do you like to read the textbook? If not, why not?

Using these and other questions or a series of statements requiring the students' reactions should be of value to teachers. In the example that follows, students would be asked to indicate whether they strongly agree, agree, are neutral, disagree, or strongly disagree to the following statements.

1. In my opinion, this textbook is not worth using in class.
2. This textbook helps me learn.
3. This textbook encourages me to use other resources.
4. This textbook doesn't interest me at all.
5. This textbook stimulates me to explore other aspects of the subject.
6. This textbook helps answer some questions I had about the subject.
7. This textbook is one of the best I ever used in school.
8. This textbook is colorful, attractive, and has a variety of print and pictures.
9. This textbook has interesting things to do at the end of each chapter.
10. This textbook is one I would recommend to my friends.

A third example asks the students to check those words that tell how they feel about any instructional resource from worksheets to transparencies. One writes the item to be evaluated on the line and then checks the words that apply.

*(Item)*_____

____ challenging	____ too difficult
____ stimulating	____ terrible
____ colorful	____ successful
____ thought-provoking	____ boring
	____ clear
____ too easy	____ readable
____ worthless	____ well organized
____ important	____ valuable
____ demanding	____ exciting
____ interesting	____ dull
____ asks good questions	____ profitable

These suggestions are recommended as ways of involving students in the evaluation of instructional materials. In the words of one social studies teacher, and as a summary of the major point of this section, "We spent thousands of dollars two years ago for textbooks that are too difficult for students to read, for films that are less than interesting, and for workbooks that even I wouldn't want to do. Obviously, something is wrong with the way we do things around here."

A FINAL COMMENT

Evaluation is an integral part of curriculum improvement. No administrator or teacher has the time, energy, or resources to evaluate the total curriculum annually. However, programs that make up the school curricula can be evaluated if and when teachers and principals establish priorities. Each year the faculty should ask itself what one program needs to be improved?

As the list of references suggests, no single chapter can be a comprehensive review of curriculum evaluation. Other chapters in this book contribute to the content in this chapter. For example, the chapter discussing the evaluation of the student activities program, in essence, provides ideas for evaluating one aspect of the curricula. Sections of most chapters have ideas that contribute to curriculum evaluation. It was the purpose of this chapter to share some ideas that principals and others would find useful when evaluating programs and instructional materials.

EVALUATION INSTRUMENTS

"Sample Instrument from Open Access Curriculum Evaluation." L. Craig Wilson. *The Open Access Curriculum.* Boston: Allyn and Bacon, 1971, pp. 282–283.

This twenty-statement instrument evaluates the extent of agreement or disagreement on curriculum matters. For example, the instrument was used in a high school to determine the degree of access provided by the curriculum. It can serve as a model for developing similar kinds of instruments as well as serving as a useful instrument in itself.

Music Program Checklist. Eunice B. Meske. "My School Has A Good Music Program—I Think!" *Bulletin of the National Association of Secondary School Principals* 59 (October 1975): 5–12.

The author provides a checklist of thirty items describing a good music program. Each item is rated by the user of the instrument as "yes," "to some extent," and "no."

"Guidelines to Evaluate the English Component in the Elementary Program." *Language Arts* 53 (October 1976): 828–838.

These useful and valuable guidelines, developed by a committee of the National Council of Teachers of English, provide a statement of concerns followed by a series of questions under the following categories: general aspects of the language arts, listening, speaking, reading, and writing. The question format provides an excellent format for elementary principals and teachers planning to assess their language arts curriculum.

"A Checklist for Appraising a School's Program." J. Galen Saylor and William M. Alexander. *Curriculum Planning for Modern Schools.* New York: Holt, Rinehart and Winston, 1966, pp. 254–256.

The authors have designed a list of criteria against which a principal and teachers can compare the school's instructional program. There are seven major criteria with four to six additional statements per category representing the "marks of a good curriculum."

"Guidelines for Self-Assessment of Secondary-School Science Programs—Five booklets." National Science Teachers Association, 1742 Connecticut Ave., N.W., Washington, D.C. 20009.

1. Our School's Science Curriculum (12 pages)
2. Our School's Science Teachers (12 pages)
3. Science Student/Teacher Interactions in Our Schools (9 pages)

4. Science Facilities and Teaching Conditions in Our Schools (16 pages)

5. Preface/Directions for Use/Report Form (33 pages)

These five booklets provide an excellent example of evaluation materials published by some subject matter organizations. These five booklets are valuable to secondary science teachers interested in a self-evaluation of their science programs. Each booklet assesses a particular aspect of the science program (curriculum, teaching, facilities, etc.) utilizing a rating scale that solicits a response regarding "desirability" and "achievement" recorded on a matrix. For example, Booklet Four contains twenty-one statements regarding science facilities and teaching conditions; each statement is followed by a matrix (desirability-achievement) upon which the respondent rates each variable. Summary forms, ideas, and suggestions for using the results are provided in Booklet Five.

"Evaluation Checklist for Appraising the Quality of Art Education Programs." *Art Education Framework*. Sacramento: California State Department of Education, 1971.

This evaluation checklist enables one to appraise the quality of existing art education programs. Following each statement of what a quality art education program contains is a three-item rating scale—operational, planned, none.

"A Checklist for Evaluating a Social Studies Program." Washington, D.C.: National Council for the Social Studies.

Fifty-seven questions abstracted from guidelines developed by an NCSS task force are useful for evaluating a social studies program at a given grade level or in a school. Each question is rated in one of three ways: strongly, moderately, or hardly at all. Following each question is one or more of the following letters: R, T, S, C, O. These letters suggest sources for answering each question: R—curriculum materials; T—teachers; S—students;

C—parents and community; O—classroom and out-of-classroom observation. The resulting profile may highlight patterns, such as lack of materials, inadequate student involvement, etc., that may be useful for social studies program improvement.

"Criteria for Assessing School Reading Programs: K–12." The Connecticut Association for Reading Renewal, Hartford, Connecticut, 1970. (28 pages.)

This booklet contains a series of instruments to help a school faculty evaluate current reading education practices with the intent of finding areas needing improvement. A questionnaire is provided for each of the following areas: systemwide and individual school background information, survey of individual teachers, K–primary programs, elementary reading program, content-area reading program, independent reading program, remedial/corrective reading program, and summarizing evaluations, commendations, recommendations.

"Program Audit Review Instrument." Lesley H. Browder, Jr., William A. Atkins, Jr., and Egin Kaya. *Developing an Educationally Accountable Program*. Berkeley, California: McCutchan Publishing Co., 1973.

This instrument is "intended as a guide for the examination of audit reports in determining the quality of an educational program audit that has been performed." School principals and others will find the instrument useful in examining the work of an auditor (evaluator) regarding functions, critique of the evaluation plan, assessment of the evaluation process, and verification of evaluation results. With modification, the instrument could be used by school principals and evaluation committees in their roles as auditors of individual school programs.

ENDNOTES

1. William J. Gephart, "Who Will Engage in Curriculum Evaluation?" *Educational Leadership* 35 (January 1978): 256.

2. For a comprehensive list of multiple criterion measures for evaluating school programs, see the appendix of Newton S. Metfissel and William B. Michael, "A Paradigm Involving Multiple Criterion Measures for the Evaluation of the Effectiveness of School Programs," *Educational and Psychological Measurement* 27 (1967): 931–943.

3. For an excellent discussion on research designs, see Donald T. Campbell and Julian C. Stanley, "Experimental and Quasi-Experimental Designs for Research and Teaching," in *Handbook for Research on Teaching*, ed. N. L. Gage (Chicago: Rand McNally and Co., 1963), Chapter 5.

4. The International Reading Association also publishes a "Stereotypes Packet."

SELECTED REFERENCES

Apple, Michael W.; Subkoviak, Michael J.; and Lufler, Henry S., Jr., eds. *Educational Evaluation: Analysis and Responsibility*. Berkeley, Calif.: McCutchan Publishing Corp., 1974.

Banks, James A., "Evaluating and Selecting Ethnic Studies Materials." *Educational Leadership* 31 (April 1974): 593–596.

Berg, Harry D., ed. *Evaluation in the Social Studies*. Washington, D.C.: National Council for the Social Studies, 1965.

Bloom, Benjamin S.; Hastings, J. T.; and Madaus, G. F., eds. *Handbook On Formative and Summative Evaluation of Student Learning*. New York: McGraw-Hill, 1971.

Borich, Gary D., ed. *Evaluating Educational Programs and Products*. Englewood Cliffs, N.J.: Educational Technology Publications, 1974.

Educational Leadership 35 (January 1978). (The theme of this issue is curriculum evaluation.)

Grobman, Hulda. "Curriculum Evaluation." *Journal of Educational Research* 64 (July/August 1971): 436–442.

Hass, Glen. *Curriculum Planning: A New Approach*. Boston: Allyn & Bacon, 1977.

Hogben, Donald. "Curriculum Development and Evaluation: The Need To Look Beyond Behavioral Objectives." *Teachers College Record* 74 (May 1973): 529–536.

House, Ernest, et al. *School Evaluation: The Politics and Process*. Berkeley, Calif.: McCutchan Publishing Corporation, 1973.

Joint Committee of National Education Association and Association of American Publishers. *Selecting Instructional Materials for Purchase*. Washington, D.C.: National Education Association, 1972.

Jordon, K. Forbis. "Program Improvement through School Evaluation." *Educational Leadership* 34 (January 1977): 273–275.

Klein, M. Frances. *About Learning Materials*. Washington, D.C.: Association for Supervision and Curriculum Development, 1978.

Kindred, Leslie W.; Wolotkiewicz, Rita J.; Mickelson, John M.; Coplein, Leonard; and Dyson, Ernest. *Middle School Curriculum: A Practitioner's Handbook*. Boston: Allyn and Bacon, 1976.

Lewy, Arich, ed. *Handbook of Curriculum Evaluation*. New York: Longman, 1977.

Oliver, Albert I. *Curriculum Improvement: A Guide to Problems, Principles, and Process*. New York: Harper and Row, 1977.

Orlosky, Donald E., and Smith, B. Othanel. *Curriculum Development: Issues and Insights*. Chicago: Rand McNally, 1978.

Popham, W. James. *Educational Evaluation*. Englewood Cliffs, N.J.: Prentice-Hall, 1975.

Procedures for Textbook and Instructional Materials Selection. Arlington, Va.: Educational Research Service, 1977.

Provus, Malcolm M. "The Discrepancy Evaluation Model." In *Readings In Curriculum Evaluation*, ed. Peter Taylor and Davis Cowley. Dubuque, Iowa: W. C. Brown, 1972.

Roberts, Arthur D., ed. *Educational Innovation: Alternatives in Curriculum and Instruction*. Boston: Allyn and Bacon, 1975.

Rubin, Louis J., ed. *Curriculum Handbook: Administration and Theory*. Boston: Allyn and Bacon, 1977.

Rubin, Louis J., ed. *Curriculum Handbook: The Disciplines, Current Movements and Instructional Methodology*. Boston: Allyn and Bacon, 1977.

Rubin, Louis J., ed. *Life Skills in School and Society.* Washington, D.C.: Association for Supervision and Curriculum Development, 1969.

Stake, Robert E., ed. *Evaluating and Arts in Education: A Progressive Approach.* Columbus, Ohio: Charles E. Merrill, 1975.

Staples, Ezra. *Impact of Decentralization on Curriculum: Selected Viewpoints.* Washington, D.C.: Association for Supervision and Curriculum Development, 1976.

Stradley, William E. *Administrator's Guide to an Individualized Performance Results Curriculum.* New York: The Center for Applied Research in Education, 1973.

Tuckman, Bruce W. *Evaluating Instructional Programs.* Boston: Allyn and Bacon, 1979.

Webster, William J. *Evaluation of Instructional Materials.* Washington, D.C.: Association for Educational Communications & Technology, 1976.

Willis, George, ed. *Qualitative Evaluation: Concepts and Cases in Curriculum Criticism.* Berkeley, Calif.: McCutchan Publishing Corp., 1978.

Worthen, Blaine R. "Characteristics of Good Evaluation Studies." *Journal of Research and Development in Education* 10 (Spring 1977): 3–20.

Zenger, Weldon F., and Zenger, Sharon K. *Writing and Evaluating Curriculum Guides.* Belmont, Calif.: Fearon Publishers, 1973.

8

EVALUATING
THE STUDENT
ACTIVITIES
PROGRAM

At the core of every true talent there is an awareness of the difficulties inherent in any achievement, and the confidence that by persistence and patience something worthwhile will be realized.

Eric Hoffer

The word traditionally used for describing this program has been *extracurricular*. However, the preferable term, *student activities program* implies that the program is no "extra" but rather an integral part of the total school program.

It is not unusual to think of the student activities program as a secondary school program only. However, elementary and middle schools can and should have student activities programs as part of the total school program, including such activities as student government, athletics, clubs, bands, choruses, to a name a few. For this and other reasons, the term *student activities programs* will include both levels of education unless otherwise indicated specifically or by the content of certain sections of this chapter.

Most textbooks on school administration describe the student activities program in a single chapter, devoting one or two paragraphs to evaluation. The discussion in this chapter will focus on ways for school principals to evaluate existing programs with guidelines presented for organizing and administering such programs.

EVALUATING SCHOOL ACTIVITIES: SOME IDEAS

Elementary and secondary principals have responsibilities regarding the evaluation of the student activities programs in their school. The student activities program is an important part of the total educational program of a school and as such deserves periodic evaluation based on the criteria of effectiveness. Effectiveness, in this sense, means that you as the school principal and your faculty evaluate in terms of:

- The goals of the student activities program
- The objectives of each activity within the program
- The opportunities offered to every student
- The kinds of learning experiences provided in each activity
- The number of participating students
- The attitude of students, teachers, and parents toward the program
- The budgetary considerations
- The limiting factors such as participation, space, interest, and supervision
- The per pupil expenditures, income, debts; expenditures of each activity
- The extent to which school personnel and the community work together to meet program goals.

Some questions you and others might ask concerning the student activities program in your school include:

1. Is the student activities program achieving its goals and objectives?
2. What are the opinions and attitudes of students and parents toward current activities in the program?
3. What are the opinions and attitudes of teachers and moderators toward the school activities programs?
4. What is the cost of operating the student activities program? The cost for each activity?
5. Is the money and time spent in student activities worth the results?
6. What activity is having problems, needs revision, or needs attention of the principal and faculty?

These and other questions can form part of an evaluation plan that may be implemented by an advisory council, or an in-school committee of teachers, students, and administrators, or by the principal.

Assessing Moderator and Student Views

Examples of questionnaires designed to obtain information from students and moderators are shown in Figures 8-1 and 8-2. While questionnaires of this type will provide information of value, one should be reminded of the equal value of observing each activity and making an analysis; of holding conferences with students in each activity; and of consulting with moderators individually and as a group to determine progress, strengths, weaknesses, needs, etc.

As many principals know, not all advisers/moderators want this responsibility, particularly after they have been teaching for several years. Nothing can detract from the effectiveness and value of an activity than to have an adviser who lacks the motivation and interest to guide and supervise students in the activity. Therefore, self-evaluation by an adviser would contribute to ways to improve the student activities program. Figure 8-3 shows a device that can be used for adviser self-evaluation.

EVALUATING SPECIFIC ACTIVITIES

The examples that follow illustrate ways you may use to evaluate specific activities such as the student council, school assemblies, school fairs, and school publications. It is not intended that each example be used alone; that is, evaluating each activity requires several methods (observation, checklists, conferences, etc.) and a plan to analyze the information, discuss results, and implement changes when necessary.

Student Council

The earlier we get children and young people involved in the government of the school, the quicker they will learn their rights and more importantly their responsibilities. They may even come to appreciate the problems and processes of decision making in a democracy and the role of principals and teachers in operating a school.

Figure 8–1
Student Evaluation: School Activities

School:_____ Date:_____

Directions: Please answer each question in order to help us evaluate the effectiveness of the particular activity identified.

1. Name of organization:_____
2. Are you an ____officer ____member ____representative ____nonmember?
3. Purpose of organization as you know it:

4. Do you feel the organization ____achieves, ____partially achieves, ____does not achieve, its purpose or objectives?
5. If you are not a member, please indicate why:

6. If you are a member, do you attend ____all, ____most, ____some, ____none of the meetings?
7. Do you feel most members of the organization are ____very interested, ____very active, ____somewhat active, ____indifferent?
8. Do you feel the moderator of the organization is ____very interested, ____somewhat interested, ____indifferent to its success?
9. Do you feel that the organization's moderator and officers cooperate to serve the needs and interests of its members? ____Definitely ____Somewhat ____Not at all
10. What suggestions do you have for improving this organization?

The degree of student involvement will vary according to the level of the school (elementary or secondary) and the age, skills, and talents of the student body. The process should begin in the lower elementary grades where children become involved in the governance of their classroom—clean-up work, attendance, distribution and collection of supplies and materials, classroom management, class officers (elected each month), hall monitors, etc. In upper elementary grades students can serve, via the election process, on the principal's advisory council where they can be encouraged to make recommendations about policies, procedures, rules, regulations, assemblies, programs, projects, etc.

At the secondary level the process becomes more sophisticated but nevertheless as valuable in developing student leadership, student firsthand knowledge and experiences in representative democracy, as well as other goals resulting from student council participation. Again the council serves as a recommending body to the administration, electing its officers via democratic procedures, and planning and implementing programs, activities, and services.

Three groups should be involved in a periodic evaluation of the student council; again, the degree and extent of the evaluation will depend on the level of the school in which the council operates. The three groups include the student council itself,

Figure 8–2
Moderator Evaluation: School Activities

Name:_____ Date:_____
Moderator of (organization):_____

1. Organization's Objectives:

2. Requirements for Membership:

3. Procedures for Selection of Officers:

4. Frequency of Meetings:_____
5. Number of Members:_____ Number of Active Members:_____
6. List the specific activities the organization has engaged in this year:
    a.

    b.

    c.

7. Do you feel the organization is achieving its objectives? Explain:

8. Identify difficulties you find moderating this organization.

9. How is the organization financed?

10. How is the money used?

11. Who keeps the financial records?

12. What suggestions can you offer for improving the organization?

Figure 8-3
Evaluation Sheet for Activity Adviser

1. Am I interested in my activities assignment?_____
2. Do I attempt to inspire student interest in activities?_____
3. Do I believe that activities participation can be of great value?_____
4. Do I yield my "teacher" role to become a partner in the activity?_____
5. Do I provide ideas and leadership subtly?_____
6. Do I attend meetings regularly and arrive promptly?_____
7. Do I earn and keep the respect and confidence of the group?_____
8. Am I following administrative policy and decisions, and at the same time aiding students in understanding and respecting these decisions?_____
9. Do I maintain an adequate personality at neither extreme?_____
10. Do I keep a sense of humor and good nature at all times?_____
11. Do I exercise a good sense of relative values; stress only those things really important and valuable?_____
12. Do I give adequate preparation, time, and thought to my group's activities; keep aware of their progress and needs?_____
13. Do I try to expand my effectiveness in activities?_____
14. Do I try not to become discouraged easily, even if students do?_____
15. Do I ever consider when I might be wrong and admit it?_____
16. Do I have the courage to try something new?_____
17. Do I try to understand and observe regulations and procedures related to activities?_____
18. Do I evaluate activities constantly with a view toward change where the need is indicated?_____

James R. Marks, Emery Stoops, and Joyce King-Stoops, *Handbook of Educational Supervision: A Guide for the Practitioner* (Boston: Allyn and Bacon, 1971), pp. 493–494.

who should engage in a self-evaluation; the student-body, the recipients and beneficiaries of the council's work; and the administration and faculty.

To assist each of these three groups in the evaluation process, the following rating scale is provided (Figure 8–4). The items have been categorized into two broad areas, student council organization and student council activities and services. One of the reasons for this is that although a student council may be well organized, they may not, for one reason or another, be delivering the services and activities expected by the student body and others. Other items can be added to meet the situations of a particular school.

This example and other evaluation methods should be used to answer such questions as: Are there ways to improve the student council? Does the student body understand and accept the purpose and function of the student council? Is the student council attaining the objectives established for it?

Assembly-Type Activities

School assemblies, once a popular activity, have declined for several reasons, particularly in large schools. Principals discovered that the behavior of students detracted from the value of assembly pro-

Figure 8–4
Evaluation of Student Council

Directions: Circle the number that best describes your feelings.

Student Council Organization

	Adequate/ Satisfactory			Inadequate/ Unsatisfactory	
1. Student council objectives are compatible with the goals of the school's student activities program.	1	2	3	4	5
2. Student council objectives are published in several school publications.	1	2	3	4	5
3. Student council has a constitution and by-laws.	1	2	3	4	5
4. Student council conducts its own elections and meetings.	1	2	3	4	5
5. Student council uses democratic election procedures.	1	2	3	4	5
6. Student council and moderator are left to decide procedures for electing officers.	1	2	3	4	5
7. Student council understands its "limits" of responsibility as delegated by the principal.	1	2	3	4	5
8. Student council moderator guides and supervises activities, meetings, services.	1	2	3	4	5
9. Student council provides all students the opportunity to be elected.	1	2	3	4	5
10. Student council members are elected by the entire student body.	1	2	3	4	5

Student Council Services/Activities

11. Student council uses the committee structure to carry out its services and activities.	1	2	3	4	5
12. Student council seeks and receives faculty and administrative support for its activities and services.	1	2	3	4	5
13. Student council seeks and receives student body support for its activities and services.	1	2	3	4	5
14. Student council has procedures for soliciting and solving real student problems.	1	2	3	4	5
15. Student council involves itself with academic as well as nonacademic problems.	1	2	3	4	5
16. Student council attends to problems of student behavior in school and at school functions.	1	2	3	4	5
17. Student council attends to matters relating to school publications.	1	2	3	4	5
18. Student council involves itself with nonacademic awards and honors.	1	2	3	4	5

grams. Many schools did not have auditoriums that could house the entire student body. However, in small- and medium-sized high schools and in many elementary and middle schools assembly-type activities are still considered a worthwhile activity.

There is much to be said for assembly-type activities that bring the entire student body together or significant portions thereof. Many schools have assemblies for subgroups within the student body, such as all freshmen, students in tenth and eleventh grade social studies, intermediate grades students, and the like.

Principals and teachers recognize the value of assembly-type activities as an expansion of knowledge and content of the regular curriculum, an opportunity to interest and motivate students, a chance to promote large audience behavior habits, and a method of promoting school spirit.

Several recommendations should be considered when organizing assembly-type activities:

1. Establish a student assembly committee; this can be a subcommittee of the student council but it should include both teachers and students.
2. Establish procedures that insure that assembly-type activities are properly planned, organized, directed, and evaluated.
3. Establish procedures that insure that teachers prepare students for the type of program to be presented.
4. Establish procedures that insure that most, if not all, assembly-type activities are planned well in advance and are listed in the school's activity calendar.
5. Establish procedures (and publish them in student handbooks) for student behavior in assemblies.

There are a variety of assembly-type activities worth considering:

1. Subject matter departments, particularly in high schools, should suggest programs to the assembly committee such as science programs, musical programs, and so on.

2. Films, motion pictures.
3. Lectures, discussions by locally or nationally famous people.
4. Demonstrations and exhibits.
5. Debates, panel discussions, forums on a variety of problems and issues.
6. Formal ceremonies—patriotic, awards, graduation.
7. Student demonstrations, exhibits, and council activities.
8. Rallies, "pep" assemblies.
9. Dramatizations and musical groups and programs.

School assemblies provide an opportunity for the entire student body or large groups of students to come together for educational and recreational purposes. Thus, the evaluation of assembly activities is important and should be assigned to the Assembly Committee if you create one or by some other group, including yourself, if you don't use the Assembly Committee recommendation.

The checklist shown in Figure 8–5 can be used for assessing the organization and administration of assembly-type activities.

School Fairs

One of the activities that can enrich the curriculum and encourage students to apply what they are learning in various subject matter areas is school fairs. Whether the activity is a total school activity, a departmental activity, or an activity confined to one or more classrooms, the objectives are the same

- To develop a greater interest in the subject matter
- To balance subject matter learning with an opportunity for creative expression
- To develop a student's problem-solving skills through experimentation with various materials
- To promote community interest in the content students are learning at school by exhibiting the work of all students.

Figure 8–5
School Assemblies: A Checklist

We Do	We Don't	We Should	
____	____	____	have an assembly committee.
____	____	____	have school assembly policies and procedures.
____	____	____	have an assembly calendar.
____	____	____	have students involved in assembly planning.
____	____	____	publicize the program before and after the assembly.
____	____	____	have a welcoming committee to greet guests.
____	____	____	have criteria for evaluating assembly programs.
____	____	____	have teachers discuss with students behavior rules for assembly programs.
____	____	____	keep records of each assembly program.
____	____	____	make an effort to start and finish the assembly program on time.
____	____	____	assign blocks of seats to each class.
____	____	____	have the program presided over by students.
____	____	____	have a fire drill exercise while the students are in the assembly program.
____	____	____	have a policy about student attendance at assemblies.

Fairs, then, should be evaluated in light of these four objectives. The questions in Figure 8–6 can serve as a checklist for evaluating fairs in your school.

School Publications

Most schools, particularly those at the secondary level, provide opportunities for students to publish their own newspapers, yearbooks, and magazines. Student publications have been seen historically as methods for students to apply skills learned in the curriculum, as an opportunity to develop self-expression and creative writing abilities, and as a learning experience that benefits the individual student, the student body, and the school. These publications receive financial support from the school budget, student activities fees, advertising revenue, and/or community sponsorship.

The discussion in this section will be limited to the evaluation of school newspapers, not from a content point of view but from the principal's viewpoint—how his or her policies and procedures affect newspaper content and publication. A school newspaper is a valuable asset to both elementary and secondary schools. It provides a valuable learning experience for students, be they interested in editorializing, reporting, printing, or handling the business aspects of the newspaper. In addition, a school newspaper can serve as a focus for student ideas, opinions, and concerns; it can be the vehicle for reporting school events, announcements, and activities; it can entertain; it can interpret happenings; and it can promote and improve school-community relations. It can also damage school-community relations and be a major headache for the principal and faculty.

The turbulent sixties brought a new emphasis to the content of school newspapers. Rather than reflecting the content prescribed by administrators and teachers, student editors and reporters began reporting, editorializing, criticizing everything and everybody, and using words that were less than

Figure 8–6
Checklist for Evaluating School Fairs

Directions: Place a checkmark on the appropriate line.

	Outstanding	A Great Deal	Moderately	Very Little	Not at All
1. Did the project show that students understand principles of the subject matter?	___	___	___	___	___
2. Did the work with projects result in a clarification of classroom instruction?	___	___	___	___	___
3. Did students' interest in fair projects stimulate inquiry?	___	___	___	___	___
4. Did student-initiated learning result from the projects?	___	___	___	___	___
5. To what extent were students involved in the discovery process?	___	___	___	___	___
6. Were better students challenged?	___	___	___	___	___
7. Because of the fair did the teacher(s) discover unsuspected talent?	___	___	___	___	___
8. Did the exhibits given evidence of:					
a. mastery of skills?	___	___	___	___	___
b. neatness?	___	___	___	___	___
c. accuracy?	___	___	___	___	___
d. creativity?	___	___	___	___	___
9. Were the students able to explain their own projects satisfactorily?	___	___	___	___	___
10. Did students use instructional tools (scientific equipment, art materials, etc.) in a knowledgeable manner?	___	___	___	___	___
11. Did the projects reveal originality and creative thinking?	___	___	___	___	___
12. To what extent did students draw conclusions from their own observations?	___	___	___	___	___
13. To what degree did interest in the projects stimulate self-evaluation in the students?	___	___	___	___	___
14. How did parents respond in terms of attendance at the fair?	___	___	___	___	___
15. Did the fair create community interest beyond families who had students in the fair?	___	___	___	___	___
16. To what extent were the comments of visitors favorable?	___	___	___	___	___
17. Has the fair stimulated interest in other areas of school involvement?	___	___	___	___	___
18. Has it encouraged better parent-teacher cooperation?	___	___	___	___	___
19. Has the fair resulted in improving school-community relations?	___	___	___	___	___
20. What suggestions do you have for future school fairs?					

complimentary and often "profane" to say the least. From reporting student attitudes, opinions, and activities regarding sex and drugs to criticizing school personnel and programs, newspaper staffs across the country "discovered" the freedom of the press. And in most cases where the students have been challenged in the courts, the courts have responded to the dangers of censorship by ruling in favor of the students.

With these circumstances in mind, it would be to your benefit, as principal, to examine your procedures regarding the student newspaper. In addition, an evaluation of the publication every other year would be of value to you, the adviser, and the newspaper staff.

The following questions serve as a means of self-evaluating how you currently administer the student newspaper. Each question is a guideline that requires your attention:[1]

1. Has your school board adopted policies that define what school publications are?
2. Has your school board adopted policies that do not violate the First Amendment?
3. Do you have publication guidelines and procedures that reflect the policies of the school board?
4. Do your guidelines detail the rights and responsibilities of student editors and reporters?
5. Do students receive a copy of these rights and responsibilities before being assigned to a publication?
6. Do your journalism teachers, publication advisers, and students know the tenets and ethics of good journalism?
7. Do your guidelines state explicitly what the school expects from its publications?
8. Do you, the advisers, and students know the "exceptions" to the First Amendment protecting students' rights to publish material? (Example: libel, privacy, etc.)
9. Have you established a publications advisory committee?

10. Does this committee include students, advisers, teachers, parents, and others? (Example: local newspaper personnel, lawyer, etc.)
11. Are the responsibilities of the advisory committee described, in writing, for members and others?
12. Do the responsibilities include:
    a. recommending policies and procedures?
    b. mediating censorship disputes?
    c. reviewing articles and editorials before publications?
    d. evaluating and improving the newspapers?
13. Are the qualifications for selecting students to serve on the newspaper explained in writing? (Example: minimum grade point average, years in school, interests, etc.)
14. Are the budgetary procedures recommended in chapter four applied to this activity?
15. Does the newspaper staff receive the necessary supplies and equipment to do their job effectively?
16. Are students able to work on preparing the newspaper during school hours?

It is obvious that these questions are applicable to other student publications besides the school newspaper. The student press should be, under your guidance, a compliment to the school curriculum and an enrichment to student learning, not a vehicle that creates complaints and controversy.

Should you, the faculty adviser, or student staff be interested in obtaining student views and perceptions of the school newspaper, two suggestions may be useful. One procedure is to have the editors run a small blocked column asking "How Are We Doing?" Students respond to this question using a coupon under the question that requires a written response. A second way is to send out a questionnaire to students, teachers, parents, and others who receive the publication soliciting their views, perceptions, and recommendations. Figure 8–7 shows a sample questionnaire.

Figure 8–7
Student Newspaper Rating Scale

Directions: Please help us publish a better school newspaper by giving us your views of the present newspaper. Place a check on the space that tells how you rate the item. Also take a few minutes to answer the questions. Your name is not necessary.

How would you rate the school
newspaper regarding:

	Excellent	*Good*	*Fair*	*Poor*
1. Overall	____	____	____	____
2. Style, format	____	____	____	____
3. Print	____	____	____	____
4. News coverage	____	____	____	____
5. Sports coverage	____	____	____	____
6. Coverage of social activities	____	____	____	____
7. Coverage of club, organization activities	____	____	____	____
8. Advertising used	____	____	____	____
9. Reviews	____	____	____	____
10. Editorials	____	____	____	____
11. Student columns	____	____	____	____
12. Other (specify)_____	____	____	____	____

13. What do you like best about our school newspaper?

14. What do you like least about our school newspaper?

15. What suggestions do you have for improving our school newspaper?

EVALUATING THE ATHLETIC PROGRAM

There are two kinds of athletic programs offered in today's secondary schools: intramural and interschool sports. At the elementary level, the program is usually restricted (and properly so) to intramural sports. The quality of both programs is related to program objectives, program organization and administration, program activities, and program finances and facilities. The purpose in this section is to provide school principals with a framework for evaluating both the intramural and interschool athletic programs and the personnel responsible for each program.

Many of the suggestions for evaluating the student activities program discussed in the previous sections of this chapter are applicable to the evaluation of the athletic program. For example, the role of the principal (supporting, supervising, organizing, staffing, scheduling, financing, and evaluating) remains critical to program effectiveness as does the principal's use of self-evaluation suggestions. Yet, both programs are highlighted for three reasons. One, participation in both is usually greater than in other activities and is increasing as girls are provided greater athletic opportunities. Two, there is a dramatic increase in adult interest and appreciation of physical activity (running, jogging, swimming) and dual sports (tennis, racquet-ball) which permeates the school's athletic program. Three, interschool sports remain the most costly yet publically supported extra-class activity. It contributes to school publicity, to school and community spirit, and to the needs, interests, and skills of its participants. Thus, the programs deserve the rigors and benefits occurring from periodic evaluation. The evaluation should be made in terms of its objectives, focuses, degree of student participation, school-community factors, and instruction-coaching. Its organizational factors include scheduling, health, and safety standards.

Objectives

The importance of establishing and evaluating a program in terms of its objectives cannot be over emphasized. Therefore, the following questions about the objectives of the athletic program are worthy of your consideration and that of the personnel conducting the athletic program.

1. Is there a statement of objectives for the intra-mural and interschool athletic programs?
2. If so, is it in writing and does it "flow" from the school district's statements on goals and objectives? If not, why doesn't your school have a written set of objectives for the athletic program? Do you plan to do anything about this?
3. Are the objectives used by personnel to plan the program, the activities?
4. Are the objectives updated periodically to reflect changes in individuals and community needs and interests?
5. Are the objectives used by personnel to evaluate the program and activities?

There are many objectives proposed by a variety of individuals and associations. For principals who administer schools without athletic program objectives, or for those with objectives who would like to compare objectives, the following set of objectives are offered.

The objectives of the athletic program are to help *all* students:

- Learn skills that may contribute to wiser use of their leisure time
- Learn rules and regulations governing a variety of sports
- Learn sportsmanship and self-control
- Learn the pleasures and disappointments of competing against oneself or an opponent
- Learn the techniques and finesse required for exemplary performance in a particular sport
- Develop, to the best of their abilities, skills and talents in one or more sports
- Try activities that are not normally included in interschool competition or in physical education classes
- Develop positive attitudes toward recreational and competition sports
- Develop attitudes and interests toward physical and mental well-being
- Develop a positive attitude about themsevles
- Develop a positive attitude toward school.

This list is not inclusive, but the point is that outcomes should reflect the knowledges, skills, and attitudes you and your staff wish to offer students in the athletic program. The emphasis is on all students including the "atypical" students. The emphasis reflects an ideal since there are a variety of factors that will prevent all students from participating.

One suggestion for summarizing the degree to which the objectives have been attained is to prepare a scale that will enable you to compare results over a three-year period based upon evidence collected regarding each objective (Figure 8–8). Comparing third year assessments of each objective with the first year's evidence you can place a checkmark on the extent to which the objectives have been attained.

Figure 8–8
Measurement Scale for Goal Attainment

	Intramurals			Interschool		
	Great	Moderate	Little	Great	Moderate	Little
Objective 1: Increased student participation	___	___	___	___	___	___
Objective 2: Worthy use of leisure time	___	___	___	___	___	___
Objective 3: Variety of activities	___	___	___	___	___	___
Objective 4: Sportmanship and self-control	___	___	___	___	___	___
Objective 5: Knowledge of rules and regulations	___	___	___	___	___	___
Objective 6: Competition	___	___	___	___	___	___
Objective 7: Application of learning	___	___	___	___	___	___
Objective 8: Attitude towards physical activity/sports	___	___	___	___	___	___
Objective 9: Well-being	___	___	___	___	___	___
Objective 10: Self-concept	___	___	___	___	___	___
Objective 11: Attitude towards school	___	___	___	___	___	___

Two requirements are essential. First, you and the advisers/coaches should have, after examining the evidence collected during the first year, established criteria/standards/specific parameters for each objective. For example, you and your group may decide that efforts will be made during the next three years to increase student participation in intramural sports by 70 percent or by a specific number of students. Then you can translate the degree of attainment, based on the evidence collected, into "great" if you reached the objective, "moderate" if you came close, or "little" if the participation increase was minimal. Second, as suggested, you need to use a variety of methods and instruments for obtaining the evidence.

Organization and Administration

As principal, you obviously delegate most of the organizational and administrative responsibilities to competent personnel such as the recreation director, athletic director, director of intramural activities, and/or activity advisers. Yet the delegation of these responsibilities is limited since, by the nature of your position, you must make decisions regarding the schedule, the finances, the facilities, and the supervision and evaluation of programs and personnel. How well you accomplish these responsibilities has a direct effect on whether the athletic program and its personnel will meet its objectives. Therefore, the evaluation checklist that follows (Figure 8–9) is designed to help you assess the extent to which you meet the implied standards. Note that the standards in the checklist are examples and are not intended to be an exhaustive list of standards that include every detail for organizing and administering the athletic program. However, you can evaluate your athletic program using these standards. The list does not include many statements about evaluation of personnel because this topic will be discussed in the section that follows. Also, many of the intramural statements are applicable to the interschool athletic program and are not restated therein.

Figure 8-9
Intramural/Interschool Checklist

Intramural Program

	Yes	*No*
1. The program is operated according to school board policies.	___	___
2. The program is governed by written policies.	___	___
3. The school board finances the program completely.	___	___
4. The program is governed by written rules and regulations.	___	___
5. All concerned parties have copies of or access to the written policies, rules, and regulations.	___	___
6. The program is governed by an advisory council of students, parents, and teachers.	___	___
7. The program is evaluated regularly in terms of its objectives.	___	___
8. Activities are selected according to the age, grade level, interests, and needs of students.	___	___
9. Activities are offered within financial and personnel limitations.	___	___
10. The administration and faculty recognize and appreciate the value of intramurals as part of the total school program.	___	___
11. Complete records are required for all activities, inspections, schedules, etc.	___	___
12. Activities are scheduled to make maximum use of facilities.	___	___
13. Activities are scheduled to accommodate as many students as possible.	___	___
14. Activities are supervised by competent personnel.	___	___
15. The health and safety of participants is a major concern.	___	___
16. Competent, trained officials are used to officiate intramural competition.	___	___
17. Every student who wishes to participate is able to do so.	___	___
18. Every student who does participate must complete a physical examination.	___	___
19. Athletic equipment and apparatus are inspected regularly.	___	___
20. Athletic facilities (showers, bleachers, etc.) are inspected regularly.	___	___
21. The program does not discriminate in its offerings or participation between boys and girls.	___	___
22. There is effective communication between the principal and intramural personnel.	___	___
23. An annual report is required of each activity adviser and/or director of the program.	___	___
24. The principal has scheduled regular supervisory visits to the activities.	___	___
25. Each activity adviser and/or director is provided a job description and salary statement.	___	___

(cont.)

Interschool Program

	Yes	No
1. All coaches and assistants are qualified to coach the assigned sport.	___	___
2. Coaches are required to be in attendance to supervise all practices and contests.	___	___
3. The program is evaluated regularly by coaches, athletic director, and principal.	___	___
4. On-call medical services are available at all contests/games.	___	___
5. Medical services are available at all contests/games.	___	___
6. Written parental permission is required for all participating students.	___	___
7. Girls' sports are provided the same resources, proportionately, as boys' sports.	___	___
8. Requirements for participation in a sport are in writing and available for those interested.	___	___
9. Practice and game schedules do not interfere with the regular school program.	___	___
10. Participants are not exempt from physical education classes.	___	___
11. No student—spectator or participant—is excluded from interschool contests/games because of financial reasons.	___	___
12. Official association contracts are used for scheduling contests/games.	___	___
13. Qualified officials are provided contracts for officiating games/contests.	___	___
14. Efforts are made to insure crowd control and sportsmanlike conduct at contests/games.	___	___
15. Association standards are used to evaluate programs and personnel.	___	___
16. Monies collected from this program are returned to the general school fund.	___	___
17. Coaches/directors are expected to file periodic reports regarding receipts and expenditures.	___	___
18. Internal audits are conducted annually.	___	___
19. Students participating in all sports are provided with proper equipment.	___	___
20. All participants are required to be properly insured.	___	___
21. State eligibility requirements are implemented for each sport.	___	___

EVALUATING ATHLETIC PROGRAM PERSONNEL

Coaches, assistant coaches, intramural activities advisers, and other personnel responsible for carrying out the school's athletic program should be supervised and evaluated regularly. This can be done by the principal, the coaching staff, the school's athletic council, the athletic director, and/or the assistant principal. The use of self-evaluation and supervisor evaluation techniques (observation, etc.) and instruments should be utilized.

Criteria by which coaches and advisers could be evaluated would include such factors as organizational ability, administrative ability, on-field

/court supervision and behavior, selecting and encouraging student participation, relationships with players and other students, relationships with administration and faculty, performance standards during practices and competitions, attitudes and support of other school programs, and relationships with professional associations, parents, and the public.

The literature presents many traits of successful coaches which are applicable to intramural advisers as well and which may be used as a basis for the evaluation. Included among these traits are:

- A knowledge of the sport—the basics, the changes, the innovations
- The ability to analyze and evaluate game situations and make appropriate decisions
- Demonstrated respect for his or her own and opponents' players and coaches
- A dedication to assignment and responsibilities
- Demonstrated honesty, integrity, sincerity
- An eagerness and enthusiasm for the sport(s) he or she coaches
- An enjoyment of and commitment to his or her work
- The ability to place winning and losing in the proper perspective
- The valuing of team and individual effort and discipline.[2]

These traits and some of the recommendations made for the evaluation of teachers and other personnel in the previous chapters may be useful for the evaluation of coaches and intramural advisers. Many schools use a combination of self-evaluation and supervision-evaluation techniques. Both techniques are recommended and illustrated here, but no technique should be used without pre- and post-conferences. Many districts require a pre-conference between the coach/adviser and the principal/designee to review the previous years' work and performance and to establish some objectives for the up-coming year. The use of checklists for self-evaluation and supervisor-evaluation remains the most popular method of evaluation. A self-evaluation instrument for use by coaches is shown in Figure 8–10. A self-evaluation instrument for use by intramural activity advisers is included in Figure 8–11. Frequency of use and the sharing of results of these instruments should be determined during the pre-conference.

Information from these instruments and observational methods can be useful in post-conferences with coaches and intramural advisers. Many school districts have coaches' evaluation forms; a composite of several is shown in Figure 8–12. With some modifications, the form can also be used to help you evaluate intramural advisers.

The evaluation form (Figure 8–12) enables the principal to develop a profile of her or his evaluation of a coach. This profile can be retained and then lines of a different color can be drawn at the next evaluation to help the principal and coach note changes. Additional items can be added under each category.

In addition to paper and pencil checklists, the use of audiotape and/or videotape recordings of coaches' behaviors at practice and in game situations would be informative. If the purpose of coaches' evaluation is to change behavior, or to improve it if necessary, then it seems that they require the same scrutiny as classroom teachers. The use of audiotape and videotape recordings was suggested for classroom teachers and is recommended here. An analysis of the written checklists and of the tapes will provide excellent content for discussion, for planning behavior change, during post-conferences.

EVALUATING ACTIVITY ADVISERS

Every activity adviser in your school should have a job description. The purpose of a job description is that it lets each adviser know what is expected of each person. The job description serves as the basis for the evaluation. It makes clear to both you and

Figure 8-10
Self-Evaluation Form for Coaches

Name:_____ Date:_____ School:_____

Directions: Circle the number that best describes how you rate your performance on the criteria listed. "1" is poor performance, "3" is average performance, and "5" is outstanding performance.

Part I

I rate my performance regarding _____ as:

1. records and reports	1	2	3	4	5
2. relationship with coaching staff	1	2	3	4	5
3. relationship with players	1	2	3	4	5
4. relationship with other players and coaches	1	2	3	4	5
5. relationship with administration	1	2	3	4	5
6. relationship with faculty/staff	1	2	3	4	5
7. relationship with parents and public	1	2	3	4	5
8. ability to coach the sport	1	2	3	4	5
9. ability to be a leader	1	2	3	4	5
10. cooperation/consideration	1	2	3	4	5
11. acceptance of suggestions/criticisms	1	2	3	4	5
12. effectiveness of practice sessions	1	2	3	4	5
13. preparation of players for the game	1	2	3	4	5
14. behavior at games	1	2	3	4	5
15. sportsmanship	1	2	3	4	5
16. financial responsibilities	1	2	3	4	5
17. supervisory responsibilities	1	2	3	4	5
18. motivational and teaching responsibilities	1	2	3	4	5
19. other (specify)	1	2	3	4	5

Part II

Directions: Complete each of the following incomplete sentences.

1. In general, I think I am . . .

2. From my perceptions of my coaching staff, I think they would . . .

3. The community seems to . . .

4. It appears to me that the administration of this school . . .

5. The problem(s) with the athletic program at this school . . .

(cont.)

6. Some of my strengths are . . .

7. Some of my weaknesses are . . .

8. If I were to plan self-improvement objectives, I would include . . .

Figure 8–11
Athletic Activity Adviser Self-Evaluation Form

Activity Advisor for:_____ Date:_____

Name:_____ School:_____

Directions: Please answer the following questions by making a check.

	Yes	No
1. Do you have a job description for this activity?	___	___
2. Are you paid extra for this activity?	___	___
3. If no, are you compensated in some other way?	___	___
4. Is this activity part of your regular teaching load?	___	___
5. Would you supervise this activity if you had a choice?	___	___

6. What self-improvements do you feel are necessary?

7. How would you rate yourself on the following?

	Excellent	Good	Fair	Poor
a. Knowledge of the activity	___	___	___	___
b. Supervision of students	___	___	___	___
c. Performance in carrying out tasks in job description	___	___	___	___
d. Self-confidence	___	___	___	___
e. Training and experience	___	___	___	___
f. Willingness to spend the extra hours required	___	___	___	___
g. Interest and enthusiasm	___	___	___	___
h. Communication with administrative and athletic personnel	___	___	___	___
i. Relationship with students in your activity	___	___	___	___
j. Methods of stimulating student interest	___	___	___	___
k. Planning and scheduling activities	___	___	___	___
l. Other (specify)_____	___	___	___	___
m. Overall rating	___	___	___	___

Figure 8–12
Coaches' Evaluation Form

Coach's Name:_____ Principal/Supervisor:_____

Date:_____ Activity/Sport:_____

Personal Qualities	_Poor_		_Average_		_Excellent_
1. Character	0	25	50	75	100
2. Personal habits	0	25	50	75	100
3. Cooperative relationships	0	25	50	75	100
4. Appearance	0	25	50	75	100
5. Health	0	25	50	75	100
6. Enthusiasm	0	25	50	75	100
7. Communication	0	25	50	75	100

Professional Qualities					
8. Interest in coaching	0	25	50	75	100
9. Dedication to job	0	25	50	75	100
10. Willingness to work	0	25	50	75	100
11. Knowledge of sport she or he is coaching	0	25	50	75	100
12. Sets an example for students and others	0	25	50	75	100
13. Knowledge of physical training/conditioning	0	25	50	75	100
14. Attitude toward self-improvement	0	25	50	75	100
15. Attends association and clinic meetings	0	25	50	75	100
16. Motivates players	0	25	50	75	100
17. Takes the initiative to get things done	0	25	50	75	100
18. Administrative duties	0	25	50	75	100
19. Supervisory duties	0	25	50	75	100
20. Conduct during practice sessions	0	25	50	75	100
21. Conduct during games	0	25	50	75	100
22. Discipline—firm, fair, consistent	0	25	50	75	100
23. Concern for health and safety of players	0	25	50	75	100
24. Organization of staff	0	25	50	75	100
25. Instructional techniques, methods	0	25	50	75	100
26. Promotes teamwork, spirit	0	25	50	75	100
27. Delegates tasks to assistants	0	25	50	75	100
28. Sportsmanship	0	25	50	75	100
29. Care and responsibility for supplies and equipment	0	25	50	75	100
30. Scheduling of practices, games	0	25	50	75	100

Comments:

Principal's/Supervisor's Signature:_____ Date:_____

Coach's Signature:_____ Date:_____

the adviser what expectations, tasks, responsibilities will serve as the basis for the evaluation. The result should lead to less misunderstandings, fewer disagreements about what and what should not be evaluated, and a greater potential for improvement of performance. The job description you provide each adviser should include, at minimum, the following information:

- The title of the position
- The person to whom the adviser reports
- A "mission" statement or the school district's goals for including the activity in its program
- The objectives for the activity in your school's program
- Your school's policies and procedures regarding the organization and administration of the activity
- A specific list of the adviser's task and responsibilities which may include: (1) financial, (2) supervision, (3) organization, (4) reports and records, (5) active membership lists, (6) handbook preparation, and (7) publicity
- Criteria for the evaluation—agreed upon by you and the adviser;
- Evaluation procedures including checklists, observations, and conferences
- Annual report about the activity, its evaluation, and recommendations.

Rather than provide you with another evaluation form, the list of sample items that follow can be used as part of an evaluation checklist you and the adviser design. Items should be selected on the basis of the kind of activity and the job description you develop.

1. ____ This adviser demonstrates respect for students, teachers, and others involved in the activity.
2. ____ This adviser assumes responsibility for his or her own conduct.
3. ____ This adviser assumes responsibility for using democratic procedures in the organization and administration of the activity.
4. ____ This adviser demonstrates a respect for excellence in organizing and administering the activity.
5. ____ This adviser adequately interprets the activity to others when the occasion demands.
6. ____ This adviser accepts constructive criticism and willingly attempts to makes changes.
7. ____ This adviser accepts recognition graciously and shares it with the students in the activity.
8. ____ This adviser has a minimum number of absences because of illness.
9. ____ This adviser is calm and mature in reacting to situations concerning the activity.
10. ____ This adviser actively participates in professional in-service and other programs to improve knowledge and skills in this activity.
11. ____ This adviser effectively leads students in the governance of activity business.
12. ____ This adviser devotes the time necessary to administer this activity.
13. ____ This adviser stimulates student interest in the activity.
14. ____ This adviser is rated highly by students in the activity.
15. ____ This adviser supervises student in all aspects of the activity.
16. ____ This adviser cooperates with the administration and faculty in administering this activity.
17. ____ This adviser demonstrates interest and enthusiasm in the activity.
18. ____ This adviser communicates effectively with students in the activity.
19. ____ This adviser has a positive attitude toward self-improvement.
20. ____ This adviser demonstrates confidence in students' abilities to carry out responsibilities in this activity.
21. ____ This adviser has positive, personal characteristics (sense of humor, respectful, patience, good natured, etc.)

22. _____ This adviser effectively implements administrative policies and decisions.
23. _____ This adviser demonstrates an awareness of needs and interests of students in this activity.
24. _____ This adviser evaluates activity progress, plans, and procedures regularly.
25. _____ This adviser shares evaluation results with students, faculty, and administration.
26. _____ This adviser is not easily discouraged.
27. _____ This adviser requires students to meet high standards of work in this activity.
28. _____ This adviser engages in effective short- and long-range planning.
29. _____ This adviser effectively updates the activity handbook.
30. _____ This adviser willingly tries out new ideas for the activity.
31. _____ This adviser listens to the opinions and suggestions of others.
32. _____ This adviser has made this activity a valuable part of the students' total school program.
33. _____ This adviser demonstrates that students know and understand their rights, responsibilities, and limitations.
34. _____ This adviser respects the rights and confidences of students in the activity.
35. _____ This adviser attends all activity meetings regularly and promptly.
36. _____ This adviser demonstrates ability to lead students toward attaining activity objectives.
37. _____ This adviser evaluates with the intent to improve.
38. _____ This adviser has been a major factor for increasing student participation in the activity.
39. _____ This adviser demonstrates skill in developing the talents of students.
40. _____ This adviser meets administrative deadlines promptly.
41. _____ This adviser files a complete and comprehensive annual report.

A FINAL COMMENT

An effective and comprehensive student activities program should contribute to the accomplishment of some of the school's objectives. In addition, it should help enhance the academic program and contribute to school spirit and morale. There are few out-of-the classroom activities that provide students with leadership opportunities, chances to practice citizenship and sportsmanship skills, ways to develop self-discipline and team-play, and opportunities to develop life-long sport and leisure time activities as does the student activities program.

The school principal should continuously examine the student activities program in relation to the school's objectives. He should look for leaders (coaches, advisers) of each activity who are well-trained, competent, willing to do the work and spend the time required, and who are interested and enthusiastic about the activity. Program quality will be directly related to the quality of instruction and supervision provided by student activity personnel.

The leadership in each school must help faculty, students, and parents maintain a proper perspective between the student activities program and the instructional program, between interschool (where a few participate) and in-student activities and requirements of the instructional program, and between the cost of each event and its worth to students.

EVALUATION INSTRUMENTS

Three resources are described that you, athletic personnel, and activity advisers may find useful in program evaluation.

"Evaluating Your Program." Muriel S. Kalin and Regina Benson. *The Effective Student Activities Program.* West Nyack, N.Y.: Parker Publishing Co., 1971, Chapter 14.

In this chapter the author provides evaluative questions for each student activity program including student and class government, club and tutorial programs, team and cheerleaders, publications and productions, and the like. The school principal can arrange these in checklist fashion to evaluate each activity.

"An Evaluation Blank." Adolph Unruh. *School Activities* 21 (October 1949): 43–44.

The author provides a rating scale that may be used to evaluate a debate, speaking and music contests, and other student activities. The speaker evaluation scale enables the student and teachers to rate a speaker on two qualities: individual and technique.

"Evaluating Your Athletic Program—Title IX Compliance." *Complying with Title IX—Implementing Institutional Self-Evaluation.* Martha Matthews and Shirley McCune. Resources Center on Sex Roles in Education, Washington, D.C.: National Foundation For the Development of Education.

This athletic checklist, reprinted in *Nation's Schools Report* (February 28, 1977), contains twenty-three questions (with yes-no rating scale) that is useful to principals, counselors, and athletic directors to determine athletic program compliance with regulations in Title IX.

Evaluation of Student Activities. Arthur C. Hearn. Washington, D.C.: National Association of Secondary School Principals, 1966.

This forty-page pamphlet discusses the need for, and principles and objectives of student activities. An evaluation scale of thirty-two criteria is provided with each criterion followed by two or more questions and a five-point rating scale. Principals and/or student-faculty committees will find the instrument valuable for assessing a school's student activities program.

ENDNOTES

1. The first eight questions are based on two articles by M. Chester Nolte, "School Board vs. The Student Press," *American School Board Journal* 165 (February 1978): 23–25; and "The Student Press and the Ways You Can Control It," *American School Board Journal* 165 (March 1978): 35–36.

2. Matthew C. Resnick and Carl E. Erickson, *Intercollegiate And Interscholastic Athletics For Men and Women* (Reading, Mass.: Addison-Wesley, 1975), pp. 243–244.

SELECTED REFERENCES

Allen, Howard W., and Ganneder, Bruce. "Student Perceptions About Student Activities." *High School Journal* 60 (October 1976): 10–16.

Beatty, Thomas B. *Secondary School Activities.* New York: McGraw-Hill, 1954.

Crum, Lewis R. "Evaluation of An Activities Program." *School Activities* 26 (April 1955): 243–247.

Forsythe, Charles E., and Keller, Irvin A. *Administration of High School Athletics.* Englewood Cliffs, N.J.: Prentice-Hall, 1977.

Frederick, Robert W. *The Third Curiculum.* New York: Appleton-Century-Crofts, 1959, Chapter 13.

Hare, Alexander P. "Evaluation of Extra-Curriculum Activities." *School Review* 63 (March 1955): 164–168.

Hoffman, Michael. "Strong Activity Program Eases Transition to Junior High." *Bulletin of the National Association of Secondary School Principals* 62 (April 1978): 120–122.

McKown, Harry C. *Extracurricular Activities.* New York: MacMillan Co., 1952.

National Commission On Resources For Youth. *New Roles For Youth in the School And Community.* New York: Citation Press, 1974.

Robbins, Jerry H., and Williams, Stirling B., Jr. *Student Activities in the Innovative School.* Minneapolis, Minn.: Burgess Publishing, 1969.

9

EVALUATING PUPIL PERSONNEL SERVICES AND PERSONNEL

What is crucial is that we agree on the need to respect and enhance the uniqueness of each of our charges, to reinforce his often fragile sense of worth, and to strengthen his ability to function in his own best interests, as well as in the best interests of society.

Bruno Bettelheim

A principal's roles and responsibilities for organizing, administering, and supervising pupil personnel services and staff will vary in direct proportion to the number of students and teachers, the kinds and extent of existing services, and the availability of administrative assistance (i.e., a director of pupil personnel services). But size does not detract from the principal's responsibility to see to it that the program is one of quality and that personnel effectively provide services approved by the school board. What Reiton and McDougall say for the counseling program may be applicable to the entire range of pupil personnel services; namely, that the school principal is one of the major factors in the success of a counseling program and that he or she must be considered the "counselor's counselor."[1]

This chapter, then, is designed to help you assess some aspects of pupil personnel services and staff. The major programs to be discussed include counseling and guidance services, social and psychological services, and health services.

ORGANIZING FOR EVALUATION

The nature and scope of pupil personnel services suggest that the principal needs the cooperation of the instructional and personnel service staff, the administrative supervisers, as well as student and parents. Your charge is to administer what pupil personnel services you have to the best of your abilities and, if necessary, to continually keep program and service needs before the school board, other administrators, and the public.

You should appoint a committee to help you evaluate pupil personnel programs and services.

Committee membership should include teachers, parents, students (if a high school), and pupil personnel staff. The number of members of the committee depends upon the number of faculty and personnel staff and the school's student enrollment. Nine committee members should be the limit, however. Subcommittees can be appointed if the work load appears burdensome. The charge of the committee should be to assess the pupil personnel program and services using the following framework:

Program goals/objectives. Specific statements, in measurable terms if possible, should be identified as an indication of what the program intends to accomplish. In other words, each program within the school's total pupil personnel offerings should have clearly defined statements of goals and objectives. The committee's task, should these not exist, is to work on obtaining program goals and objectives from pupil personnel staff.

Program and personnel evaluation. There are several guidelines that the committee should consider when developing plans for the evaluation of pupil personnel programs and its personnel:

1. The evaluation should be made in terms of the stated goals and objectives.
2. The evaluation instruments selected should be valid and reliable.
3. The evaluative procedures should involve those who are working with the program on a daily basis and who have a firsthand knowledge of how the program operates.
4. The evaluation should be planned, ongoing, and provide an annual review of progress and problems.
5. The evaluation plan may include one or more of the following methods:
   a. Discrepancy methods. Once standards, goals, and/or objectives are established for the entire program or each service within the program, standards are used to assess actual performance in terms of design, installation, personnel, programs, and cost.[2]

In other words, the committee sets out to find out how well the program and personnel are doing what they set out to do—the application of the standards to actual performance.

   b. Before and after methods. Once the goals and objectives are identified, the committee may wish to find out how effective a certain program is (such as work-study program) in relation to its objectives—the reasons for establishing such a program. Assuming that the work-study program did not previously exist, the committee can measure certain factors before and after the program (end of the first year), such as the number of participants, the attitudes of participants toward the program, the attitudes of employers toward the program, the skills students learned, and other factors relating to the objectives of the program. During the second year of the program, evaluation data can be compared to the data collected before the program began and to data collected at the end of the first year with the intent toward program improvement.
   c. Comparison methods. Once the goals and objectives are identified, the committee may wish to compare one group of students in a program with another group of students not in the program; or they can make comparisons against some existing norms; or they may wish to compare programs and services in their school to school of similar size, locations, etc.

Feedback and follow-through. The committee must use the evaluative data. To collect data and not use it for program and personnel improvement is a waste of time and energy. Personnel involved in pupil personnel programs should be given the data and the results to help them in decision making, program planning and development, and continuous evaluation planning. To paraphrase a famous quotation, "evaluative data keeps no better than fish''; it must be used to provide feedback to those who are responsible for program development and implementation.

A CHECKLIST FOR THE EVALUATION OF SERVICES

As you and others examine and evaluate the pupil personnel services offered in your school, it may be helpful to assess all services in relation to specific questions. In the checklist that follows (Figure 9-1), questions are provided to assess counseling and guidance services, social and pyschological services, and health and welfare services. This checklist may be given to the committee or to members providing each service to be used as a self-evaluation instrument. Specific questions should be added by your pupil personnel staff under each major category to reflect indicators peculiar to the school's programs and services.

Figure 9-1
Evaluation of Services

Directions: Circle the number that represents your feelings. The scale ranges from 5 (yes, definitely) to 0 (no, not at all).

A. Are Services Comprehensive?

1. Do the programs include counseling and guidance services, social and psychological services, health and welfare services?   5 4 3 2 1 0
2. Are the objectives for each service stated in writing?   5 4 3 2 1 0
3. Is the budget adequate to support each service?   5 4 3 2 1 0
4. Do the services attempt to help teachers work with students of differing abilities, talents, needs, and problems?   5 4 3 2 1 0
5. Do the services include opportunities for individual, small-group, and large-group counseling?   5 4 3 2 1 0
6. Do the services provide students and others with educational, vocational, and other appropriate information?   5 4 3 2 1 0
7. Do the services provide studies (descriptive, experimental, longitudinal, short-term) of school clientele?   5 4 3 2 1 0

B. Are Services Accessible?

1. Are services available to all students in the school?   5 4 3 2 1 0
2. Are services offered by appointment only?   5 4 3 2 1 0
3. Are services available without an appointment?   5 4 3 2 1 0
4. Can students, parents, and teachers review records and reports with a minimum of "red-tape"?   5 4 3 2 1 0
5. Do physical facilities promote the accessibility and use of the services?   5 4 3 2 1 0
6. Are services available to parents and teachers at times convenient to them?   5 4 3 2 1 0
7. Can students visit service centers/areas unannounced and use information or seek consultation?   5 4 3 2 1 0
8. Are students informed about their assessment/evaluative data and encouraged to ask questions and discuss results?   5 4 3 2 1 0

(cont.)

C. Are Services Coordinated?

   1. Do personnel in each service meet regularly to coordinate activities?   5 4 3 2 1 0

   2. Is the organization and administration of the services such that they contribute to program effectiveness and efficiency?   5 4 3 2 1 0

   3. Are classroom teachers provided opportunities to become actively involved in services provided students?   5 4 3 2 1 0

   4. Are written policies concerning procedures, responsibilities, referrals, etc., available for each service?   5 4 3 2 1 0

   5. Are student records comprehensive, reliable, and coordinated among the services?   5 4 3 2 1 0

   6. Are duplicative and repetitive data, record collection, and storage minimized?   5 4 3 2 1 0

   7. Do all services insure confidentiality of student records and reports?   5 4 3 2 1 0

D. Are Services Continuous?

   1. Is the budget adequate to support each service each year?   5 4 3 2 1 0

   2. Are there sufficient supplies and equipment for continuous delivery of each service?   5 4 3 2 1 0

   3. Do service personnel meet with teachers and administrators regularly to inform them of students with special needs, problems, etc.?   5 4 3 2 1 0

   4. Are records and reports maintained in a way that is easily retrievable and accessible?   5 4 3 2 1 0

   5. Are student records and reports regularly reviewed for planning assistance to students?   5 4 3 2 1 0

E. Are Services Evaluated?

   1. Are committees formed to evaluate each service?   5 4 3 2 1 0

   2. Are services evaluated annually?   5 4 3 2 1 0

   3. Are service personnel evaluated annually?   5 4 3 2 1 0

   4. Is each service required to file an annual report?   5 4 3 2 1 0

   5. Are evaluative data used by each service area to plan improvements?   5 4 3 2 1 0

   6. Are evaluation plans developed from the objectives of each program?   5 4 3 2 1 0

F. Are Services Personnel Qualified?

   1. Is leadership provided by personnel in each service?   5 4 3 2 1 0

   2. Are personnel in each service certified to carry out their tasks?   5 4 3 2 1 0

   3. Do personnel engage in activities to update their skills?   5 4 3 2 1 0

   4. Is there evidence of staff activity in continuing their education?   5 4 3 2 1 0

   5. Do personnel demonstrate skill and talent in carrying out their tasks?   5 4 3 2 1 0

EVALUATING SCHOOL COUNSELORS

Evaluation of school counselors must be based upon an understanding of their roles and responsibilities. You will recall a discussion, in an earlier chapter, of the various perceptions people have about the role of the principal. This same condition exists for school counselors. Principals, teachers, and parents tend to view counselors' roles and responsibilities differently. This has led one author to conclude that the inability or unwillingness of counselors to effectively inform administrators about their particular skills has made their role a major topic of debate.[3]

To assist you and your faculty, a review of the major responsibilities of school counselors is recommended before you proceed with your evaluation plans.[4] Using the roles statements listed in these resources, the principal and/or director of guidance services may wish to implement a competency-level counselor evaluation program. One plan would require the counselor and principal/supervisor to:

- Develop a list of performance objectives
- Establish criteria to be used to determine effectiveness in relation to these objectives and other factors such as the school setting, counselor-counselee load, funds, etc.
- Design or select evaluation instruments that would measure the extent to which the performance objectives have been achieved
- Arrange for pre- and post-conferences and feedback sessions
- Analyze the results of the evaluation to determine strengths and weaknesses
- Plan strategies for improving performance and for implementing the next phase of performance evaluation.[5]

Evaluating Relationships and Responsibilities

Evaluating the work of school counselors must focus upon the quality of their relationships with others as well as their effectiveness in performing tasks.

Figure 9–2 is one example of a scale that combines both self-evaluation and principal/supervisor evaluation of relationships with others. The scale should be completed by the counselor and principal/supervisor separately. Either party can summarize the results and use the comparative data for discussion during the conference.

One may wish to specify tasks under each of the relationships listed thus providing more detailed information for use in conferences. For example, the scale could be rewritten to specify items under each category:

- Motivates students to seek counseling
- Is sensitive to students needs
- Has good rapport with all groups of students
- Encourages groups of students to use available resources.

A variety of instruments may be designed to evaluate the effectiveness of a counselor's performance relative to specific responsibilities. Counselors and the principal/supervisor could develop their own set of performance objectives and then develop a scale that would rate each counselor's performance on a particular responsibility or objective.

EVALUATING HEALTH SERVICES

School health services are an important adjunct to the school's health education program. Health services implement many of the concepts and content of the health curriculum. Health education and health services have as their major objectives the concept of "wellness"; that is, a way of living designed to help one achieve potential for well being including four dimensions—nutrition, physical awareness, stress reduction, and self-responsibility.[6]

Programs and services that promote positive health attitudes and knowledge with an emphasis on care and prevention may contribute to the decrease or elimination of unhealthy practices such as

Figure 9-2
Evaluating Counselor Relationships

Counselor's Name:_____ Evaluator's Name:_____ Date:_____

Relationships	Self-Evaluation			Principal/Supervisor Evaluation		
	Poor	Average	Exceptional	Poor	Average	Exceptional
1. Work with individual student	___	___	___	___	___	___
2. Work with groups of students	___	___	___	___	___	___
3. Work with parents	___	___	___	___	___	___
4. Work with teachers	___	___	___	___	___	___
5. Work with principal	___	___	___	___	___	___
6. Work with school personnel	___	___	___	___	___	___
7. Work with colleagues in guidance department	___	___	___	___	___	___
8. Work with community personnel	___	___	___	___	___	___
9. Work with guidance personnel in other schools	___	___	___	___	___	___
10. Work with other administrators	___	___	___	___	___	___

Items rated as poor:

Items rated as exceptional:

Recommendations for improvement:

Commendations:

_____   _____
    Signature of Counselor   Signature of Principal/Supervisor

poor nutritional practices, failure to exercise, and the use of alcohol, tobacco, and drugs. However, many school districts, reacting to budget limitations, have sought other ways of providing health services rather than decreasing existing services. Greater reliance on community health services, the local health department, paramedical personnel, and visiting nurses, are but a few examples. Some districts have developed health teams, many have decided to assign the school nurse, psychologist, dental hygienist (or other members of the team if one exists) to several schools on a rotating schedule. Regardless of the means used to deliver the necessary health services, it is imperative that a goal-directed (with measurable objectives) school health program and accompanying services be designed so

that appropriate measuring instruments can be used to determine the effectiveness of these programs and services. The school principal's roles and responsibilities for leadership in this area is crucial to its success. The same is true for the school nurse who, working closely with the school principal, faculty, and other school members, functions to advise, evaluate, organize, and integrate.

Two examples for evaluating the health services offered in your school will be described. In each of these examples, it is best that the evaluation be done by a committee representing faculty, health personnel, and adminstrators. Another procedure would be to have the faculty, the administration, and the health service staff evaluate health services separately, and then compare the results.

Regardless of how you decide to organize for evaluating health services, the intent should be to improve these services within the parameters created by budget limitations, the number of personnel, community resources, and the like.

The first example requires an analysis of current practices as well as determining what could be done, which in essence, provides ideas for the improvement of health services. Four questions should be answered for each of the ten factors listed. The four questions are:

1. Where are we currently?
2. How well are we doing currently?
3. How well could we be doing it?
4. Where would we like to be?

The ten factors that each of these questions could be applied to include health service:

- Objectives
- Offerings
- Organization
- Administration
- Budget
- Personnel
- Facilities
- Resources
- Needs
- Improvements.

Another way to evaluate school health services is to use a checklist similar to that shown in Figure 9-3.

Figure 9-3
School Health Services Checklist

	Yes	No
1. The school health services are based upon specific measurable objectives.	___	___
2. The objectives are understood by faculty and administrators.	___	___
3. The objectives are understood by students and parents.	___	___
4. School health personnel are provided written descriptions of their job and expectations.	___	___
5. School health personnel are supervised and evaluated periodically throughout the school year.	___	___
6. School health personnel are accessible to faculty, students, and administrators.	___	___
7. The services offered meet the health needs of students.	___	___
8. Health services are evaluated periodically with the results used for planning improvements.	___	___
9. Faculty and community view the services as a valuable adjunct to the total school program.	___	___
10. Health service offerings make use of community resources.	___	___
11. School health services are organized in such a way that the potential for achieving objectives are great.	___	___
12. School health services are administered in such a way that the potential for achieving objectives are great.	___	___
13. Plans for the continuous evaluation of school health services have been developed.	___	___
14. Achievements, failures, and school health service activities are identified in an annual report.	___	___
15. Achievements, failures, and activities of health services are reported to parents and public.	___	___

EVALUATING SOCIAL AND PSYCHOLOGICAL SERVICES

In most school districts the school social worker and the school psychologist work out of the central office and visit individual schools on a scheduled basis and are "on call" in case of special needs or emergencies. Personnel who divide their time among several schools find it difficult to develop the human and professional attachments that one finds among faculty and staff assigned to a specific school. In addition, the sharing of professional services among several schools can easily lead to misunderstandings by principals and teachers about roles and responsibilities.

It is apparent that the building principal take the lead in developing an attitude of acceptance of the social worker and school psychologist. To do this requires that you, as the building principal, know the roles and responsibilities of the school social worker and school psychologist. Once you understand their roles and responsibilities, it is important that you develop policies and procedures that govern their work and clearly define, in writing (for them as well as the faculty and staff), the job they are expected to perform in your school with students, teachers, and parents.

Principal and Faculty Self-Evaluation

In order for you and your faculty to better understand and appreciate roles and responsibilities, and utilize services provided by the school social worker and the school psychologist, ten questions are presented for self-evaluation and discussion at faculty meetings. Each question includes some information that may be utilized to guide the discussion:

Question 1: How would you (principal-teacher) rate your knowledge of the role and responsibilities of the school social worker?

The responsibilities include:

1. Working with students who have social and emotional difficulties or other school adjustment problems

2. Working with the parents of students who have been referred for help
3. Conducting home visitations and reporting conditions and circumstances to principal and specific teachers
4. Constructing family histories and making other psychosocial assessments.
5. Serving as a liaison between the school and community social service agencies.
6. Interpreting services provided by him or her to teachers, parents, and the community.[7]

Question 2: How would you (principal-teacher) rate your knowledge of the role and responsibilities of the school psychologist?

The responsibilities include:

1. Helping students with emotional problems and educational maladjustments
1. Performing diagnostic (testing) services
2. Helping teachers understand the meaning of group test results
3. Working as an effective member of the diagnostic/prescription team
4. Working with teachers for improving the classroom climate and procedures to maximize student academic and personal growth
5. Working with teachers to develop curriculum and programs for maximizing student learning
6. Demonstrating concern for the mental health of teachers and students
7. Serving as a liaison between the school and community
8. Preparing appropriate case studies with diagnostic write-ups, data analysis, counseling activities, and plans of action
9. Interpreting case study to personnel at staff conferences
10. Conducting continuous evaluations of student programs and, where appropriate, revising suggested remediation.[8]

Question 3: Do you (principal) have a written sample that teachers receive describing students who may be eligible for social work or psychological services?

As principal, you should help the social worker and school psychologist provide teachers with descriptions of the kinds of student problems, behaviors, and maladjustments that they are qualified to work with. This process contributes to the discussion and helps teachers become more aware of who does what and why.

Question 4: Do you (principal) have written procedures that describe exactly how students are to be referred to either the social worker or the school psychologist?

Clear, step-by-step procedures cooperatively developed by you and the school social worker and psychologist can contribute teacher understanding and use of each specialized service. It can also promote a positive attitude toward personnel and the services performed because it lists procedures that are precise and contribute to a team effort rather than an individual responsibility.

Question 5: Do you (principal) use a team approach to study specific referrals?

In many school districts the concept of a multidisciplinary team has made significant con-tributions for helping specific students and their parents understand and cope with their particular needs. The "M-team" may include teachers, school social worker, school psychologist, principal, school nurse, and others selected for their specialities.

Question 6: Do you (principal) insure that adequate records and reports are developed and maintained?

It is important that school policies regarding student records and reports be created, properly administered, and periodically evaluated as suggested in an earlier chapter.

Question 7: Do you (principal) and your faculty evaluate, annually, the social work and psychological services provided students, teachers, and parents in your school?

Like other services provided school personnel, you and the faculty should evaluate services rendered by the school social worker and the school psychologist. Some information can be gleaned from the evaluation of their performance. An example of an evaluation scale is shown in Figure 9–4.

Figure 9–4
Evaluating Services: A Form for Principals and Teachers

	Out-standing	Satis-factory	Needs Improving*	Unsatis-factory*
1. How would you rate the social services this school receives? *Explain:	——	——	——	——
2. How would you rate the psychological services this school receives? *Explain:	——	——	——	——
3. How would you rate our procedures for referring students to either of these two services? *Explain:	——	——	——	——

(cont.)

	Out-standing	Satis-factory	Needs Improving*	Unsatis-factory*
4. How would you rate the effectiveness of our M-team (multidisciplinary) approach? *Explain:	——	——	——	——
5. How would you rate the contributions/suggestions of the school social worker to the M-team? *Explain:	——	——	——	——
6. How would you rate the contributions/suggestions of the school psychologist to the M-team? *Explain:	——	——	——	——
7. How would you rate the services provided by the social worker in helping individual teachers? *Explain:	——	——	——	——

____Check here if you have been a recipient of this service.

8. How would you rate the services provided by the school psychologist in helping individual teachers? *Explain:	——	——	——	——

____Check here if you have been a recipient of this service.

9. How would you rate the services provided by the social worker in helping individual students? *Explain:	——	——	——	——
10. How would you rate the services provided by the school psychologist in helping individual students? *Explain:	——	——	——	——

11. Explain any questions you have answered "Needs Improving" or "Unsatisfactory."

EVALUATING SOCIAL, PSYCHOLOGICAL, AND HEALTH SERVICE PERSONNEL

Personnel in each of these three services must be evaluated regarding the performance of their tasks stated in their job descriptions and in any other documents detailing expectations. There are tasks specific to the school nurse that are not applicable to the school psychologist nor the school social worker. Therefore, it is important, in any evaluation scheme, to include the tasks that are unique to the position being evaluated.

The evaluation instrument in Figure 9–5 may be used as a self-evaluation instrument, an administrator evaluation instrument, and a teacher evaluation instrument. Teacher evaluation of social, psychological, and health service personnel is important because teachers are a valuable source of information about the effectiveness of these personnel and the quality of services provided them

and their students. The instrument provides you and the person being evaluated the opportunity to write in specific performance tasks to be evaluated (five examples are provided for a school psychologist). The principal should meet individually with the school nurse, school psychologist, and school social worker to develop a list of specific performance statements related to the job description. At the same time, other items suggested in Part II of Figure 9–5 can also be examined. Part II was designed to examine factors common to all three positions.

Many school districts have specific kinds of rating scales and checklists instruments for evaluating social, psychological, and health service personnel. Whether one uses the instrument in Figure 9–5, a locally constructed instrument, or a commercially prepared instrument (including instruments suggested in the literature), it is appropriate to recall the discussion about the purpose and proce-

Figure 9–5
Sample Form for Evaluating a School Nurse, Psychologist, or Social Worker

Name:_____ Title:_____ Date:_____

Evaluator's Name:_____ School:_____

Date of Evaluation:_____ _____ _____ _____

Directions: Place a check in the box after each statement which expresses your assessment/judgment of that statement.

Part I: Performance	Commendable	Satisfactory	Needs Improving	Poor/ Unsatisfactory
1. Assists teachers in interpreting group and individual test data	___	___	___	___
2. Assists teachers in planning, developing, and evaluating special education needs of certain children	___	___	___	___
3. Confers with parents regarding special needs of their child and how to provide these needs	___	___	___	___
4. Serves as a liaison between the school, parents, and community resource personnel	___	___	___	___
5. Engages in effective individual and group counseling services with students	___	___	___	___
6. Other	___	___	___	___

(cont.)

Part II: Personnel/Professional Qualities	Commendable	Satisfactory	Needs Improving	Poor/ Unsatisfactory
1. Calm in emergency situations	___	___	___	___
2. Efficient in carrying out tasks	___	___	___	___
3. Effective in carrying out tasks	___	___	___	___
4. Resourceful	___	___	___	___
5. Cooperative	___	___	___	___
6. Accessible to teachers	___	___	___	___
7. Accessible to parents	___	___	___	___
8. Job knowledge	___	___	___	___
9. Professional development	___	___	___	___
10. Dependable	___	___	___	___
11. Leadership	___	___	___	___
12. Promotes team spirit	___	___	___	___
13. Effectiveness with students	___	___	___	___
14. Effectiveness with teachers	___	___	___	___
15. Counseling/communication ability	___	___	___	___

Areas of Strength:

Areas of Weakness:

Specific Improvements To Be Tried:

_____   _____
(Signature of supervisor)   (Signature of person being evaluated)

_____   _____
(Date)   (Date)

dures for supervising and evaluating personnel. The importance of pre-evaluation and post-evaluation conferences should not be overlooked by the school principal. In other words, pupil service personnel should be afforded the same courtesies and opportunities in performance evaluation as those provided teachers.

A FINAL COMMENT

In this day and age, when children and teenagers need, more than ever, the benefits provided by counseling and guidance, social work, psychological, and health services, the principal's task of ad-ministering, coordinating, delivering, and evaluating these services takes on added importance. The task is complicated by the fact that most pupil personnel services are located in a department in the central office or in a central service agency. This situation leads to a staff that is part-time in a particular school both in practice and people's perceptions. Dividing their time among many schools, pupil personnel staff are often misunderstood regarding their roles, their work, and their contributions. This situation adds to the responsibilities faced by school principals with regard to the organization, administration, and supervision of pupil personnel services.

EVALUATION INSTRUMENTS

Several instruments may be of value to you, your faculty and pupil personnel staff:

> Jonathan Sandoval and Nadine M. Lambert. "Instruments For Evaluating School Psychologists' Functioning and Service." *Psychology in the Schools* 14 (April 1977): 172–179.

This article describes and provides examples of five data-collection instruments useful in evaluative efforts. Included are (1) a vignette-based questionnaire, (2) a role-model questionnaire, (3) a services-received questionnaire, (4) a teacher interview, and (5) a nonobtrusive measures.

> "Counselor Image Questionnaire." Educator Feedback Center, School of Education, Western Michigan University, Kalmazoo.

This seventeen-item questionnaire uses a checklist format ranging from "rarely" to "almost always" to assess one's opinion regarding a counselor's helpfulness, skill, attitude, competence, and the like. Two open-ended questions are also included.

> Franklin F. Zeran and Anthony C. Riccio. "A Checklist for the Analysis of Existing High School Guidance Programs." *Organization and Administration of Guidance Services.* Chicago: Rand McNally and Co., 1962, pp. 152–158.

This checklist is designed to help principals and pupil personnel staff conduct a preliminary assessment of the status of guidance services in their school. It is composed of four parts: an overview of the comprehensiveness of five guidance services, a detailed analysis of each of the five, a comment section for each of the five services, and an assessment of the organization and administration of the guidance program.

> Arthur L. Benson, ed. *Criteria for Evaluating Guidance Programs in Secondary Schools* and *How to Use the Criteria for Evaluating Guidance Programs in Secondary Schools.* Washington, D.C.: Federal Security Agency, Office of Education, 1949.

Both guides provide a school principal and the guidance staff with evaluative material for measuring the many elements of a secondary school's guidance program and personnel.

> *Program for Evaluation of Guidance (PEG).* Columbus, Ohio: Department of Education, Division of Guidance and Testing, State of Ohio, 1967.

The manual describing this cooperative evaluation program includes such useful instruments as the "Secondary School Guidance Program Inventory," "Student Inventory of Guidance Awareness," and others.

> J. Purvis. "How to Evaluate K–8 Guidance Programs." *Nation's Schools* 91 (May 1973): 43–44.

The author provides a useful checklist for evaluating elementary school guidance programs. There are fifty-three items, each requiring a "yes" or "no" answer with categories such as services to teachers, students, administrators, and parents; facilities, equipment, and material evaluation; and the like.

> Edward F. DeRoche and Jeffrey S. Kaiser *Complete Guide to Administering School Support Services.* West Nyack, N.Y.: Parker Publishing Co., 1980.

The authors offer the following instruments for evaluating pupil personnel services and personnel:

Evaluating Services
Counselor's Self-Evaluation Form
Counselor Education Form
School Psychologist Performance Evaluation Form
Social Worker Services Evaluation Form

ENDNOTES

1. Henry M. Reiton and William P. McDougall, "How To Make A Counseling Program Work," *Nation's Schools* 77 (April 1966): 65–67.

2. Gerald Pine, "Evaluating School Counseling Programs: Retrospect and Prospect," *Measurement and Evaluation in Guidance* 8 (October 1975): 136–144.

3. Eugene T. Buckner, "Accountable to Whom? The Counselor's Dilemma," *Measurement and Evaluation in Guidance* 8 (October 1974): 189.

4. See, for example, Jackie Lamb and Roger Deschenes, "The Unique Role of the Elementary School Counselor," *Elementary School Guidance and Counseling* 8 (March 1974): 219–223; Mary Ryan and Carol Reynolds, "The Unique Role of the Middle/Junior High School Counselor," *Elementary School Guidance and Counseling* 8 (March 1974): 216–218; and ASCA Governing Board, "The Role of the Secondary School Counselor," *The School Counselor* 21 (May 1974): 380–386.

5. M. M. Guber, "Performance-based Counseling: Accountability or Liability?" *The School Counselor* 21 (March 1974): 296–302.

6. See, for example, Halbert L. Dunn, "What High Level Wellness Means," *Health Values: Achieving High-Level Wellness* 1 (January/February 1977): 9–16; John Travis, *Wellness Workbook(s) for Health Professionals* (Mill Valley, California: The Wellness Resource Center, 1977); and Lydia Ratcliff, *Health Hazard Appraisal: Clues for a Healthier Lifestyle* (New York: Public Affairs Committee, 1978).

7. Edward F. DeRoche, "Responsibilities of the School Social Worker," *National Elementary Principal* 43 (April 1963): 50–52.

8. Emery Stoops; Max Rafferty; and Russell E. Johnson, *Handbook of Educational Administration: A Guide for the Practitioner* (Boston: Allyn and Bacon, 1975), p. 569; and Richard A. Gorton, *School Administration: Challenge and Opportunity for Leadership* (Dubuque, Iowa: W. C. Brown Co., 1976), p. 307.

SELECTED REFERENCES

Ballast, Daniel L., and Shoemaker, Ronald L. *Guidance Program Development.* Springfield, Ill.: Charles C. Thomas, 1978.

Brown, Jeannette A., and Kameen, Marilyn C. *Organizing and Evaluating School Guidance Services: Why, What, and How.* Monterey, Calif.: Brooks/Cole Publishers, 1977.

Burck, H. D., and Peterson, G. W. "Needed: More Evaluation, Not Research." *Personnel and Guidance Journal* 53 (April 1975): 563–569.

Crabbs, Susan K., and Crabbs, Michael A. "Accountability: Who Does What to Whom, When, Where, and How?" *The School Counselor* 25 (November 1977): 104–109.

Evaluation: A Forum for Human Services Decision-Makers. Minneapolis, Minn.: Minnesota Medical Research Foundation, Program Evaluation Research Center, Quarterly Magazine.

Fairchild, Thomas N. "Accountability: Practical Suggestions for School Psychologists." *Journal of School Psychology* 13 (Summer 1975): 149–159.

Glicken, Morley D. "Counseling Effectiveness Assessment: A Practical Solution." *The School Counselor* 25 (January 1978): 196–198.

Humes, C. W. "Accountability: A Boon to Guidance." *Personnel and Guidance Journal* 51 (October 1972): 21–26.

Keirsey, D., and Bates, M. *Results Systems Management: The Human Side of Accountability.* Monograph No. 6. Fullerton, Calif.: California Personnel and Guidance Association, 1972.

Marcotte, Donald G. "Accountability in Internal Communications." *Bulletin of the National Association of Secondary School Principals* 62 (January 1978): 138–142.

Measurement and Evaluation in Guidance 8 (October 1975). (The theme of this issue is measurement and evaluation of guidance.)

Muro, James J., and Dinkmeyer, Don C. *Counseling in the Elementary and Middle Schools: A Pragmatic Approach.* Dubuque, Iowa: W. C. Brown, 1977.

O'Hare, R. W., and Lasser, B. *Evaluating Pupil Personnel Programs.* Monograph No. 2. Fullerton, Calif.: California Personnel and Guidance Association, 1971.

Siegel, B. "Evaluating a Guidance Counselor." *The School Counselor* 16 (February 1969): 309–311.

Sullivan, H. J., and O'Hare, R. W., eds. *Accountability in Pupil Personnel Service: A Process Guide for the Development of Objectives.* Monograph No. 3. Fullerton, Calif.: California Personnel and Guidance Association, 1971.

Weinrach, Stephen G. "How Effective Am I? Five Easy Steps to Self-Evaluation." *The School Counselor* 22 (January 1975): 202–205.

10

EVALUATING AND IMPROVING SCHOOL-COMMUNITY RELATIONS

The key unit for educational change is the individual school, with its principal, teachers, students, parents, and community setting.

John Goodlad

There is a difference between school-community relations and public relations. A school district may need to engage in public relations—a one-way communication process designed to "sell" or inform without feedback. Public relations does inform the citizenry about the schools' educational programs, activities, finances, and the like, but when it is done, little if any feedback from the community is expected. School-community relations, on the other hand, is a term that I feel is best applied to individual schools within a district. School-community relations focuses upon the quality of interaction and participation by the parents and public (people without children in your school) in a school's attendance area. The differences between the two terms may seem like hair-splitting but a principal who has an effective school-community relations program does not have to engage in public relations activities. For example, the principal of the school which my children attend does not have to "sell" the school's program, activities, needs, etc., because the parents do it for him. The basic reason the parents engage in the "selling" of the school is a direct result of their active participation in the educational program of their children. These parents are tuned-in to what is happening at the school, are actively involved with teachers, are requested to participate in decision making and thus "sell" the school, informally, in their discussions and relationship with others in the community.

PRINCIPAL'S RESPONSIBILITIES AND PLANS

The principal has the major responsibility for organizing and implementing a plan for an effective school-community relations program. The ten responsibilities that follow can be used as the basis for the organizational plan:

1. The principal should know the public and parents in her or his school's attendance area.
2. The principal should know the school district and the community in which the school is a part.
3. The principal should establish leadership practices involving faculty and staff that promote effective school-community relationships.
4. The principal should promote a team effort for improving school-community relations by creating a representative advisory council.
5. The principal should use the advisory council and its subcommittees for implementing an effective, well-planned school-community relations program.
6. The principal should provide in-service education opportunities for faculty, staff, advisory council members, and others involved in the program.
7. The principal and advisory council should use a variety of communication resources in its program.
8. The principal and advisory council should create opportunities and use methods that insure parent-public feedback.
9. The principal and advisory council should periodically evaluate the school-community relations program.
10. The principal and advisory council should use the evaluative data to improve the school-community relations program.

These responsibilities and plans will be discussed in greater detail in the content that follows. Suggestions for evaluating progress toward implementing each of these responsibilities will also be provided.

The responsibilities and plans should be based upon a sound foundation of the purposes of school-community relations which is discussed in the following section.

PURPOSES AND NEEDS: HOW DOES YOUR SCHOOL SCORE?

D. Bortner[1] has identified twelve purposes and needs underlying an effective school-community relations program, and has also developed a scale principals can use to assess how their school's operational procedures either help or hinder the attainment of each of the twelve purposes in Figure 10–1.

PRINCIPAL'S SELF-EVALUATION OF CURRENT PROGRAM

School-community relations begin in two specific places: the principal's office and the teacher's classroom. Two suggestions for examining your school-community relations program follow. You may wish to involve faculty and staff in this self-evaluation.

The first suggestion requires that you answer the question: How effective is your school-community relations program? To do this, consider:

1. Objectives. State the purposes of your school-community relations program.
2. Activities. Indicate how you have achieved these purposes to date. What have you actually done?
3. Evaluation. State how well your program or activities have achieved stated purposes. What evidence do you have?
4. Planning. What do you need to do as a result of the evaluation?

The second suggestion requires answers to fifteen questions. Each question can serve as a guideline for developing an effective program.

1. Are you aware of the needs and attitudes of parents and public in your school's attendance area?
2. Are the faculty, staff, and students making maximum use of community resources?
3. Do you have a school-community relations program plan?

Figure 10–1
How Does Your School Score?

Does your school, as it operates today, help or hinder these twelve purposes?

Twelve Purposes for a Comprehensive Public Relations Program	*Helps*	*Hinders*
1. To assure a good and appropriate education for the youth of the community.	⎯	⎯
2. To supply full and accurate information on school objectives, programs, services, problems, and needs.	⎯	⎯
3. To stimulate the people to assume a partnership of responsibility for the quality and kind of education which the school offers.	⎯	⎯
4. To involve citizens in the activities of the school.	⎯	⎯
5. To develop the interest, understanding, and confidence of the people.	⎯	⎯
6. To foster a type of public opinion and expectation which approves change and progress in education.	⎯	⎯
7. To secure adequate financial support.	⎯	⎯
8. To promote respect and enthusiasm for teachers.	⎯	⎯
9. To maintain parent interest that is typical of the elementary school.	⎯	⎯
10. To channel constructively the demands of pressure groups.	⎯	⎯
11. To establish and maintain cooperative relations and mutual understanding with (other) schools and institutions of higher education.	⎯	⎯
12. To maintain good internal staff relations.	⎯	⎯

Doyle M. Bortner, "The High School's Responsibility for Public Relations," *Bulletin of the National Association of Secondary School Principals* 44 (September 1960): 313.

4. Do you and your faculty and staff make adequate use of the media available to you?

5. Do you and your faculty and staff create situations that actively involve the parents and public in school programs and activities?

6. Do you know the percentage of parent-public participation in school affairs this past year?

7. Do you know what impact this participation has had on the school's programs and activities?

8. Are you and your faculty and staff doing everything you should to let your public know how "good" your school is?

9. Do you take annual or biannual public polls to find out the public's perceptions of your school?

10. Are the personnel in your school aware of the need and value of an effective school-community relations program?

11. Do you know what percentage of your faculty and staff participate in community affairs and organizations?

12. Does your public know the problems, needs, and issues regarding your school's programs and personnel?

13. Do you use strategies that seek feedback from parents and public regarding their perceptions of the programs, activities, personnel and other matters in your school?

14. Do you develop a yearly school-community relations activities calendar?

15. Do you use methods to examine the effectiveness of materials (newsletters, bulletins, etc.) your school sends to parents?

These questions and suggestions reinforce the ten responsibilities/plans listed in the previous section. These questions imply that there is a need for an organized school-community relations plan; that your public be queried regarding the types of programs and activities their school should be offering; that an effort be made to find out how parents and public perceive the strengths and weaknesses of your school; that parents and public react to the quality and quantity of information they receive from the school; and that periodic evaluation of the program be made to insure its improvement.

PRINCIPAL'S EVALUATION OF KNOWLEDGE OF THE COMMUNITY

Almost every textbook with chapters on school-community relations and/or public relations recommends that the principal know his or her community. This charge was also identified as one of the major responsibilities of the school principal in the previous sections of this chapter. The reasons for this are well described in the purposes and needs underlying an effective school-community relations program. You have to know your community if you expect to effectively utilize its resources. You must know the pressure groups, special interest groups, opinion makers, and the power structure if you expect to ally forces for school financial, program, and activity support. Two suggestions for evaluating your knowledge of your community follows. One is the use of a checklist, the other is a rating scale.

Know Your Community Checklist

The following checklist may be used to assess your knowledge of the community in your school's attendance area or the town or city in which your school is located. You should place an "A" in the space provided if you rate your knowledge as "adequate"; use "NI" if you feel you need more information than you currently have about a particular

item; and use "I" if you have little or no knowledge about an item.

How would you rate your knowledge of the community's:

1. ____ attitudes
2. ____ incomes
3. ____ occupations
4. ____ ethnic backgrounds
5. ____ racial composition
6. ____ educational level
7. ____ prejudices, biases
8. ____ conflicts
9. ____ problems, issues
10. ____ aspirations/goals
11. ____ elected officials
12. ____ appointed officials
13. ____ opinion makers
14. ____ media sources
15. ____ power structure
16. ____ organizational leaders/officers
17. ____ growth patterns
18. ____ graduate of your school or other schools
19. ____ mobility of the population
20. ____ health factors/problems/issues
21. ____ safety factors/problems/issues
22. ____ private and public schools
23. ____ other education institutions
24. ____ religious institutions
25. ____ service agencies
26. ____ recreational and youth programs
27. ____ adult programs
28. ____ minority groups
29. ____ special interest groups
30. ____ housing patterns
31. ____ industrial areas
32. ____ redevelopment plans
33. ____ financial and tax structure

Community Activity Scale

Principals have been encouraged and many times cajoled to be active members of the community. To help you evaluate this aspect of administration, a self-evaluation rating scale has been developed (Figure 10–2).

Figure 10–2
Principal's Community Activity Scale

Directions: Use the following scale to determine your activity in school-community relations. Scale: I do this: (1) often; (2) sometimes; (3) seldom; (4) never.

Activities	*Rating*
1. Serve as a member of a civic organization.	____
2. Initiate communication between the school and existing civic organizations.	____
3. Initiate communication between the school and other school personnel.	____
4. Plan informational meetings to acquaint the staff with the existing civic organizations.	____
5. Invite community agencies to participate in staff in-service training programs and/or parent education programs.	____
6. Study the changes taking place in the family patterns of the community.	____
7. Study the changes taking place in the educational facilities of the community.	____
8. Study the changes taking place in the cultural facilities of the community.	____
9. Study the racial and nationality make-up of residents in school attendance areas.	____
10. Study community agencies to learn about their functions and services.	____
11. Make use of the services offered by the community agencies.	____
12. Help facilitate work in the community agencies involved in the field of organized recreation and in youth activities.	____
13. Cooperate with community civic organizations in promoting better schools.	____
14. Cooperate with community civic organizations in establishing laws for protection, welfare, and education of youth.	____
15. Cooperate with community civic organizations by making school building meeting hall facilities and/or recreational facilities available to the community when need is demonstrated.	____
16. Cooperate with community civic organizations in planning new programs for community development.	____
17. Develop monthly school-community relations functions.	____
18. Use parents and others to help with the school's community relations functions.	____
19. Foster staff cooperation in encouraging students to use local cultural facilities (e.g., museums, art galleries, etc.).	____
20. Campaign with civic groups for improved health and recreational facilities.	____
21. Utilize public news media for bringing about an awareness of school programs and activities.	____
22. Utilize the public services organizations or other community agencies to enrich the school curriculum and promote school projects.	____
23. Provide school personnel with information about how to improve and promote school-community relations.	____
24. Make significant contributions to service organizations through a process of evaluation of services.	____

One of the major points to these self-evaluation suggestions is to highlight the fact that school principals can be powerful and positive influences in community affairs provided they willingly demonstrate leadership, know their community, and use its resources.

POLLING PARENTS AND PUBLIC

If you have heard it once you have heard it a thousand times—communication is a two-way process. The parents and the public in your school's attendance area need ways of communicating with the school that are informal, psychologically and socially safe, and not particularly time-consuming. As principal you are the one that has to create the methods by which the school's public can communicate with the school.

People evaluate their school everyday whether the administration or teacher likes it or not. They talk about their satisfactions and dissatisfactions about a school practice, a procedure, a teacher's behavior, an administrative decision, etc. Their discussions occur at work, at parties, on the telephone, in meetings, and over the back fence. Your job is to channel the public's ideas, questions, criticisms, and concerns into some semblance of order so that you can plan appropriately.

That plan calls for you and your faculty to develop procedures for soliciting information from parents and other citizens and then to use the information for improving school programs, activities, policies, procedures, etc.

Feedback will help you and your faculty and staff gather and summarize information that will focus attention on specific problems, help dispel rumors and misunderstandings, stimulate discussion, contribute to bringing parents and school personnel together to solve their problems, allow school personnel to organize efforts to correct or change things, and keep school personnel abreast of organized "attacks" on their school.

You and your faculty and staff have to know the community your school serves if effective communication and feedback is to be realized. Some suggestions for studying the community were presented in a preceding section of this chapter. To highlight the number and varied audiences you have in your school's attendance area, the following example by R. Olds (with a space for your analysis) follows:

Setting: 2,000-student school (high school); area of medium population density.

Inventory:

Example		Your School
160	Staff	_____
3,000	Parents	_____
25,000	Citizens in attendance area	_____
250	Community agencies, groups, churches	_____
100	University and other post-high school institutions	_____
200	Local employers	_____
2,000	Students	_____
5,000	Alumni	_____
4,000	Students in feeder schools	_____

Olds suggests that a count of 35,000 to 45,000 persons is present in many school attendance areas and that these audiences have "diverse, even conflicting, interests in the school."[2] Although the size and total audience may be smaller for your school, the diversity will probably be there and the need to communicate with and receive feedback from these people is not diminished.

SOME IDEAS FOR CONDUCTING A POLL

There are several ways you can obtain feedback from parents and others regarding their ideas, concerns, questions, and perceptions about what goes on at school.

School publications.   Place in all school publications such as the school newsletter, special activity announcements, and the like, a feedback section titled "How Are We Doing?" Leave space for parents and others to respond. If you wish, you can add two additional open-ended questions: "What are we doing right?" and "What are we doing that bothers you?"

Telephone surveys.   This is a procedure that requires the use of sampling procedures. A random sample of persons in the school attendance area could be selected. Specific questions should be listed for the callers to use. In secondary schools, this would be a good project for a sociology class; at other levels, parent volunteers could be used.

Door-to-door.   Again, a selection procedure is necessary. Students or volunteers would go to the homes with a checklist of items that would take ten to fifteen minutes to complete. They can simply ask each respondent the question and check or write in the reply on the form.

Telephone hot-line.   Advertise a "hot-line" number throughout the school's attendance area. People can call to get answers to their questions, to share their concerns, to "sound-off," to check on rumors, etc.

Local newspaper.   A letter to the editor by the principal or advisory council soliciting comments regarding specific concerns (homework, discipline, drug use, etc.) may be helpful. In addition, the principal may arrange with the editor to publish a questionnaire soliciting parent-public reaction to school programs, activities, policies, and procedures.

Meetings, forums, groups.   Feedback from parents and the public can also be elicited through contacts at meetings, by talking to groups, and by arranging forums on particular issues. The parent-teacher association remains one of the best vehicles for information about public attitudes toward the school. Forums designed to attract people to respond to specific issues is also informative. Inviting representatives to lunch or breakfast (or in an informal setting) is also effective. These methods not only provide feedback to school personnel but they also enable school personnel to react, to inform, and to influence.

Survey.   The formal or informal surveys through the use of questionnaires, opinionnaires, checklists, and scales remains one of the most popular, easy, and effective ways of eliciting information from the school's public. Two examples are provided.

Figure 10–3 shows a questionnaire designed to have parents rate the various programs offered by the school.

Figure 10–4 suggests a way that parent-public attitudes about the school can be elicited. The intent of the demographic data (Section III) is to provide an overview of the respondents—to provide data about the people the school serves.

The methods described here should not be viewed as something the principal does to *appear* to be concerned and interested in community beliefs and attitudes. The methods are designed to elicit information that can be used as both a prelude for change and as a way of communicating with the community.

POLLING PARENTS AND CITIZENS ABOUT SPECIAL EDUCATION SERVICES

You may recall that the leadership responsibilities for principals were outlined in Chapter 5. One of the responsibilities identified addressed the need for planning and implementing an evaluation of special education programs and services. To help school principals and parents assess the extent to

Figure 10-3
Parent Evaluation of School Programs

Years in school district:_____
Children attending J.D.H.S.:_____
Children graduated from J.D.H.S._____

John Doe High School: Parent Questionnaire

Purpose: This questionnaire is designed to gather information for the teachers and administrators. The data collected will be useful in providing the best possible education to your children.

Directions: Please answer each question by circling the appropriate letter. Comment whenever you wish to do so. Return this questionnaire in the self-addressed, stamped envelope provided or give it to your child to bring to his or her teacher. Scale: E—Excellent; G—Good; F—Fair; P—Poor, DK—Don't Know

1. In general, how would you rate your son's/daughter's
   education at J.D.H.S.?   E G F P DK
   Comment:

2. How would you rate the basic academic program your
   son/daughter receives?   E G F P DK
   Comment:

3. What do you think of the elective program?   E G F P DK
   Comment:

4. What do you think of the guidance program?   E G F P DK
   Comment:

5. What do you think of the athletic program?   E G F P DK
   Comment:

6. How would you evaluate discipline at this school?   E G F P DK
   Comment:

7. How would you rate the student activity program?   E G F P DK
   Comment:

(cont.)

8. How do you feel about the communication between school
   and your home?   E G F P DK
   Comment:

9. How well do you feel the parent-teacher group fulfills its
   obligation of improving cooperation between home and
   school?   E G F P DK
   Comment:

10. How would you rate the teaching in the
    a. English Dept.   E G F P DK
    b. Mathematics Dept.   E G F P DK
    c. Science Dept.   E G F P DK
    d. Foreign Language Dept.   E G F P DK
    e. Social Studies Dept.   E G F P DK
    f. Physical Education Dept.   E G F P DK
    Comment:

11. What program needs our immediate attention? Why?

12. What program seems to be our strongest? Why?

Figure 10–4
Community Attitude Scale

Purpose: This questionnaire is designed to determine your attitudes toward our school. Our study will be incomplete without your opinions.

Directions: Please answer each question as frankly and accurately as possible. Your name is not necessary. The questionnaire will only take a few minutes of your time. Please complete and return in the enclosed stamped envelope.

Section I

1. In general, what is your opinion regarding the quality of education provided by this school?
   ____excellent   ____good   ____fair   ____poor
   Comment:

2. Do you feel that the cost of education in this community could be reduced?
   ____absolutely   ____I think so   ____probably not

(cont.)

3. Do you feel that the costs could be reduced by cutting out some unnecessary courses?
____absolutely   ____I think so   ____probably not
What courses?

4. Are you generally satisfied with the education children/youth receive in this school?
____yes   ____no   ____needs improving
Comment:

5. Do you feel that the schools are trying out too many new methods, new ways of teaching, etc.?
____not at all   ____they could do more   ____too much
Comment:

Section II

Please rate this school on each of the following items. Scale: 1—Excellent; 2—Good; 3—Fair; 4—Poor; 5—Don't Know.

Administration	1	2	3	4	5
Teachers	1	2	3	4	5
Student body	1	2	3	4	5
Conduct of students	1	2	3	4	5
School discipline	1	2	3	4	5
Textbooks	1	2	3	4	5
Instructional supplies	1	2	3	4	5
Academic program	1	2	3	4	5
Community use of school facilities	1	2	3	4	5
Athletic program	1	2	3	4	5
Extracurricular activities	1	2	3	4	5
School plant	1	2	3	4	5
School site and area	1	2	3	4	5
Communication with parents	1	2	3	4	5
Communication with the community	1	2	3	4	5
General attitudes of public toward the school	1	2	3	4	5

Section III

1. Age of person completing this questionnaire:
   a. ( ) 18–20   d. ( ) 31–45
   b. ( ) 21–25   e. ( ) 46–60
   c. ( ) 26–30   f. ( ) over 60
2. Sex of person completing this questionnaire:
   a. ( ) Male   b. ( ) Female

(cont.)

3. This questionnaire has been answered by:
   a. ( ) An unmarried man, woman, widow, or widower without children.
   b. ( ) A married (or widow or widower) couple, all of whose children are below school age.
   c. ( ) A married couple (or widow or widower), some or all of whose children are of school age.
   d. ( ) A married couple (or widow or widower), all of whose children are over school age.
   e. ( ) Single person living with parents.
   f. ( ) Single person living alone.
4. Are you the major financial supporter of the family?
   a. ( ) Yes   b. ( ) No
5. If you answered "No" to question 4, are you
   a. ( ) housewife
   b. ( ) employed (working) wife
   c. ( ) single and employed
   d. ( ) unemployed male
   e. ( ) a student
   f. ( ) other, please specify_____
6. How many children in your family?
   a. ( ) None   d. ( ) Three   g. ( ) Six
   b. ( ) One   e. ( ) Four   h. ( ) Seven
   c. ( ) Two   f. ( ) Five   i. ( ) Eight
7. How many children attend the public schools?
   a. ( ) None   d. ( ) Three   g. ( ) Six
   b. ( ) One   e. ( ) Four   h. ( ) Seven
   c. ( ) Two   f. ( ) Five   i. ( ) Eight
8. Do you believe your family would make its decisions concerning public education in the same way you have in answering this questionnaire?
   a. ( ) Yes   b. ( ) No
9. Your income (combined if both husband and wife are working):
   a. ( ) Less than $5,000
   b. ( ) $5,001 to $7,500
   c. ( ) $7,501 to $10,000
   d. ( ) $10,001 to $15,000
   e. ( ) over $15,000
10. Your education (highest grade completed, either husband or wife):
    a. ( ) Elementary school only
    b. ( ) Some high school
    c. ( ) High school graduate
    d. ( ) Some college
    e. ( ) College graduate
11. Your occupation (occupation of principal wage earner):
    a. ( ) Professional (doctor, lawyer, banker, etc.)
    b. ( ) Manager, owner, government official
    c. ( ) Salesman or clerical worker
    d. ( ) Craftsman (skilled worker)
    e. ( ) Factory or mill worker (unskilled)

which the program is in compliance with one of the mandates of Public Law 94-142, specifically, providing a written educational program for each child to meet his or her unique educational needs, the National Committee for Citizens in Education has designed a survey instrument for this purpose. The questionnaire is reprinted in Figure 10–5 with permission from NCCE.

Figure 10–5
A Parent/Citizen Survey

Improving Services for Children in Special Education Public Law 94-142 (The Education for All Handicapped Children Act of 1975) is a federal law which provides for a free and appropriate public education for all handicapped children regardless of the degree or type of handicap. This law also requires that a written educational program (IEP) be developed for each child to meet his/her unique educational needs.

This questionnaire is designed to find out about the parents' views concerning one aspect of this law—the Individual Educational Plan (IEP). We value the amount of time and help you are about to give. Keep in mind that your help could improve services for children throughout the country. As one example, we plan to produce a handbook for parents on how to participate more successfully in the IEP process.

School Building:_____

School System:_____

Parent's Name:_____

Address:_____

      Street   City   State   Zip

Child's Age:____ Sex: M____ F____

What is your child's primary handicapping condition?

_____

Is your child in a public school? Yes____ No____

If NO, what type of school? i.e., parochial, private, state_____

Your phone number (would be held confidential) could be helpful to us if we want to follow up. _____

      Area Code   Number

Please answer the following questions after you have attended the meeting at which your child's IEP was developed for the coming school year.

Parts and Procedures of the Individual Educational Plan

Please circle your answer

  1. The IEP meeting was held within 30 days following evaluation of my child. If NO, please check when the IEP meeting was held following the evaluation: Yes   No

    _____   _____   _____

    2 mos. later   3 mos. later   4 mos. later

    _____   _____   _____

    5 mos. later   6 mos. later   never

  2. The information from my child's evaluation before the IEP was fair and useful for planning a program for my child.   Yes   No

                                                                        (cont.)

3. The following were present at the IEP meeting:
   a. my child   Yes   No
   b. child's teacher   Yes   No
   c. school representative (other than child's teacher)   Yes   No
   d. parent or Guardian   Yes   No
   e. other_____

4. The IEP for my child contained the following items:
   a. annual goals   Yes   No
   b. short-term objectives   Yes   No
   c. specific service(s) to be provided   Yes   No
   d. present level of performance   Yes   No
   e. date services were to begin   Yes   No
   f. ways to check my child's progress   Yes   No
   g. special materials, equipment or media   Yes   No
   h. percentage (%) of time in regular class placement   Yes   No
   i. place for me to indicate my approval   Yes   No
   j. educators informed me of how the IEP was to be developed and what would be in it   Yes   No

5. The description of my child's present educational performance in the IEP included information in all four of these areas:
   a. self-help skills (personal maintenance)   Yes   No
   b. academic skills (reading, math, etc.)   Yes   No
   c. social behavior (how s/he gets along with others, etc.)   Yes   No
   d. physical skills (coordination, running, etc.)   Yes   No

6. There were major areas of educational needs for my child which were ignored during the IEP meeting.   Yes   No

7. The short-term objectives are written as specific steps my child will achieve in the next three months or more.   Yes   No

8. The short-term objectives did seem closely related to the annual goal(s).   Yes   No

9. The annual goal(s) in the IEP did not fully meet the educational needs of my child.   Yes   No

10. The IEP clearly stated what specific service(s) my child would be receiving.   Yes   No

11. The dates for the beginning of services for my child were quite clear.   Yes   No

12. I know when the IEP services will end for my child.   Yes   No

13. The service(s) for my child in the IEP was determined by what was available rather than what was needed (for example: if a certain service was known to be needed but the final decision was made based on what the school district currently had).   Yes   No

14. A specific date was set for reviewing my child's progress under this IEP.   Yes   No

15. The method of checking my child's progress in the IEP included:
    a. how it would be checked   Yes   No
    b. when it would be checked   Yes   No
    c. who would be responsible for making sure it's done   Yes   No

(cont.)

16. Some regular class placements for my child were considered during the IEP meeting.   Yes   No

17. Every attempt was made by educators to provide services for as much time as possible in a regular classroom.   Yes   No

18. A completed copy of the IEP was:
   a. made available to me to look at   Yes   No
   b. made available to me to keep   Yes   No

19. The IEP for my child was completed before the meeting with me.   Yes   No

What Were Your Feelings About the Following:

20. Educators presented information during the IEP meeting in understandable language.   Yes   No

21. I was given the opportunity to ask questions about points I didn't understand regarding the IEP.   Yes   No

22. I was encouraged to contribute significant information to my child's IEP.   Yes   No

23. The IEP that was developed seemed to fit my child's needs.   Yes   No

24. Educators provided information that helped me understand the IEP process.   Yes   No

25. I felt like a fully participating member with the educators during the planning of the IEP.   Yes   No

26. The school which my child attends has a program for preparing parents to participate in the IEP process.   Yes   No

27. I refused to consent to the IEP.   Yes   No

28. I was given specific information on how to appeal the program assignment decisions in the IEP.   Yes   No

29. I was asked to assume costs connected to services in my child's IEP. Yes   No

30. I am hopeful that the IEP for my child will improve next year.   Yes   No

COMMUNICATION: MESSAGE AND MEDIUM

The principles and practices, as well as the self-examination recommendations, highlighted three important administrative tasks:

1. You and the faculty should know the parents and public in your school's attendance area.
2. Opportunities should be provided for parents and public to share their ideas, concerns, and questions (feedback) with school personnel. and
3. An organized school-community relations program should be developed in your school.

With the help of the advisory council, one of the components of a school-community relations program worth assessing is the current communication practices used by you in your school. How effective is your school-community relations program? Does the school's public get the message? Additional questions on this point may be helpful:

1. Do you send home most communication materials with students?
2. Do you have evidence that the information sent home via students gets to their parents?
3. Do you have methods of informing the public (other than parents) about the school?

4. How do you inform the public about school events, activities, etc.?

Many principals testify to the fact that sending communication home with the students is not one of the better ways of insuring that parents get the message. Many prefer a direct mailing. There are two advantages to mailing communication to a home. First, the message gets there. Second, it goes to home of nonparents as well. With bulk mailing rates and computer mailing lists (labels), a principal can mail material that is of interest to all people in the school attendance area at a minimum cost. Obviously, you have to be selective. There is little need to mail all residents in your area a parent handbook, but there may be a valuable service rendered by sending the public a school calendar of events.

Examining Past Practices

Once the advisory council determines whether the message is received or not, it may be worth the time and effort to examine past practices in how the message was presented. The checklist in Figure 10–6 may be helpful.

The analysis leaves the central question unanswered; namely, to what extent is the written communication sent to homes from the school judged effective by you, the council, the faculty and the staff, the parents and public? Three examples to help you answer this question follow.

Examining the Medium

Example 1.   The advisory council selects five items that were sent to parents and/or public during the past school year and asks a random sample (see Chapter 1 for sampling methods) of people to react to them. It should be noted that this procedure could also be done with teachers, students, and council members with minor changes in the form that follows.

After five items have been selected (newsletter, bulletin, school newspaper, a letter, and calendar, for example) a packet is prepared for the sample of parents to be polled. A letter explaining the purpose of the study and directions for completing and returning the questionnaire would also be included. Among the questions the council should ask include those shown in Figure 10–7.

Examining the Message: Two Examples

The idea here is to obtain feedback from the consumers of school information. Rather than use last

Figure 10–6
Communication Effectiveness Checklist

Medium	How Distributed	No. of Issues	Purpose
1. Bulletins	_____	_____	_____
2. Newsletters	_____	_____	_____
3. School newspaper	_____	_____	_____
4. Class newspaper	_____	_____	_____
5. Flyers/brochures	_____	_____	_____
6. Special announcements	_____	_____	_____
7. Handbooks	_____	_____	_____
8. Calendars	_____	_____	_____
9. Memos	_____	_____	_____
10. Other (specify)	_____	_____	_____

Figure 10-7
School Information Follow-Up Form

1. Did you receive these materials last year?
   __Yes   __No   __Not sure
2. Did you, as far as you remember, read these materials?
   __Yes   __No   __Not sure
3. As you read the materials now, does the content of all five interest your?
   __Most of it does   __Some of it does
   __Little of it does   __None of it does
   Why?

4. Which two of the five do you like best?
   __Newsletter   __Bulletin   __School Newspaper
   __Letter   __Calendar
5. Which of the two do you like least?
   __Newsletter   __Bulletin   __School Newspaper
   __Letter   __Calendar
6. Which two of the five should the school continue to send you on a regular basis?
   __Newsletter   __Bulletin   __School Newspaper
   __Letter   __Calendar
7. Which two of the five has information that is of greatest interest to you?
   __Newsletter   __Bulletin   __School Newspaper
   __Letter   __Calendar

year's materials, the council could do the assessment during the middle of the school year and use material that was sent out during the first few months of school.

Example 1. In this example a questionnaire is sent to parents and public (or a sample of) for their reactions and perceptions of the material sent to them during the year. Each principal would have to provide a statement of directions for completing and returning the questionnaire, but, in general, the questionnaire (Figure 10–8) is designed to get parent/public reaction to the material the school sent to them during the school year.

There are several questions on this sample form that are worthy of exploration. Those questions deal with the opportunity of your school's public to provide you with information about what they would like to see and hear about the school.

The emphasis in previous discussions has been on two-day communication. Some suggestions have already been provided to solicit parent-public feedback. What we want to examine here is a way of finding out what parents and public want to hear about. To do this, it is suggested that once every two to three years you or your advisory council poll parents and public about the content of the materials being sent to them, as well as solicit information about what they would like to read about. Some of the items based upon an examination of the literature suggest that the content include curriculum matters, discipline, teacher qualifications, grades and achievement, current teaching methods, school rules and regulations, school administration and organization, career and guidance information, athletic and other school events, problems and solutions, student abilities, talents, achievements, and the like. An examination of the

Figure 10-8
Parent-Public Evaluation of School's Communication Material

1. Are you generally satisfied with the printed information you received from the school during this year?
   __Very satisfied   __Somewhat satisfied   __Not satisfied

2. Do you feel that this school only sends you material when it needs your support?
   __I generally feel this way   __I sometimes feel this way.
   __I seldom feel this way.   __I never feel this way.

3. Do you feel that the information this school sends you is self-promoting, part of a public relations campaign?
   __I generally feel this way.   __I sometimes feel this way.
   __I seldom feel this way.   __I never feel this way.

4. Does the information this school sends you tell you things you really want to know about?
   __Most of it is.   __Some of it is.
   __Little of it is.   __None of it is.

5. What do you like best about the material this school sends you?

6. What do you like least about the material this school sends you?

7. What suggestions do you have to help us improve the content of the material we send you?

8. Do the materials we send you give you an opportunity to inform us about your ideas, opinions, questions, concerns?
   __Most of it does   __Some of it does   __None of it does

9. What materials cause you to communicate with this school?

10. Do you have ideas, questions, or concerns you would like to share with us at this time?
    __Definitely   __Not now, but later   __None at this time

content of the material you send to parents and public in view of this list may be interesting and informative.

Example 2. This example suggests that you or the advisory council survey parents regarding a specific piece of information sent to parents. During the first day of school, many school principals give each student an information packet for their parents. For this example, the information packet is a five-page mimeographed sheet on a variety of topics regarding school rules, regulations, programs, and activities that parents should know about (we'll call it the Parent Information Packet—PIP). The sample form in Figure 10-9 is an attempt to attain the objective.

It is important to note that it may be useful to periodically evaluate specific pieces of information sent to parents to find out if the parents reviewed them and whether or not the content was of value to them.

EVALUATING USE OF THE NEWS MEDIA

One of the best ways to get your message to the public is to use the news media. The local newspaper, in particular, is a most effective medium for you because not only will it help you communicate with the public, but many times it is a factor in

Figure 10–9
Parent Evaluation of Information Packet

Directions: Place a check mark on the line that indicates your answer/preference to the question/statement.

1. Person completing questionnaire:
   __mother   __father   __ward/guardian
2. Grade of son/daughter:
   __freshman   __sophomore   __junior   __senior
3. Did you receive the information packet given to your son/daughter the first day of school?
   __yes   __no
4. If "yes," was the information of value to you?
   __all of it was   __some of it was   __none of it was
5. Was the packet
   a. attractive?   __yes   __no
   b. readable?   __yes   __no
   c. well-organized?   __yes   __no
6. Did you understand the information regarding
   a. student fees?   __definitely   __somewhat   __no
   b. student activities?   __definitely   __somewhat   __no
   c. school board?   __definitely   __somewhat   __no
   d. school rules?   __definitely   __somewhat   __no
   e. school calendar?   __definitely   __somewhat   __no
   f. school/class schedule?   __definitely   __somewhat   __no
7. Please rate the effectiveness of this packet.
   __excellent   __good   __fair   __poor
8. What information was not in the packet that may have been helpful to you?

---

molding public opinion—hopefully in your favor. There is nothing wrong with publicity; you should seek it for your school, not for yourself. Many principals are not aggressive enough in seeking out the news media as a vehicle of public communication.

The following questions will help you or the advisory council assess your use of the news media. Each question implies a worthwhile practice.

1. How often have you sent information to your local newspaper about school programs, activities, and personnel?

2. How much of the material you send might be classified as "PR material," self-promoting material? How much of it is newsworthy and human-interest oriented?

3. Of the items you sent your local newspaper, how much of it was published?

4. Of the items that were not published, did you find out why they weren't published?

5. How often have you sent information to your local radio stations?

6. How often have you sent information to your local television stations?

7. Have you ever invited the news media to the school to cover a story, event, activity, etc.?
8. Do you know the names and telephone numbers of the editor and reporters at your local newspaper?
9. Do you know the names and telephone numbers of the community relation directors and reporters of the local radio and television stations?
10. Have you sent the news media copies of materials you send the public in your school's attendance area (and some of the material you send parents)?

CONDUCTING FOLLOW-UP STUDIES

A study of students who leave your school either to continue their education, to enter the job market, or to join the armed services serves two purposes. First, follow-up studies help you keep in contact with your graduates. Second, studies of this kind serve as another way of evaluating the school, another way of determining the extent to which the objectives have been accomplished (product evaluation).

Two kinds of follow-up studies will be described. One is a within the school district follow-up study; that is, a study of students as they progress from school to school. The other is the typical study of graduates (the alumni of the senior high school).

The purpose of follow-up studies is the same for both kinds of study. First, it will help school personnel determine the perceptions of graduates concerning their academic preparation and their attitudes, interests, and activities. Second, it will enable school personnel to trace the mobility and career choices of the student population. Third, it will provide data for decision making about curricula and personnel needs (i.e., vocational education, additional counselors). Fourth, it will provide additional information for student and parent counseling. Fifth, it will provide data for the con-

tinuous evaluation of programs and personnel. Last, it will enable the high school principal to create an active alumni association.

School to School Follow-Up Studies

Principals at the elementary, middle, and/or junior high school levels might ask the question: "Is our school doing a good job of preparing students for their next level of education?" To answer this question there appears to be three sources to investigate—teachers at the next level, parents, and students.

Figure 10–10 is an example of a scale that could be used to assess teacher opinions regarding how your school prepared its students. The intent here is not to lay blame, but rather to find out if your school is perceived to be doing an adequate job of preparation by teachers who are the recipients of the students your school educates. The scale is in three parts. Part one is an attempt to find out how teachers perceive your students' attitudes, skills, and interests; part two attempts to assess perceptions regarding subject matter preparation; and part three examines teacher comments to specific questions.

An example of a parent questionnaire appears in Figure 10–11. This questionnaire can be given to all parents of the last class in your school one or more years after that class has left the school. Again, one must be cautious about the interpretation of data received from an example such as this. Nevertheless, the information can be added to the pool of information collected to evaluate and improve school programs and personnel.

The student questionnaire can follow the format suggested for the parent questionnaire with certain modifications in directions and the wording of some of the questions. In addition to assessing students' attitudes, interests, and perceptions of their preparation and the like, each principal who decides to conduct such a study should visit the school the graduates go to and collect information regarding the following for each class every year or at least every two years:

- Average daily attendance
- Tardiness rate
- Detention rate
- Discipline notices
- Honors, recognitions

- Grades in school subjects; number and percent of A's, B's, C's, D's, F's
- Number and percent of class who participate in student activities
- Drop-out rate
- Out-of-school activities
- Other data that may help quantify student behavior, achievement, activities, and interests.

Figure 10–10
Student Follow-Up: Teacher Scale

Directions: The faculty and administrators at_____School are interested in your opinion regarding the students who leave our school and attend your school. We ask that you take a few minutes to complete this questionnaire. Your name is not necessary. Scale: HAS—High Ability-Achieving Students; MAS—Middle-Average Ability-Achieving Students; LAS—Low Ability-Achieving Students

Part I: Behavior/Attitudes/Skills

	HAS				MAS				LAS			
	Most	Some	Few	None	Most	Some	Few	None	Most	Some	Few	None
1. Courteous	___	___	___	___	___	___	___	___	___	___	___	___
2. Respectful	___	___	___	___	___	___	___	___	___	___	___	___
3. Polite	___	___	___	___	___	___	___	___	___	___	___	___
4. Positive	___	___	___	___	___	___	___	___	___	___	___	___
5. Attentive	___	___	___	___	___	___	___	___	___	___	___	___
6. Concerned	___	___	___	___	___	___	___	___	___	___	___	___
7. Independent	___	___	___	___	___	___	___	___	___	___	___	___
8. Cooperative	___	___	___	___	___	___	___	___	___	___	___	___
9. Helpful	___	___	___	___	___	___	___	___	___	___	___	___
10. Participatory	___	___	___	___	___	___	___	___	___	___	___	___
11. Creative	___	___	___	___	___	___	___	___	___	___	___	___
12. Responsible	___	___	___	___	___	___	___	___	___	___	___	___
13. Social skills/ etiquette	___	___	___	___	___	___	___	___	___	___	___	___
14. Work-study skills	___	___	___	___	___	___	___	___	___	___	___	___
15. Social interests	___	___	___	___	___	___	___	___	___	___	___	___
16. Problem-solving skills	___	___	___	___	___	___	___	___	___	___	___	___
17. Discussion skills	___	___	___	___	___	___	___	___	___	___	___	___
18. Speaking skills	___	___	___	___	___	___	___	___	___	___	___	___
19. Writing skills	___	___	___	___	___	___	___	___	___	___	___	___
20. Listening skills	___	___	___	___	___	___	___	___	___	___	___	___
21. Reading skills	___	___	___	___	___	___	___	___	___	___	___	___
22. Study skills	___	___	___	___	___	___	___	___	___	___	___	___
23. Self-concept	___	___	___	___	___	___	___	___	___	___	___	___

(cont.)

Part II: Interests

	HAS				MAS				LAS			
	Most	*Some*	*Few*	*None*	*Most*	*Some*	*Few*	*None*	*Most*	*Some*	*Few*	*None*
1. In learning	——	——	——	——	——	——	——	——	——	——	——	——
2. In school	——	——	——	——	——	——	——	——	——	——	——	——
3. In social activities	——	——	——	——	——	——	——	——	——	——	——	——
4. In student activities	——	——	——	——	——	——	——	——	——	——	——	——
5. In student government	——	——	——	——	——	——	——	——	——	——	——	——
6. In sports	——	——	——	——	——	——	——	——	——	——	——	——
7. In dances, dancing	——	——	——	——	——	——	——	——	——	——	——	——
8. In assemblies, rallies	——	——	——	——	——	——	——	——	——	——	——	——
9. In drama, plays, musicals	——	——	——	——	——	——	——	——	——	——	——	——
10. In debate, forensics	——	——	——	——	——	——	——	——	——	——	——	——
11. In films	——	——	——	——	——	——	——	——	——	——	——	——
12. In radio/TV	——	——	——	——	——	——	——	——	——	——	——	——
13. In class activities	——	——	——	——	——	——	——	——	——	——	——	——
14. In school spirit	——	——	——	——	——	——	——	——	——	——	——	——
15. In physical activities	——	——	——	——	——	——	——	——	——	——	——	——
16. In clubs, organizations	——	——	——	——	——	——	——	——	——	——	——	——
17. In student publications	——	——	——	——	——	——	——	——	——	——	——	——
18. In musical activities	——	——	——	——	——	——	——	——	——	——	——	——
19. In school/ service committees	——	——	——	——	——	——	——	——	——	——	——	——
20. In community service activities	——	——	——	——	——	——	——	——	——	——	——	——
21. In volunteer activities	——	——	——	——	——	——	——	——	——	——	——	——
22. In local, state, national politics	——	——	——	——	——	——	——	——	——	——	——	——
23. In themselves	——	——	——	——	——	——	——	——	——	——	——	——
24. In forming cliques	——	——	——	——	——	——	——	——	——	——	——	——
25. Other (specify)	——	——	——	——	——	——	——	——	——	——	——	——

(cont.)

Part III: Academic Preparation

	HAS				MAS				LAS			
	Most	Some	Few	None	Most	Some	Few	None	Most	Some	Few	None
1. Reading	—	—	—	—	—	—	—	—	—	—	—	—
2. Science	—	—	—	—	—	—	—	—	—	—	—	—
3. Social Studies	—	—	—	—	—	—	—	—	—	—	—	—
4. English	—	—	—	—	—	—	—	—	—	—	—	—
5. Mathematics	—	—	—	—	—	—	—	—	—	—	—	—
6. Music	—	—	—	—	—	—	—	—	—	—	—	—
7. Art	—	—	—	—	—	—	—	—	—	—	—	—
8. Physical Education	—	—	—	—	—	—	—	—	—	—	—	—
9. Health	—	—	—	—	—	—	—	—	—	—	—	—
10. Other (specify) _____	—	—	—	—	—	—	—	—	—	—	—	—

Part IV: Questions

1. Are you generally satisfied with the students from_____School regarding their academic preparation?

2. Are you generally satisfied with the students from_____School regarding their attitudes toward school?

3. Are you generally satisfied with the students from_____School regarding their social/personal behavior?

4. Are you generally satisfied with the students from_____School regarding their interest and attitudes toward learning?

5. Are you generally satisfied with the students from_____School regarding their learning skills?

6. What specific recommendations do you have to help us better prepare students for your program?

7. What appear to be our greatest strengths?

8. What appear to be our greatest weaknesses?

9. How would you rate the degree of personnel communication between our two schools?

10. How would you rate the degree of program articulation between our two schools?

Figure 10–11
Student Follow-Up: Parent Scale

Directions: The faculty and administrators at_____School are interested in your opinion regarding how well we prepared your child for his or her continuing education at_____School. We ask that you take a few minutes to complete this questionnaire. Your name is not necessary. Please return in the self-addressed, stamped envelope.

Part I: General

1. Number of years your child attended_____School:_____
2. Sex of your child: F_____   M_____
3. General ability of your child:
   High_____   High Average_____   Average_____   Low Average_____   Low_____
4. General achievement of your child while he or she attended_____School:
   Excellent_____   Very Good_____   Good_____   Fair_____   Poor_____

Part II: School Effects

What effect do you feel that_____School, its faculty/staff/principal and programs had on your child's:

	Effect					
	Great	Moderate	Little	None	Positive	Negative
1. attitude toward school	___	___	___	___	___	___
2. attitude toward learning	___	___	___	___	___	___
3. attitude toward teachers	___	___	___	___	___	___
4. attitude toward authority	___	___	___	___	___	___
5. attitude toward himself or herself	___	___	___	___	___	___
6. interest in school	___	___	___	___	___	___
7. interest in continuing his or her education	___	___	___	___	___	___
8. interest in reading	___	___	___	___	___	___
9. interest in student activities (council, clubs, publications, etc.)	___	___	___	___	___	___
10. interest in sports	___	___	___	___	___	___
11. interest in plays, musicals	___	___	___	___	___	___
12. interest in music, concerts	___	___	___	___	___	___
13. interest in community affairs	___	___	___	___	___	___
14. skills in doing school work	___	___	___	___	___	___
15. reading skills	___	___	___	___	___	___
16. math skills	___	___	___	___	___	___
17. ability to do school work	___	___	___	___	___	___
18. study-work skills	___	___	___	___	___	___
19. emotional skills	___	___	___	___	___	___
20. social skills	___	___	___	___	___	___
21. personality	___	___	___	___	___	___
22. skills to do homework	___	___	___	___	___	___
23. possible career choice	___	___	___	___	___	___
24. success in school	___	___	___	___	___	___
25. lack of success in school	___	___	___	___	___	___

(cont.)

Part III: Questions

1. What did you like best about the way we prepared your child for his continuing education at _____School?

2. What did you like least about the way we prepared your child for his continuing education at _____School?

3. What could we have done that you feel we didn't do to prepare your child?

4. What recommendations do you want to offer to help us do a better job?

5. What questions do you have about our progress or personnel that you feel we should answer?

Graduate-Alumni Studies

Many high school guidance departments conduct follow-up studies of their graduates. Several high schools have active alumni associations. Both activities can be of value as a means of improving school-community communications, of utilizing community resources, and for evaluation purposes.

Five-Step Follow-Up Plan

A five-step plan is recommended for high school principals who want to or are currently conducting graduate follow-up studies.

Step 1: Purposes and plans.   The following questions will be helpful in beginning a follow-up study:

1. What are your purposes? Objectives? Why do you want to conduct or why have you been conducting follow-up studies of the school's graduates?
2. What are your plans for conducting the study?
3. What is your study cycle? Every year? Every two years?
4. What methods will or do you use? Interviewing? Questionnaire?
5. Who will be responsible for tabulating the data? For summarizing the data? For interpreting the data?

6. What sampling procedures will you use? Entire population? Random sample?
7. What will it cost to do the study? Where will the money come from?

Step 2: Scope and schedule.   The following questions will help focus your attention on additional plans and procedures:

1. What geographic area will you study?
2. What class or group will be studied?
3. How will the information be solicited?
4. Who will design the questionnaire?
5. What factors will be included in the questionnaire?
6. If interviews are planned, who will do the interviewing? What questions will be asked? Who will prepare the questions?
7. When will the study be made?
8. When will the study be completed?
9. Will follow-up letters be sent to graduates who do not reply?

Step 3: Collection and tabulation.   The following questions will help you in collecting the data:

1. What attention will be given to collecting the data to avoid population or sample bias?
2. Will cross-tabulations be necessary to meet the purposes of the study?

3 Who will be responsible for tabulating the data?
4. Will the data be hand- or computer-tabulated?
5. Will the data be separated into two major response categories; one for graduates who enter college, the other for students who enter the vocational, commercial, or other occupational fields?

Step 4: Interpretation and reporting. The following questions will help you make decisions regarding the interpretation and reporting of the tabulated data:

1. Who will interpret the data?
2. How will the data be interpreted?
3. How will the data be reported?
4. Will there be several small reports or one large report?
5. What graphic materials will be provided?
6. Who will be reading the report?

7. Who will receive copies of the report?
8. What will it cost to prepare the report?

Step 5: Recommendations and action. This final step suggests, through the questions asked, that action be taken on the information collected and interpreted:

1. What specific recommendations result from the study?
2. What specific actions are necessary?
3. Who will implement the actions or recommendations?
4. What actions or recommendations will take priority?
5. What will be involved in terms of cost, personnel, and programs if all or some of the recommendations and actions are implemented?
6. In terms of the time, energy, and cost, was the follow-up study worth it?

An example of a high school follow-up questionnaire is shown in Figure 10–12.

Figure 10–12
A Sample High School Follow-Up Study Form

Name:_____ Maiden Name:_____
Present address:_____ Phone:_____ Date:_____
Year graduated:____ Male____ Female____ Married____
Single____ Divorced____

1. Present occupation category:
   Professional____ Service____ Clerical____ Technical____
   Agricultural____ Sales____ Armed Forces____
   Management____ Skilled____ Semi-Skilled____
   Unskilled____ Unemployed____

2. Income:
   Below $5,000____
   Over $5,000 but less than $10,000____
   Over $10,000 but less than $20,000____
   Over $20,000 but less than $40,000____
   Over $40,000____

(cont.)

3. Employment since graduation (list):

       Firm Name   *Type of Work*   *Time in Position*

  a. _____   _____   _____

  b. _____   _____   _____

  c. _____   _____   _____

4. Armed Services since graduation:

  Branch_____   Type of work_____

  Rank_____   Length of service_____

  Not Applicable_____

5. Education since graduation:

School/College	*Course/Major*	*Degree or Years Attended*	*Did You Graduate?*
_____	_____	_____	yes____ no____
_____	_____	_____	yes____ no____
_____	_____	_____	yes____ no____

6. Is your present job one that you thought you would be doing when you graduated from high school?

  Definitely; exactly what I planned____   Close to what I planned____

  Not even close to what I planned____   I made no plans in high school____

7. What are you currently doing? Is this a part-time or full-time job?

8. Please rate your degree of satisfaction with each of the following:

	Very Satisfied	*Satisfied*	*Not Satisfied*
a. Your high school teachers	____	____	____
b. Guidance counselors	____	____	____
c. Administrators	____	____	____
d. Coaches	____	____	____
e. Activity advisors	____	____	____
f. Academic program	____	____	____
g. Extracurricular programs	____	____	____
h. Social activities/programs	____	____	____

9. How much help did you receive from the following high school personnel in choosing and planning an occupation or school/college?

	None	*Very Little*	*Some*	*Much*	*Very Much*
a. Counselors	____	____	____	____	____
b. Teachers	____	____	____	____	____
c. Administrators	____	____	____	____	____
d. Others (specify)_____	____	____	____	____	____

(cont.)

10. How would you rate your high school education in your present job?
    No help at all_____   Very helpful_____   Gave me some background_____

11. How did your high school education help you most?

    Least?

12. What problems did you have going from high school to a job or to college?

13. What major advice would you give a high school student today?

14. What should this high school be doing to help students prepare for college or work when they graduate?

15. Please rate the value of high school courses as you look back on your preparation:

	Very Valuable	Valuable	Little Value	Worthless	Didn't Take
a. English	____	____	____	____	____
b. Social Studies	____	____	____	____	____
c. Science	____	____	____	____	____
d. Mathematics	____	____	____	____	____
e. Foreign Languages	____	____	____	____	____
f. Industrial Arts	____	____	____	____	____
g. Music	____	____	____	____	____
h. Art	____	____	____	____	____
i. Physical Education	____	____	____	____	____
j. Home Economics	____	____	____	____	____
k. Speech	____	____	____	____	____
l. Other (specify_____)	____	____	____	____	____

16. What subjects were not offered that you now feel would be of great value to you?

17. How would you rate yourself during your years in high school

	Top Quarter	Third Highest Quarter	Second Lowest Quarter	Lowest Quarter
a. Academically	____	____	____	____
b. Athletically	____	____	____	____
c. Socially	____	____	____	____
d. Reading achievement	____	____	____	____
e. Math achievement	____	____	____	____
f. Music or Art achievement	____	____	____	____
g. Confidence	____	____	____	____
h. Relationship with others	____	____	____	____

(cont.)

18. Honors and Awards:
    a. In high school:

    b. Since graduation:

19. Activities/Sports:
    a. Extracurricular activities you participated in during your high school years:

    b. Sports and other activities in which you currently participate:

20. Community activities in which you currently participate:

	Activities	Offices Hold or Have Held
a. Civic clubs/organizations	_____	_____
b. Social clubs/organizations	_____	_____
c. Religious organizations	_____	_____
d. Other (specify_____)	_____	_____

21. Are you interested in forming an alumni association?   Yes__ No__
22. Are you willing to help form an alumni association?   Yes__ No__
23. Are you interested in participating in a class reunion?   Yes__ No__
24. Are you interested in helping develop plans for a class reunion? Yes__ No__

A FINAL COMMENT

This chapter provided ideas and suggestions for evaluating and improving school-community relations. A school principal should not assume that it is the superintendent's or central office administrator's job to take the lead in school-community relations. Although certain district factors such as declining enrollments, increased criticisms of schools, and the plea for tax reductions cannot be directly influenced by a principal on a community-wide basis, there is much you can do to help your public and parents understand school needs, programs, and problems. Therefore, as the leader of the school, you should be planning a long-range program for improving school-community relations with appropriate methods for assessing the effectiveness of that program.

EVALUATION INSTRUMENTS

Here are four examples of instruments available for use in conducting parent/citizen surveys.

"Annual Education Checkup." The National Committee for Citizens in Education, Suite 410, Wilde Lake Village Green, Columbia, Maryland 21044.

This pocket-size card provides parents with a checklist for assessing their child's progress in school. Using a "yes–no" and "Need more information" scale, the card enables the parent, through a series of questions, to assess material sent home by the school; parent-teacher conferences; and school records about their children.

"Community Participant Opinion Survey." Research for Better Schools, Inc., Philadelphia, Pennsylvania.

This four-page booklet contains sixteen items designed to measure community participant problems relating to educational programs. Included in the booklet are an assessment of various program elements, opinions on program benefits, and program comparisons with standard curricular offerings. It can be completed by a respondent in about fifteen minutes.

"Evaluation Instrument for Educational Public Relations Programs." National School Public Relations Associations, 1801 North Moore Street, Arlington, Virginia 22209.

The instrument in this booklet contains thirty-six standards to help administrators and others evaluate the extent to which the school has made provisions for organizing and conducting a formal public relations program. It can be adapted by school principals to assess the individual school public relations program. Also included in the booklet are a scoring worksheet and a program standards evaluation summary form.

"A Parent /Citizen Survey: Improving Services for Children in Special Education." National Committee for Citizens in Education, Suite 410, Wilde Lake Village Green, Columbia, Maryland 21044. (Also reprinted in *NAESP Communicator* 2 (27 November 1978).

This instrument is a questionnaire which enables parents to check on their school's implementation of Public Law 94–142 (All Handicapped Children Act). The thirty-item "yes–no" checklist focuses on the parents' role in developing an individualized education plan.

ENDNOTES

1. Doyle M. Bortner, "The High School's Responsibility for Public Relations," *Bulletin of the National Association of Secondary School Principals* 44 (September 1960): 9–13.

2. Robert Olds, "The Principal's PR Role," *Bulletin of the National Association of Secondary School Principals* 58 (January 1974): 18–19.

SELECTED REFERENCES

Bryne, Robert, and Powell, Edward. *Strengthening School-Community Relations.* Reston, Va.: National Association of Secondary School Principals, 1978.

Conway, James A.; Jennings, Robert E.; and Milstein, Mike M. *Understanding Communities.* Englewood Cliffs, N.J.: Prentice-Hall, 1974.

Davis, Don. "Making Citizen Participation Work." *National Elementary School Principal* 55 (March/April 1976): 20–29.

DeNovellis, Richard L., and Lewis, Arthur J. *Schools Become Accountable: A PACT Approach.* Washington, D.C.: Association for Supervision and Curriculum Development, 1975.

Eells, Donald R. "Are Parents Really Partners in Education?" *Bulletin of the National Association of Secondary School Principals* 58 (January 1974): 26–31.

Ferguson, D. Hugh. "Can Your School Survive a Parent Evaluation?" *National Elementary School Principal* 56 (March/April 1977): 71–73.

Gordon, Ira J., and Breivogel, William F. *Building Effective Home/School Relationships.* Boston: Allyn and Bacon, 1976.

Grant, Carl A. *Community Participation in Education.* Boston: Allyn and Bacon, 1979.

How to Conduct Low Cost Surveys. Arlington, Va.: National School Public Relations Association, 1973.

Ideas for Improving Public Confidence in Public Education. Arlington, Va.: National School Public Relations Association, 1971.

Jones, William, and Stough, Charles. *A Guide to Excellence in School Public Relations.* Palm Springs, Calif.: ETC Publications, 1978.

Keys to Community Involvement. Arlington, Va.: National School Public Relations Association, 1977. Fifteen guides for improving and promoting citizen participation.

Linking Schools and the Community. Arlington, Va.: National School Public Relations Association, 1977.

Mayer, Frank C. *Public Relations for School Personnel.* Midland, Mich.: Pendell Publishing, 1974.

New York State School Boards Association. *Communications/Public Relations: A Handbook on School Community Relations.* Albany: School Boards Association, 1973.

Putting Words and Pictures about School into Print. Arlington, Va.: National School Public Relations Association, 1971.

Robinson, Thomas E.; Reinfeld, George; and Robinson, Timothy B. *101 Public Relations Activities for Schools.* Danville, Ill.: Interstate Printers and Publishers, 1976.

Theory into Practice 19 (February 1977). (The theme of this issue is home-school relations.)

Thomas, M. Donald. "How to Recognize a Gem of a School When You See One." *American School Board Journal* 162 (March 1975): 27–30.

Wolf, W. C., Jr. "Community Involvement: An Unattainable Aspiration?" *National Elementary School Principal* 55 (March/April 1976): 30–32.

INDEX